AF587536

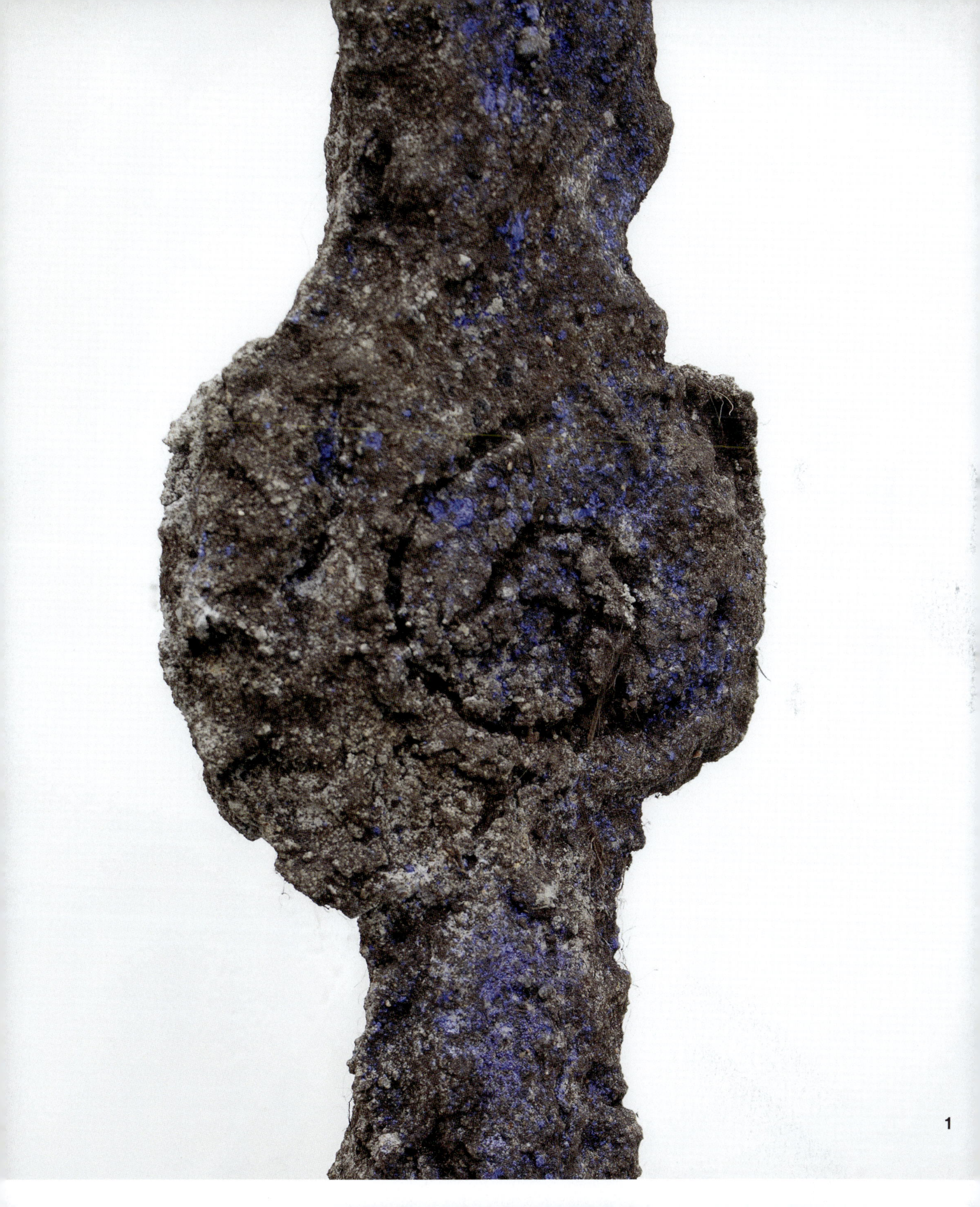

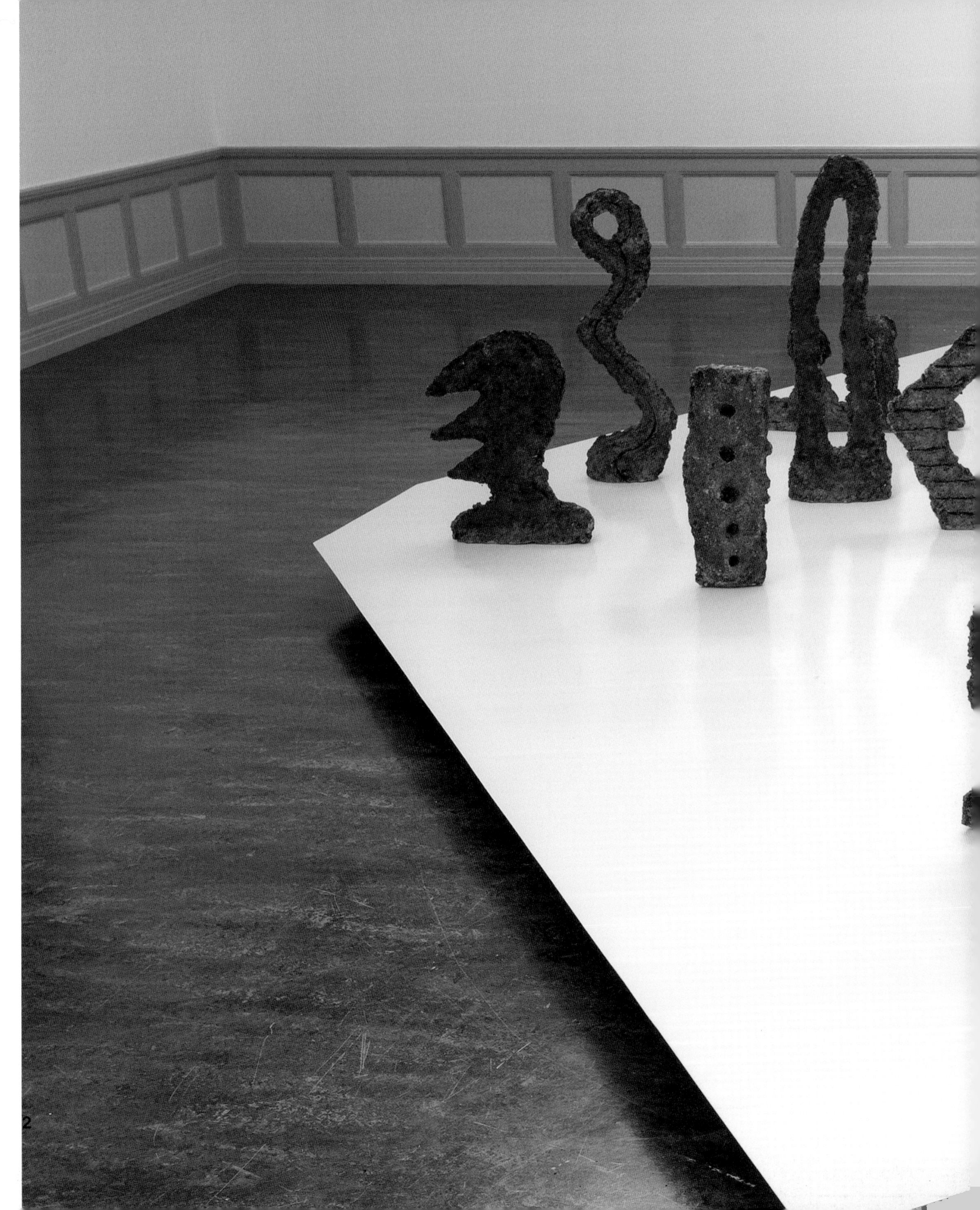

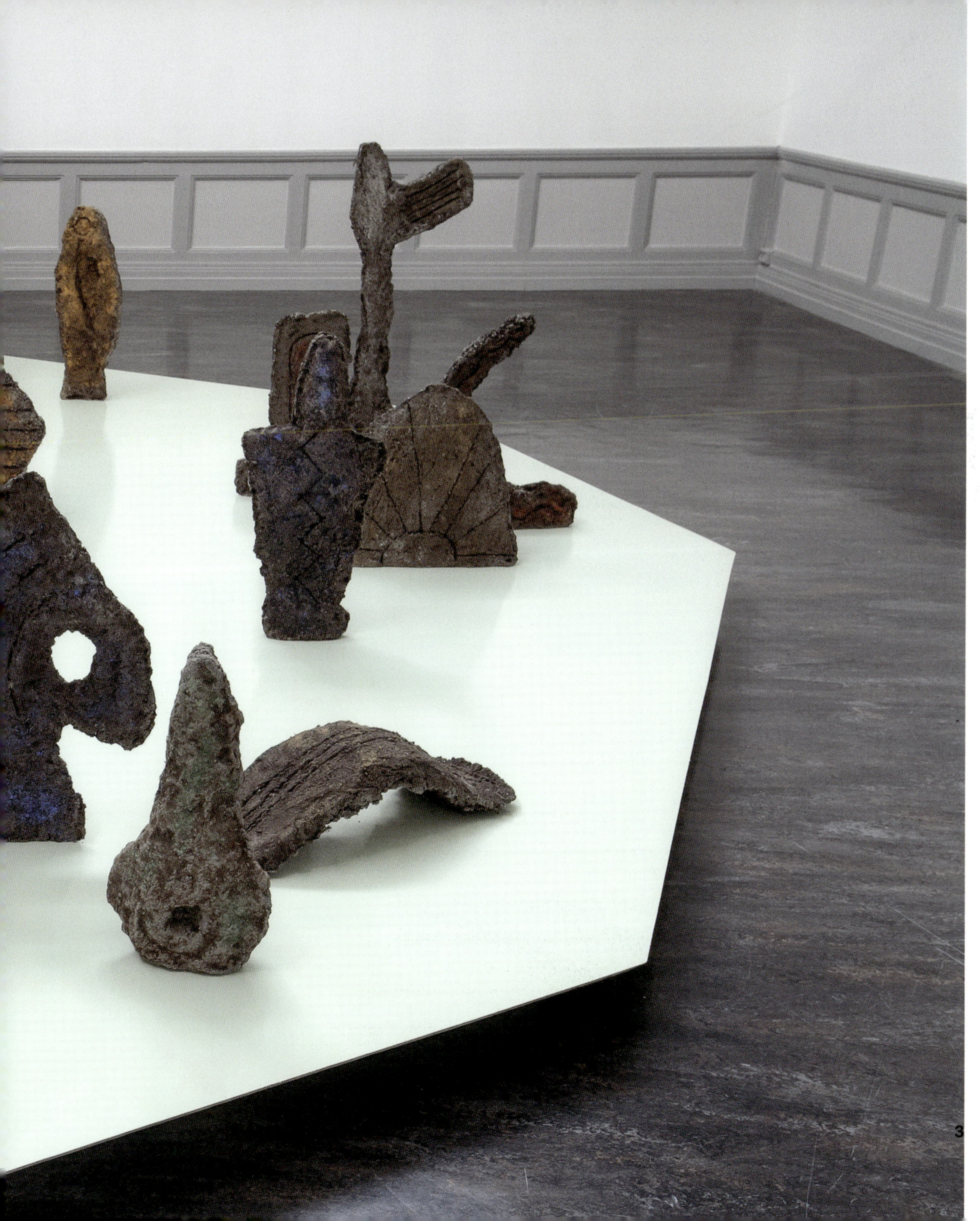

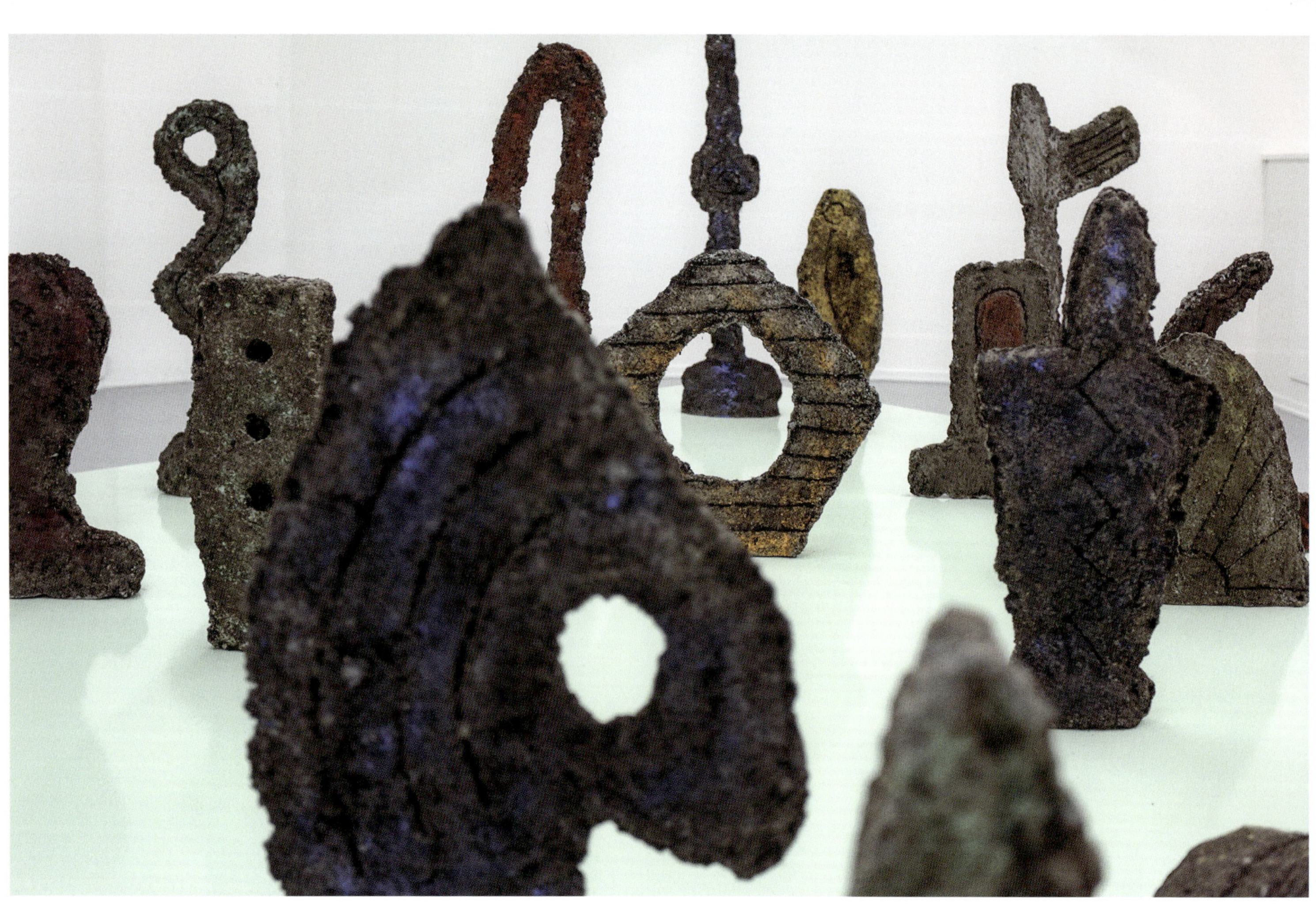

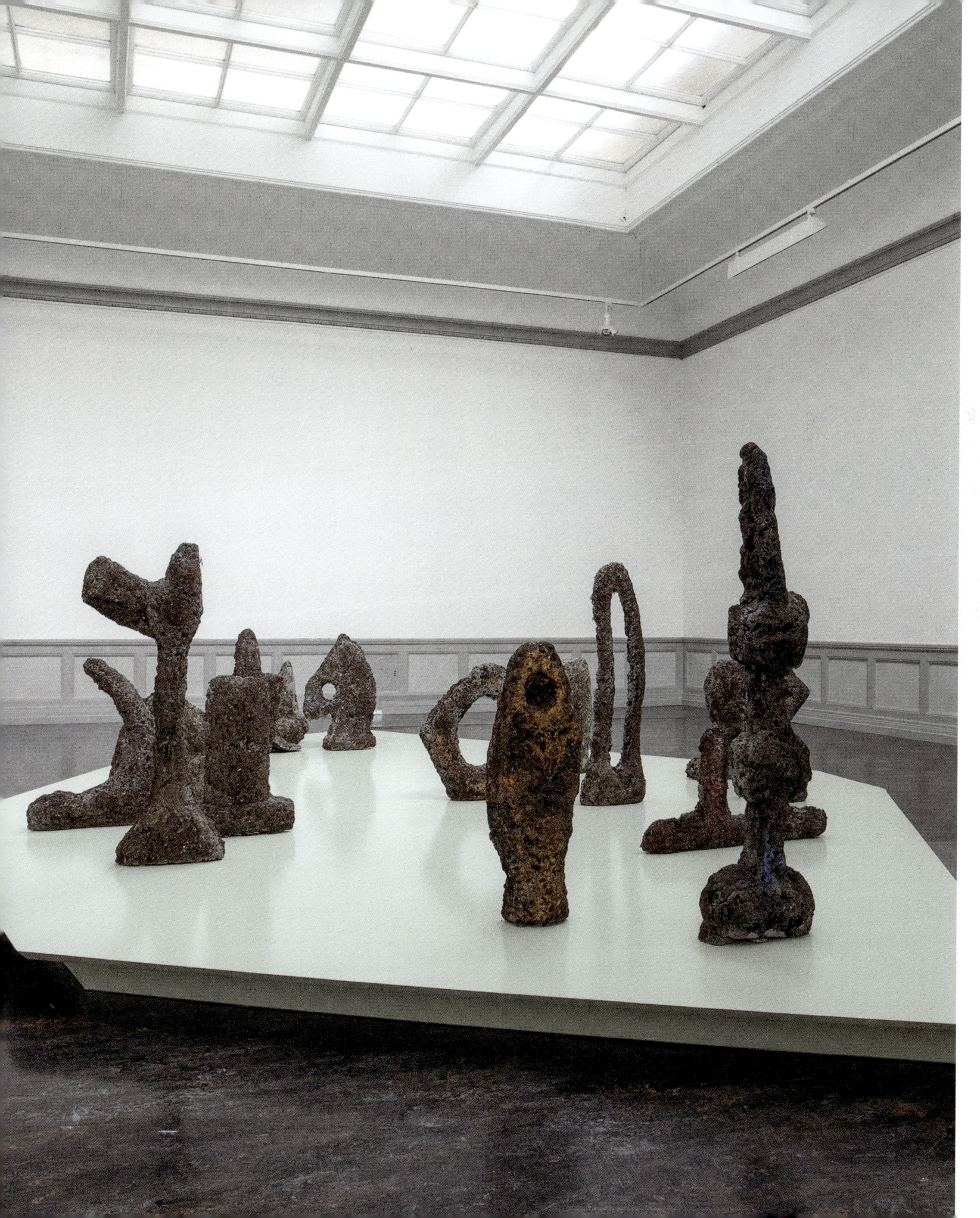

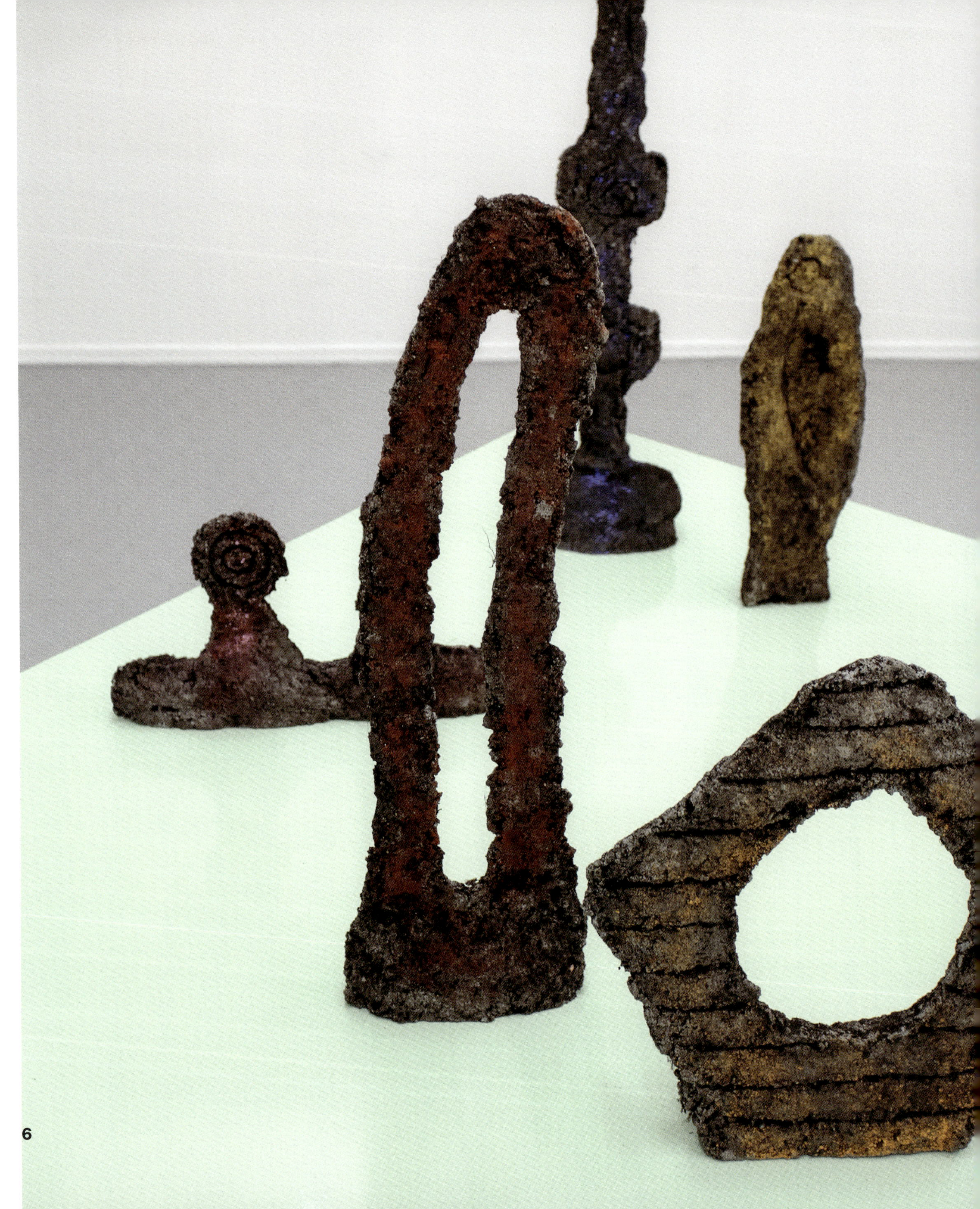

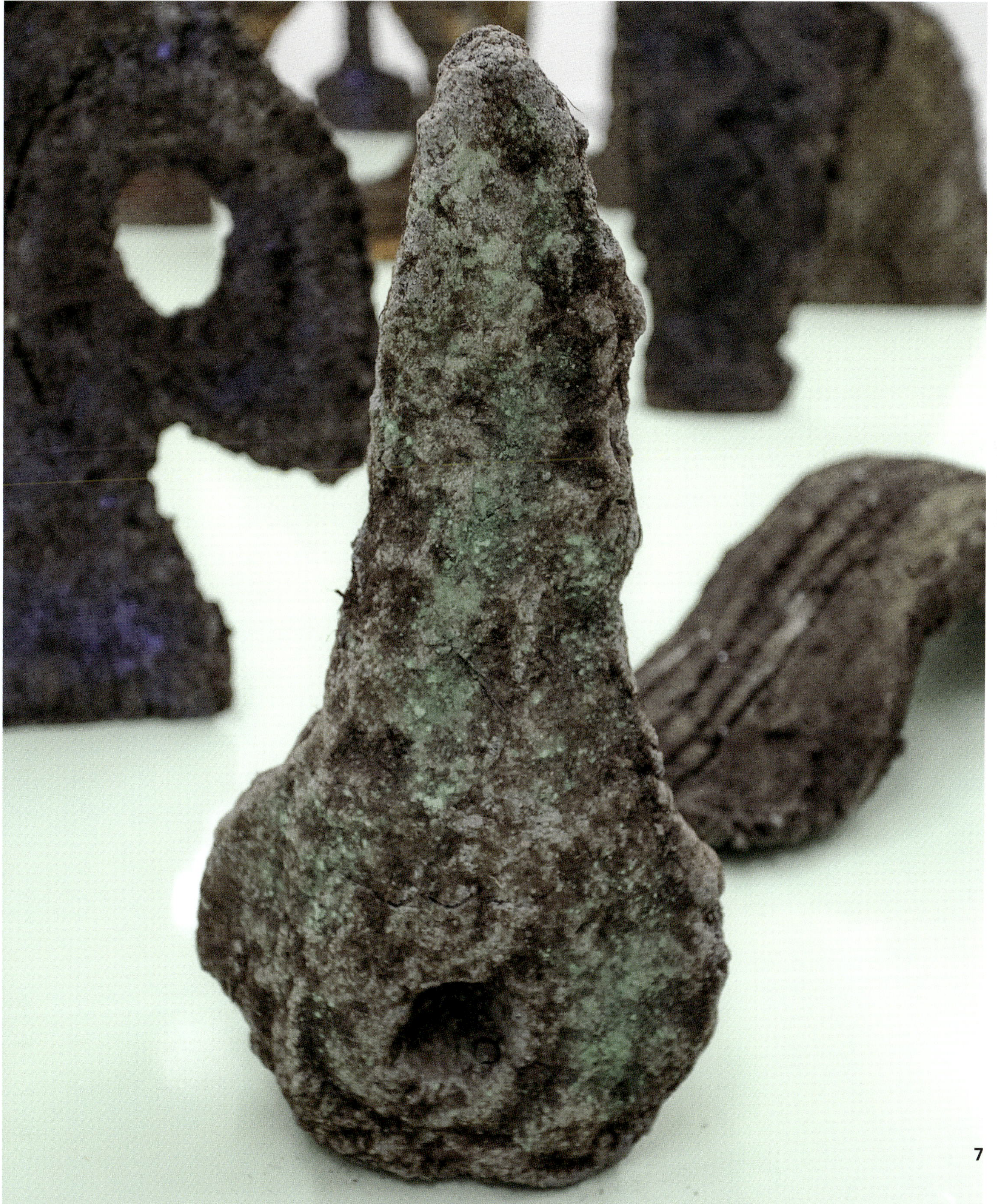

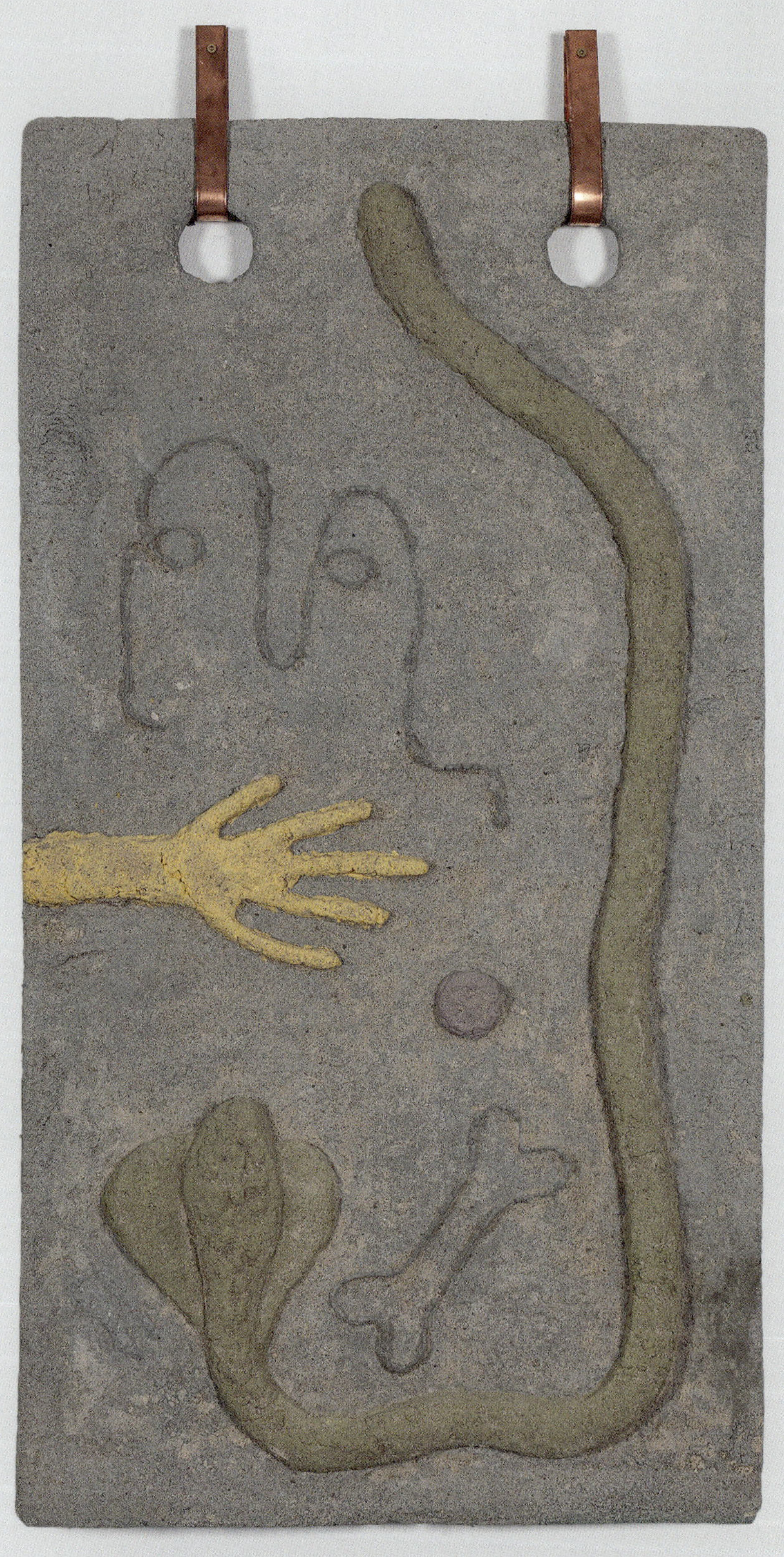

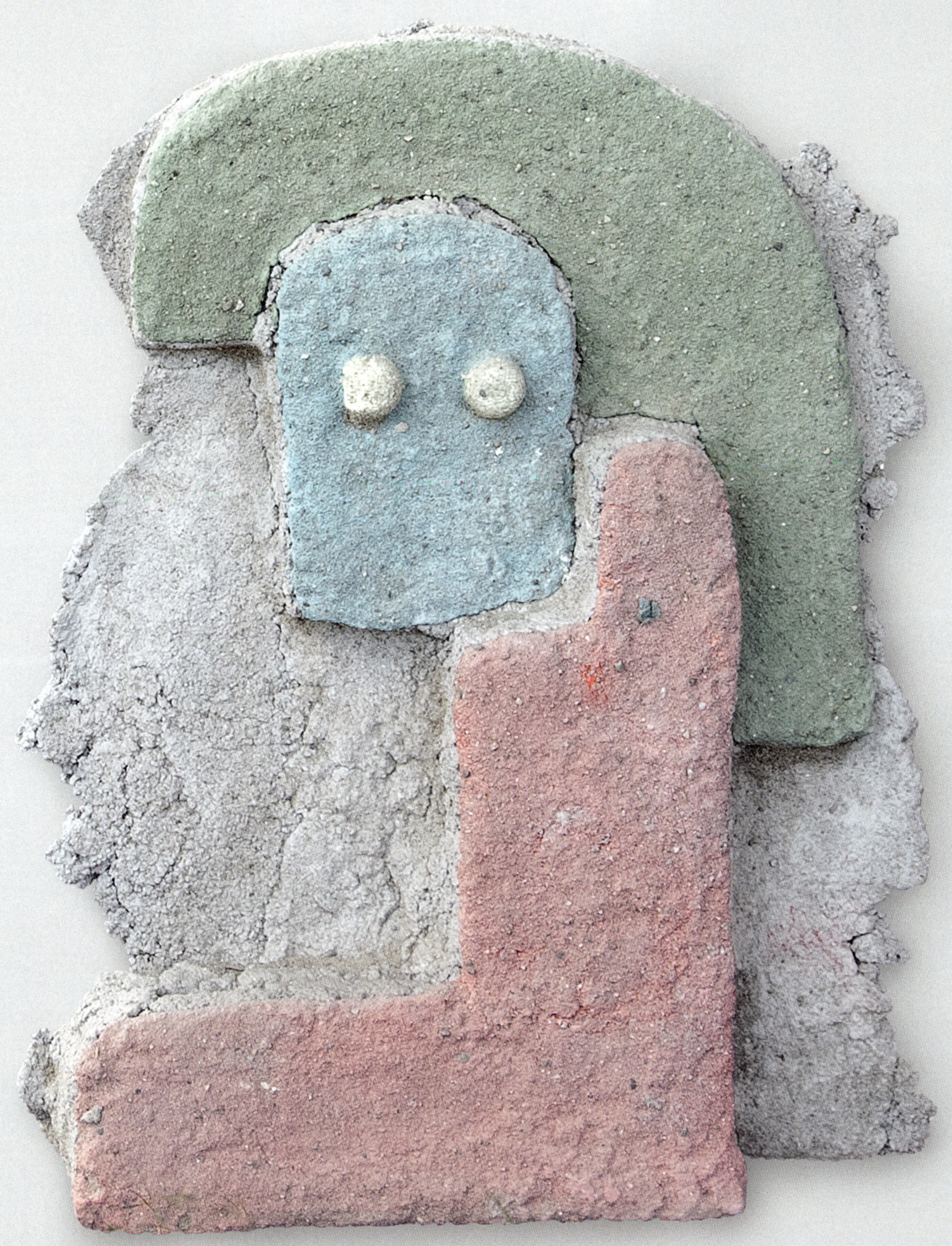

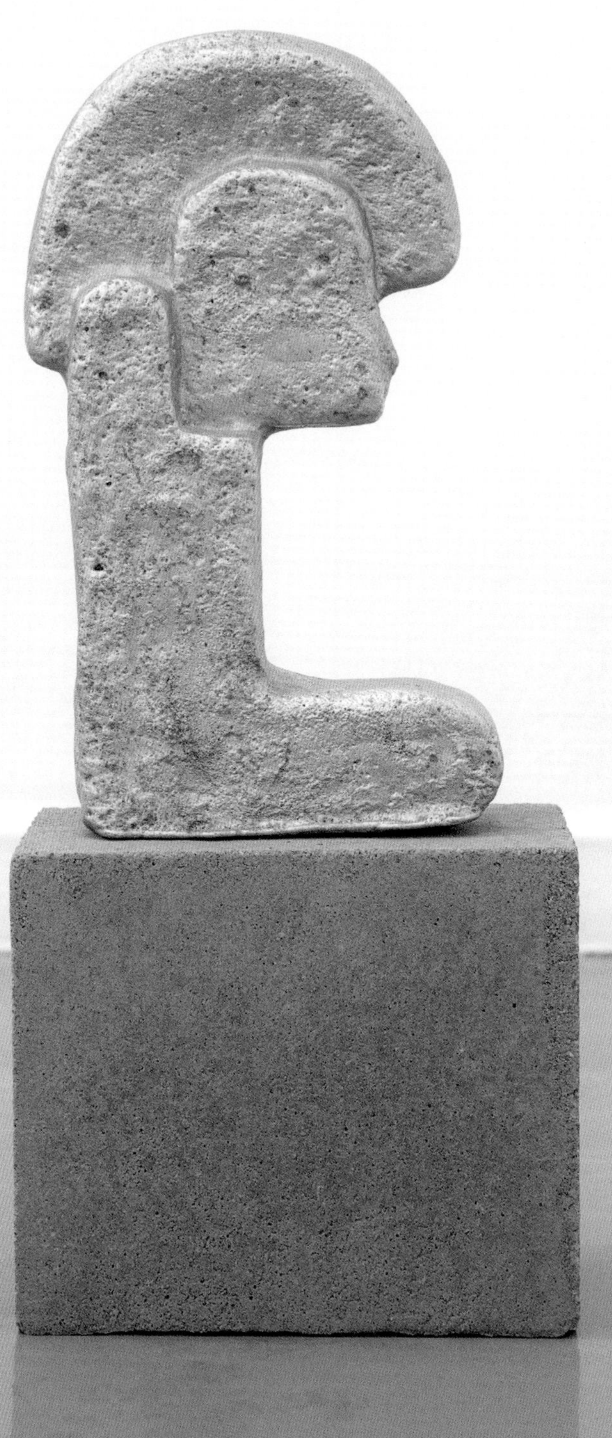

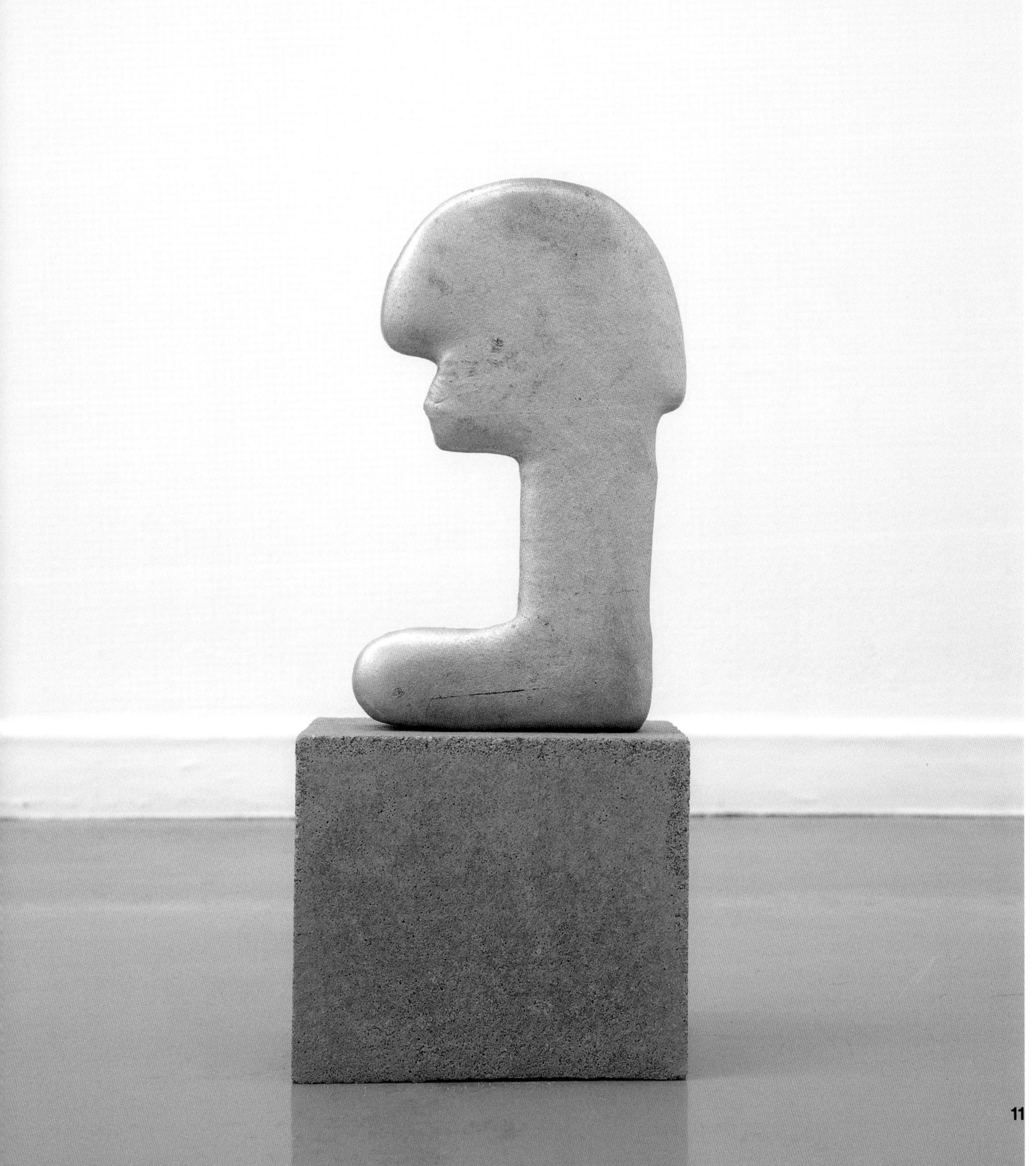

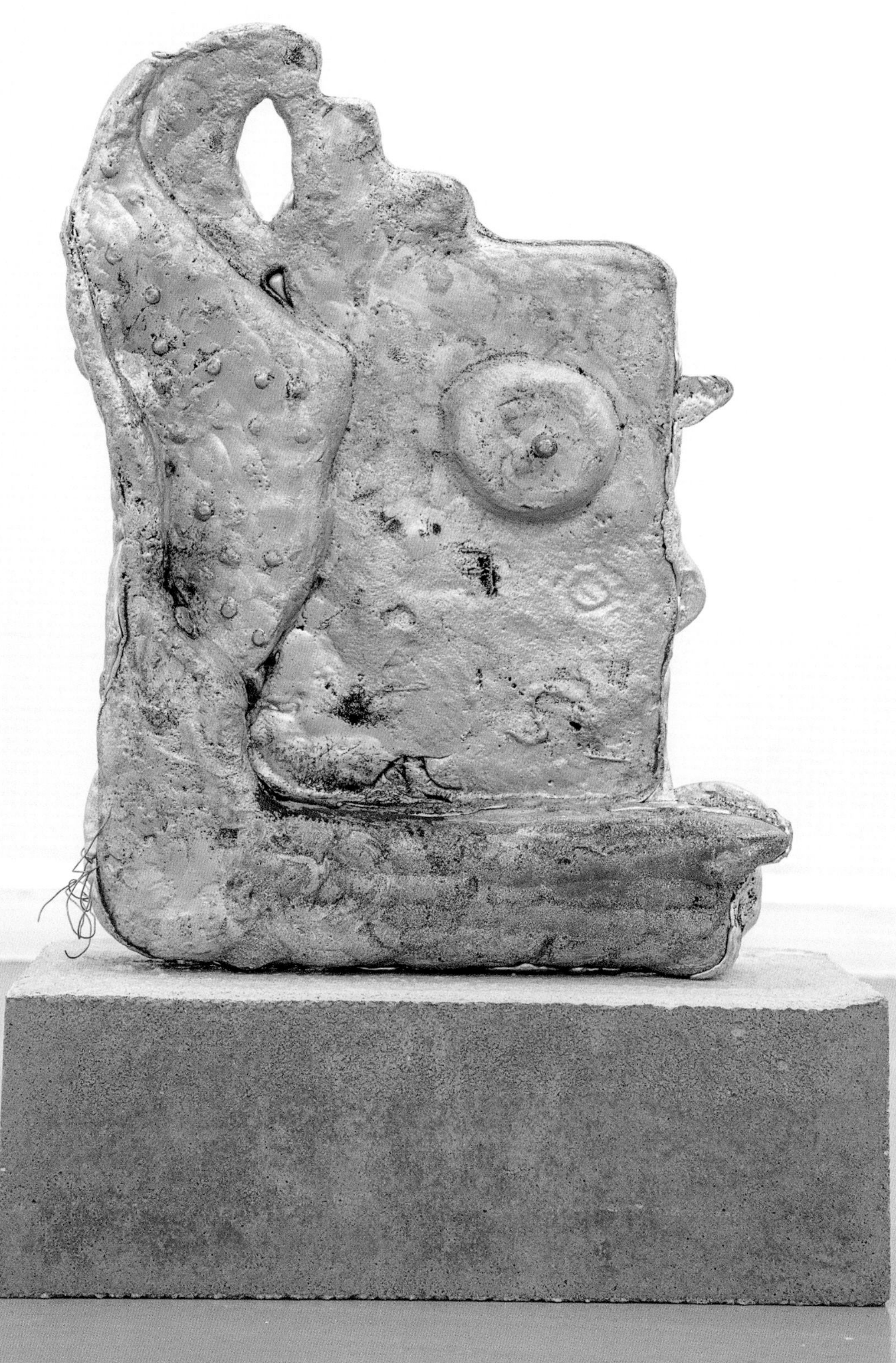

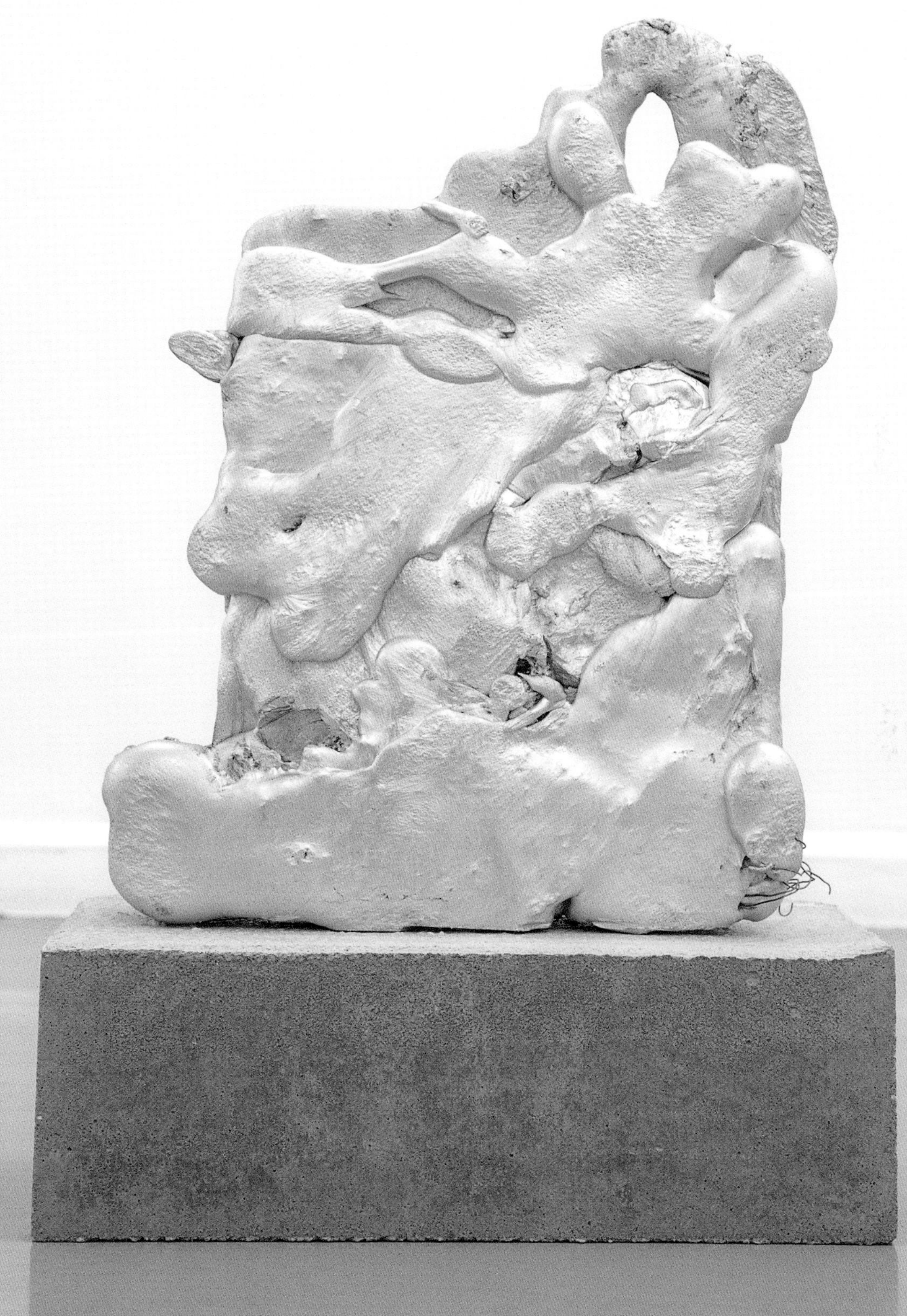

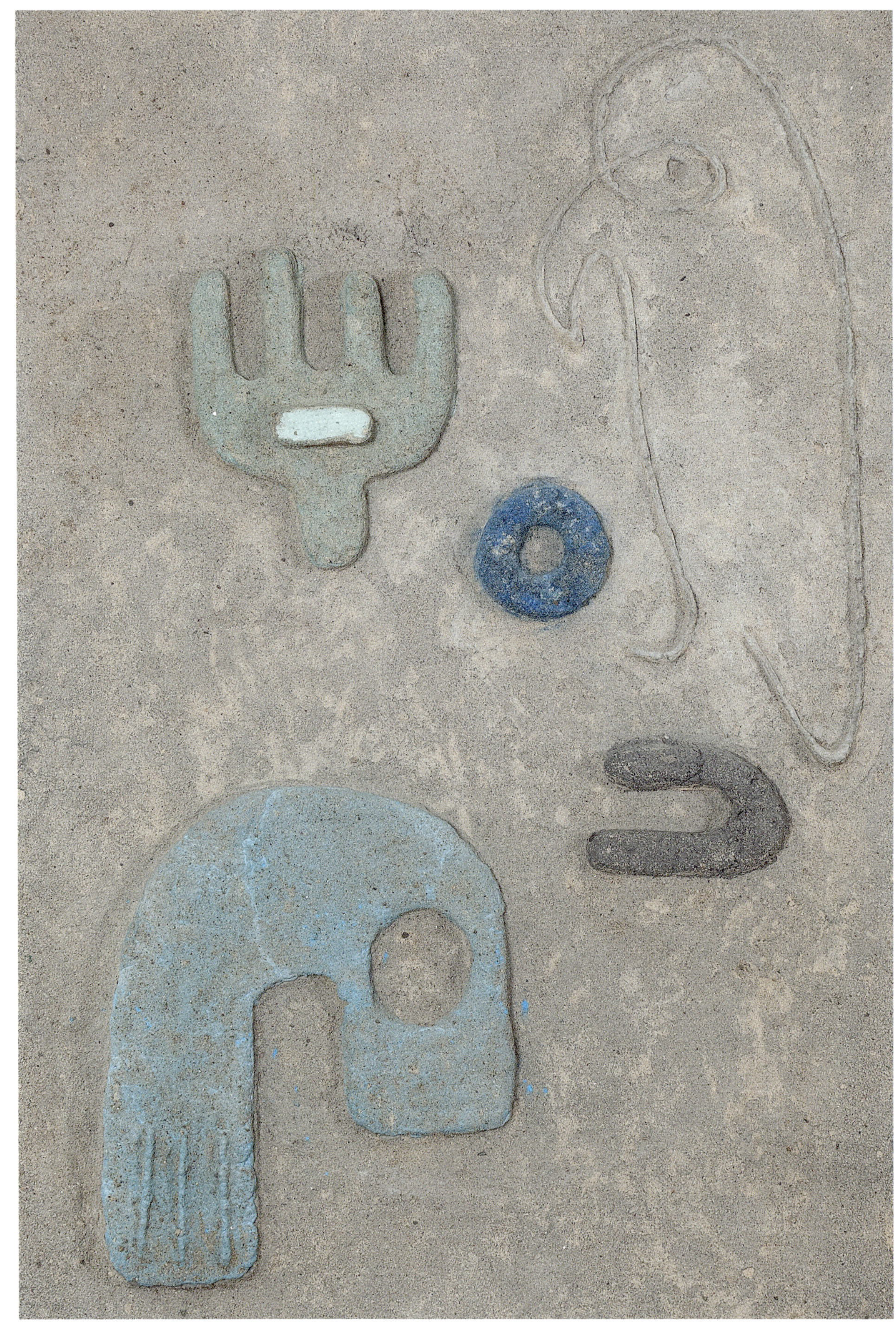

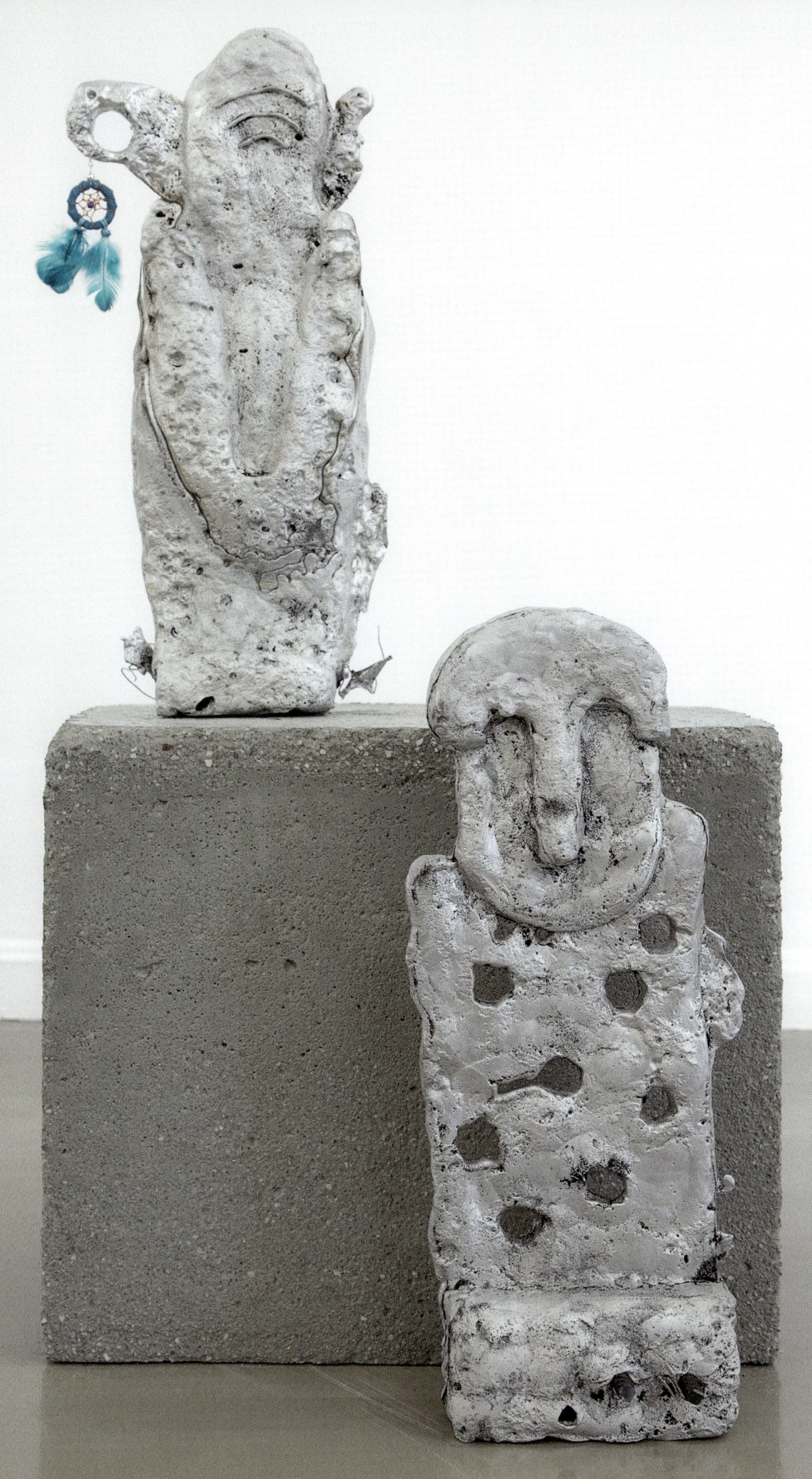

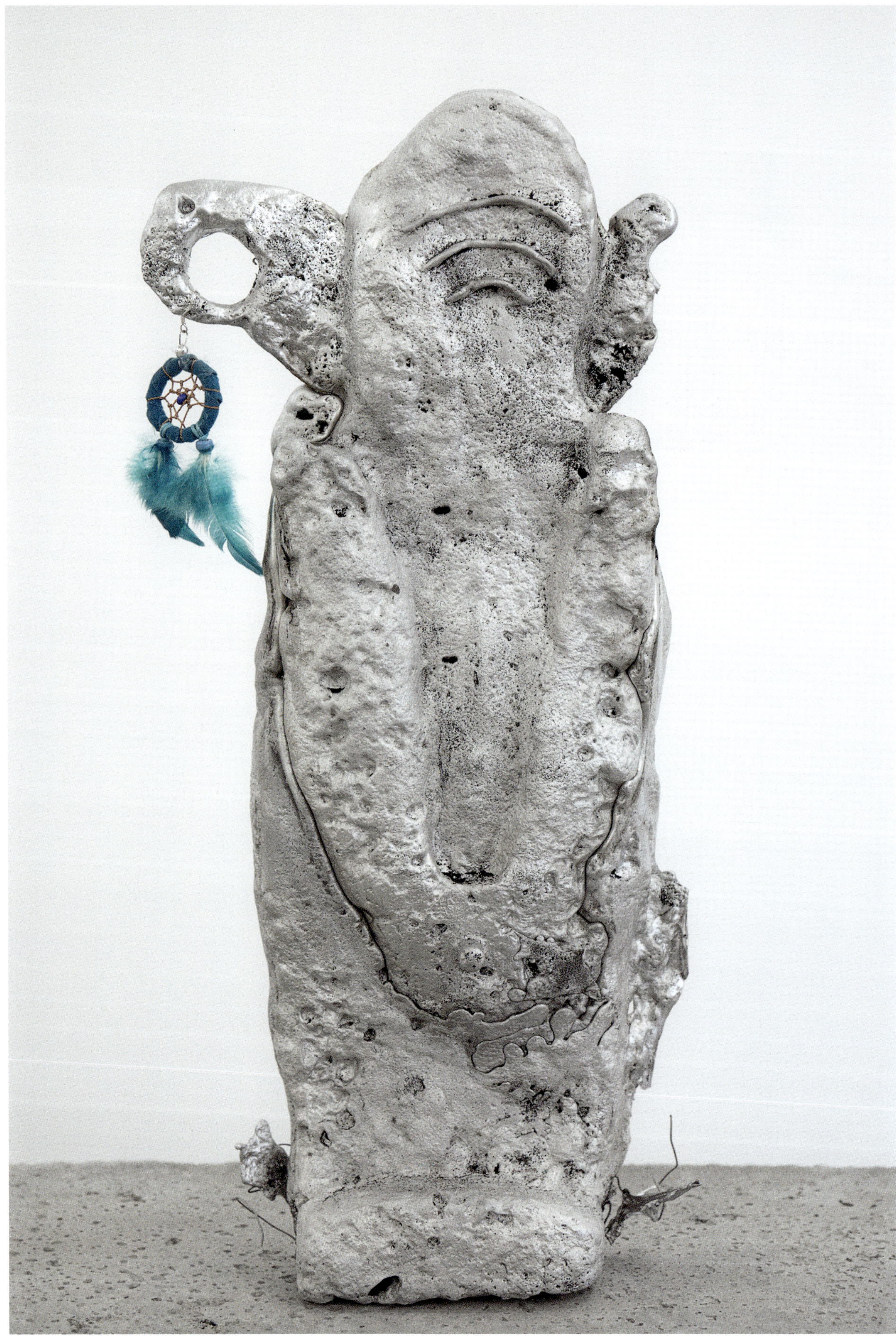

Lene Baadsvig Ørmen
0

Edited by
Mathijs van Geest

Conversations with
Jan Verwoert
Milena Høgsberg
Leah Beeferman

Text by
Ki Nurmenniemi

Published by
Lugemik &
Hordaland Kunstsenter

Contents

Foresee thy tingling thumb,
alluring tempest this way come.

Plead the forth and doubt all prior,
deep below, shall dwindle tire.

Drifting little genie urging,
feeling giddy, when backward turning.

Bolt all feasible locks,
forlorn to omit, whoever knocks.

— Lene Baadsvig Ørmen

FOREWORD

Lene Baadsvig Ørmen (zodiac sign: Gemini) is a Norwegian visual artist who has created an extensive body of sculptural works since graduating from the Oslo National Academy of the Arts in 2013. This publication presents comprehensive insights into the artist's practice and work and celebrates the formation of her career.

Whereas in her early work Lene created sculptures with an archeological dimension—raw creatures belonging to a distant past, dug up from the sand—her latest projects lean more toward shapes and objects that arrived to us from the future. Organic beings in earthly colors and sandy textures are slowly replaced by angular forms with strict lines and patterns created in steel, aluminum, and unpolished concrete. Works by Lene consist largely of raw material-focused sculptures shaped through various casting techniques that visualize the artist's continuous search for new forms and meanings.

By introducing intricate soundscapes, produced in collaboration with composer Peder Simonsen, Lene explores new strategies for her sculptures to expand and encounter an audience.

Either by looking at the past or to the future, Lene's objects reveal a strong anthropological interest. They challenge the viewer to reconsider preconceptions of the natural and the artificial, and to stretch understanding of how relationships between animals and humans have played out in different cultures and throughout time.

Strengthened by dialogue and a sharing of thoughts, this publication also explores an important social aspect of Lene's practice. Conversations with critic and writer Jan Verwoert, curator Milena Høgsberg, as well as artist Leah Beeferman, are combined with an in depth essay by curator and writer Ki Nurmenniemi. The final page of the publication is dedicated to a poem by Norwegian writer Cecilie Løveid originally written in response to Lene's exhibition Subterranea at Hordaland Kunstsenter in Bergen.

The cover of the publication features a small circular shape: we could call it the title of the book. This circular shape often appears in Lene's work in the form of an eye, a hole, a ring, a disc, a loop, a circle, and shows her fascination for linguistic and descriptive systems, particularly in an open and distorted way. Rather than a symbolic portrait of an "O" or a "0," a mathematic zero or nothingness, the circular movement on the cover that has neither beginning nor end functions as a gathering point where undefined references can come together.

Mathijs van Geest

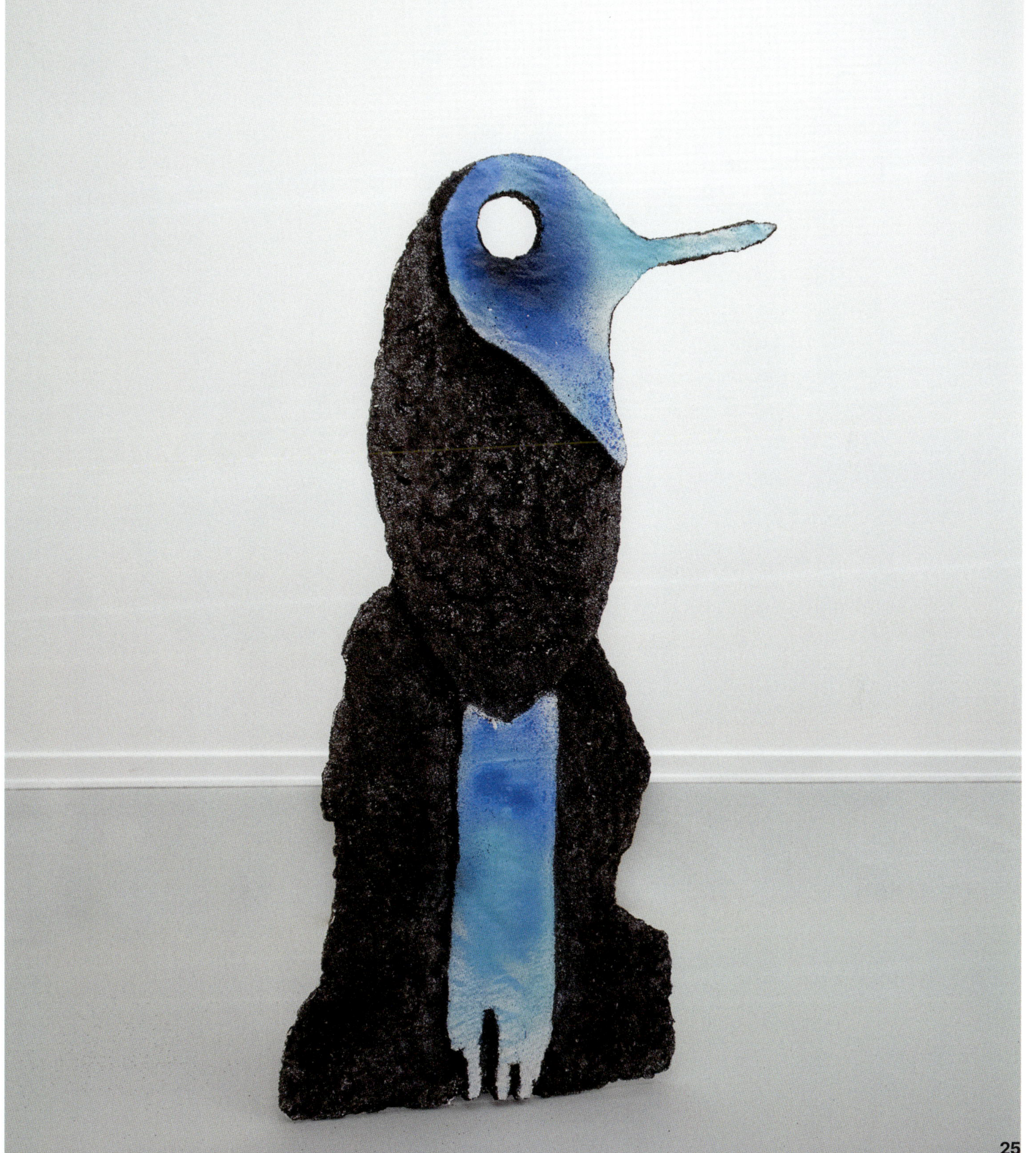

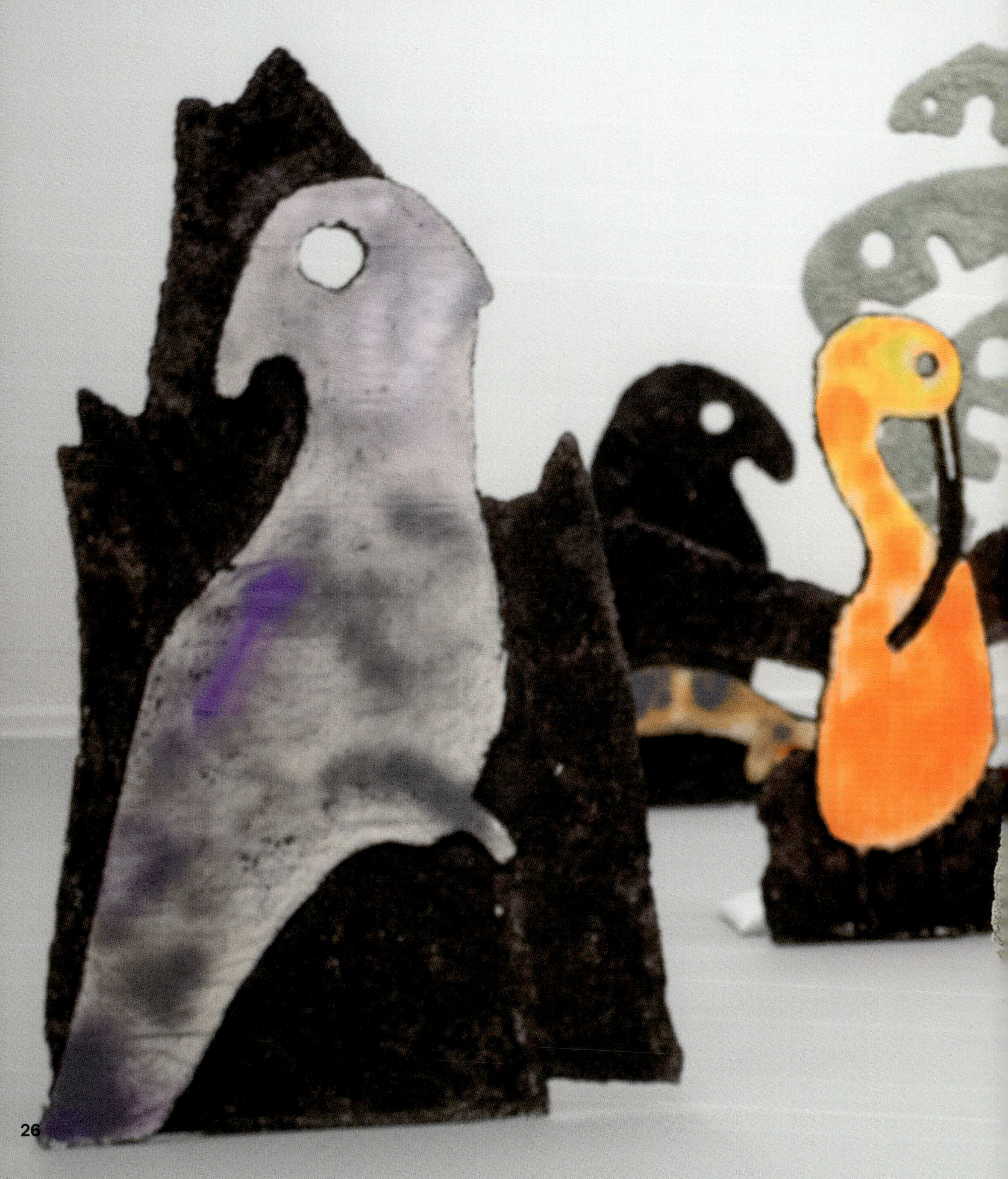

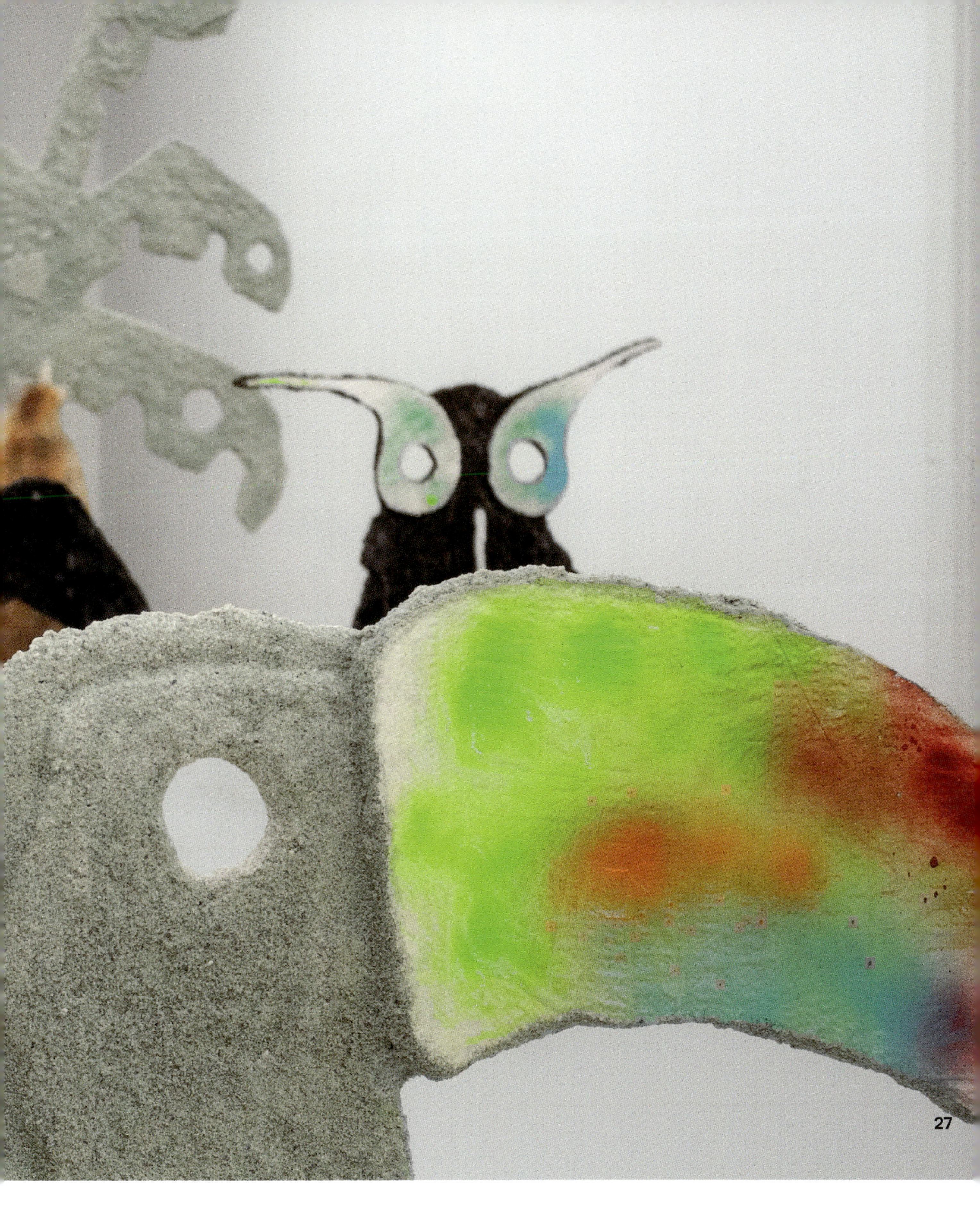

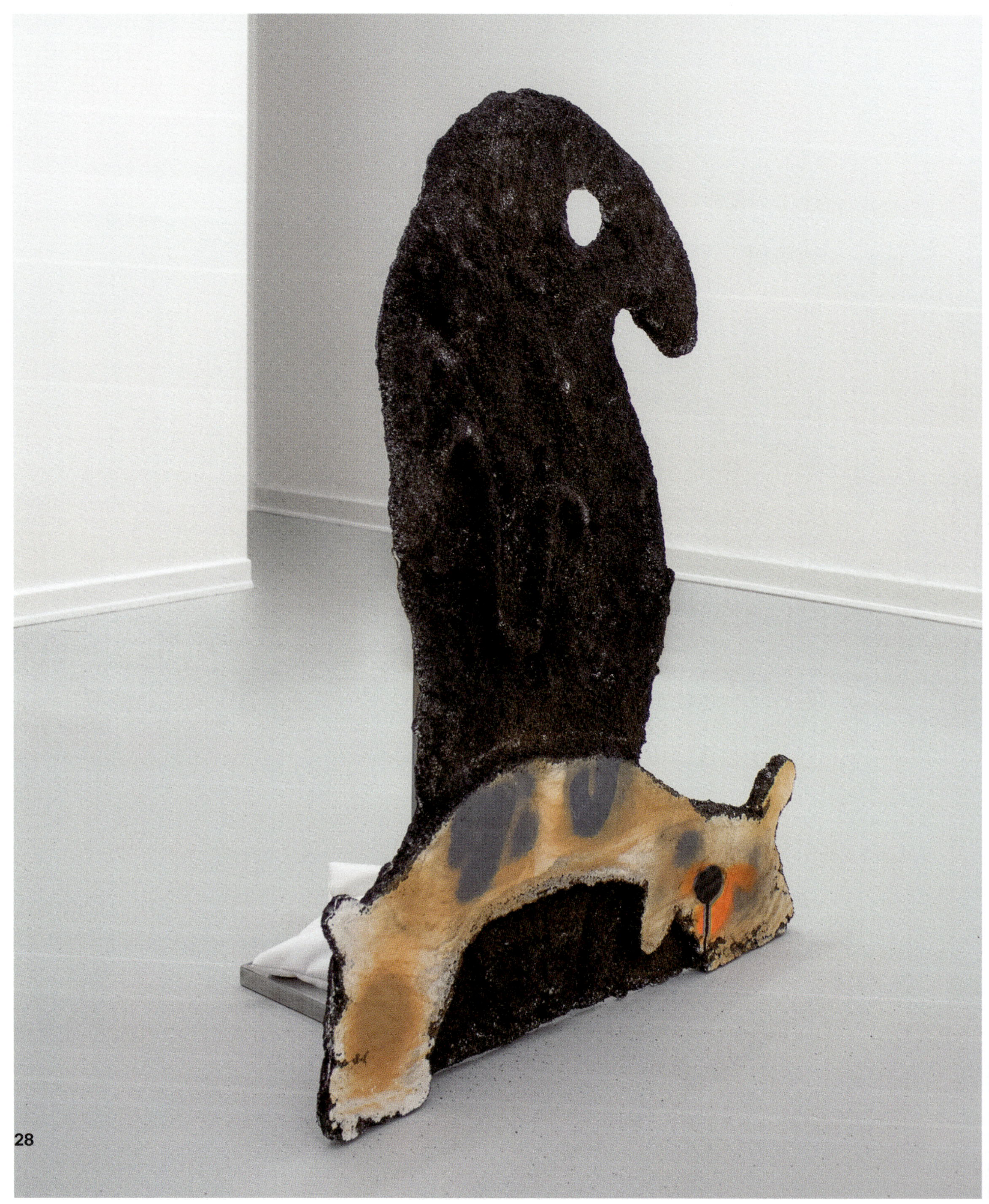

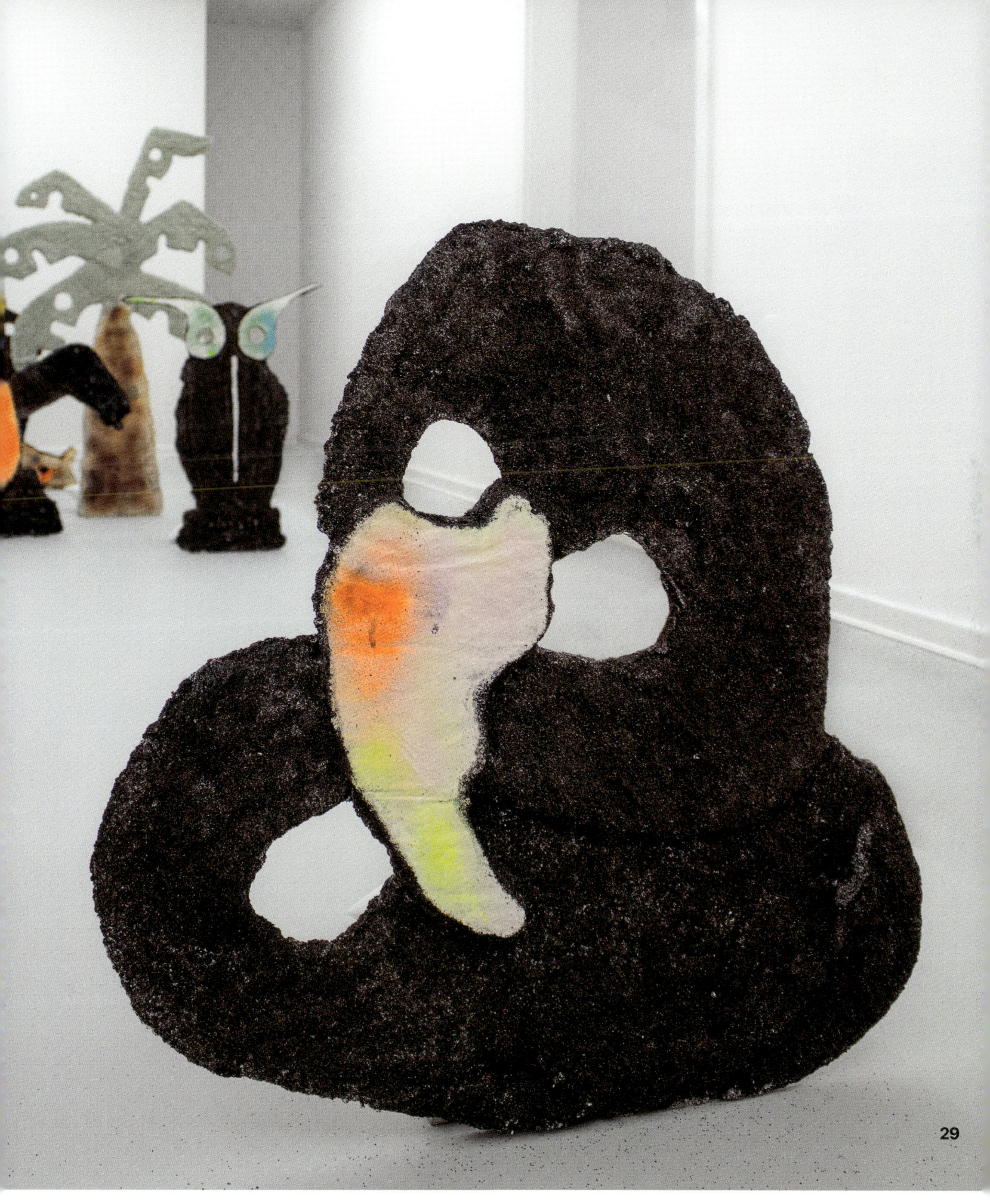

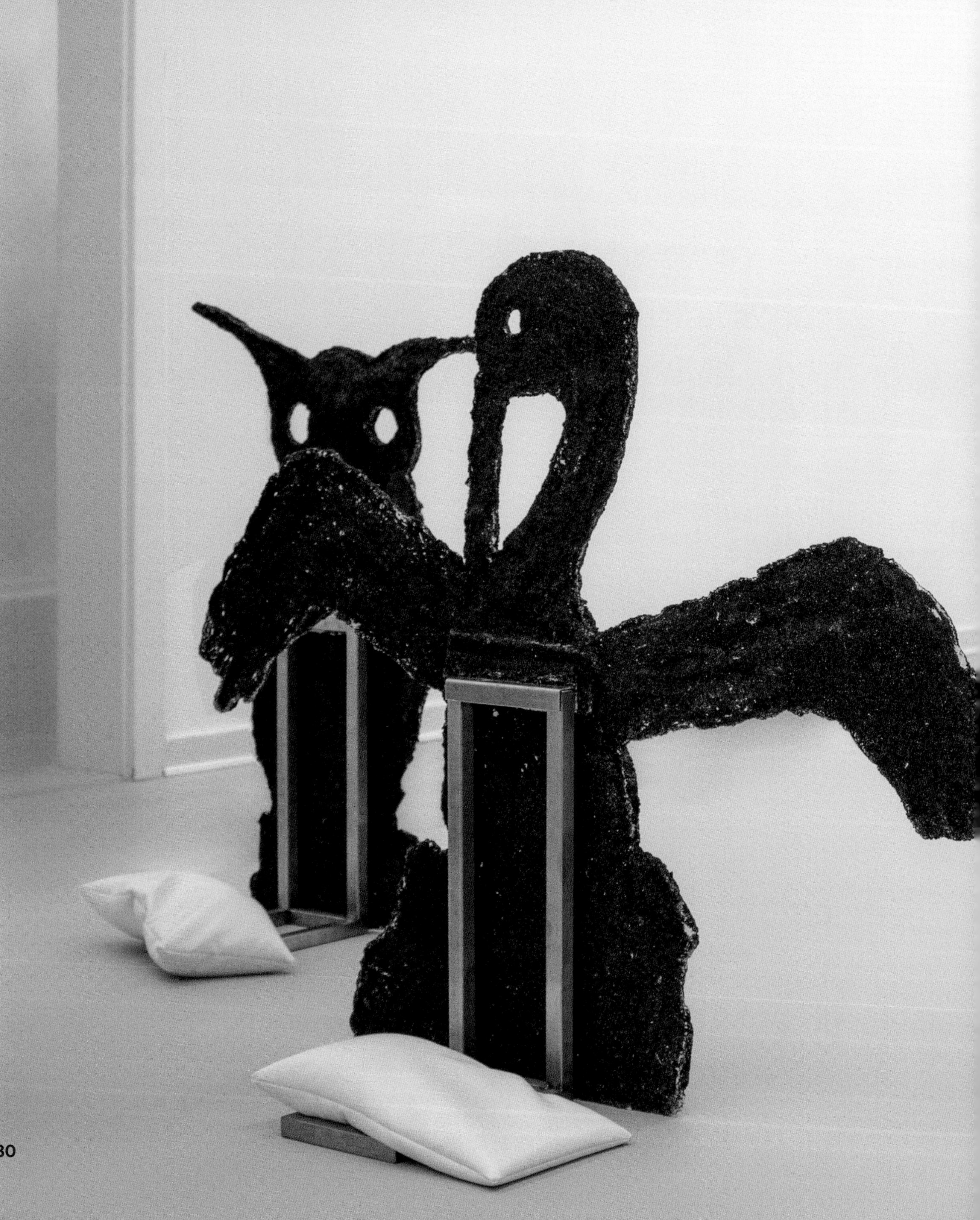

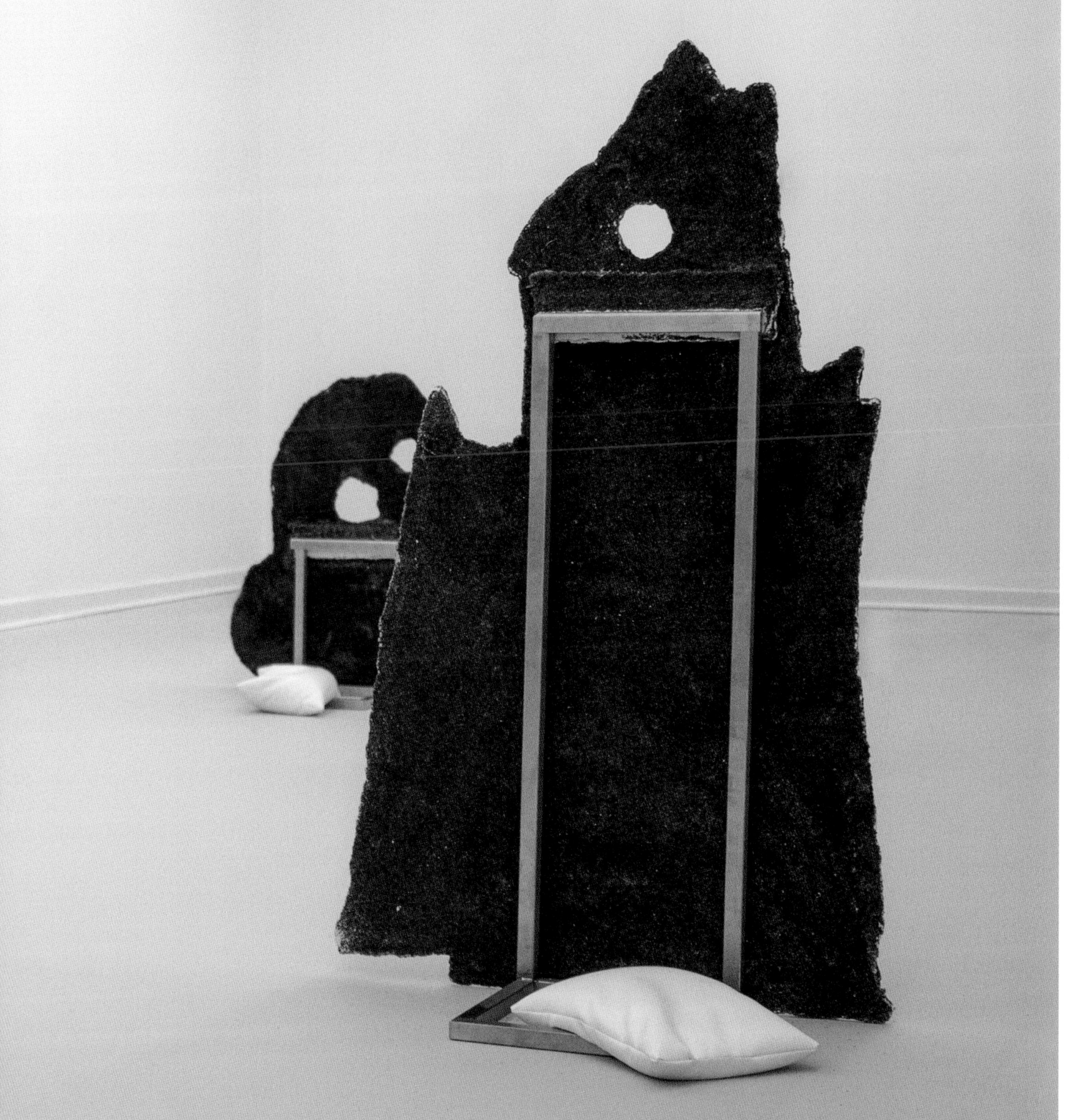

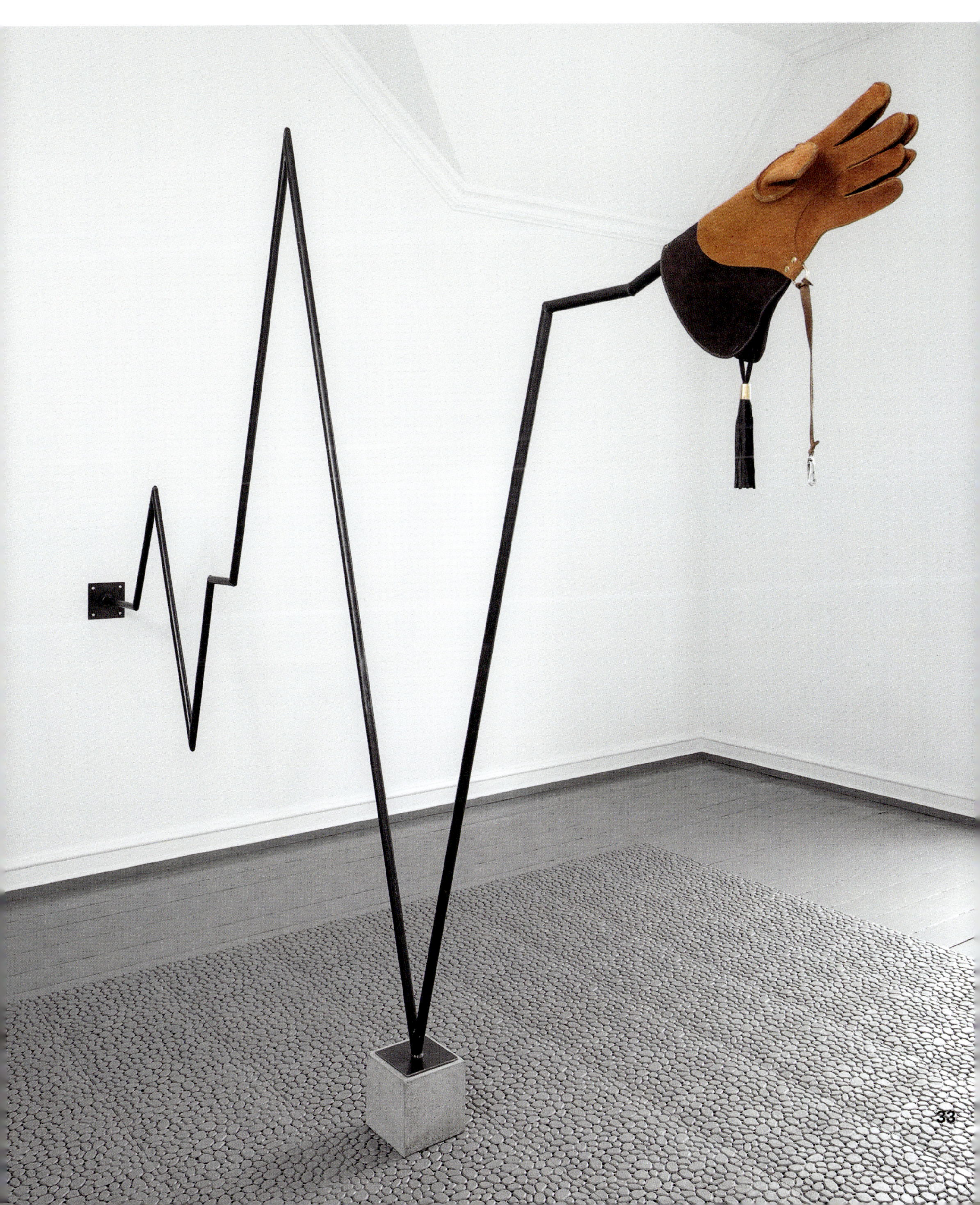

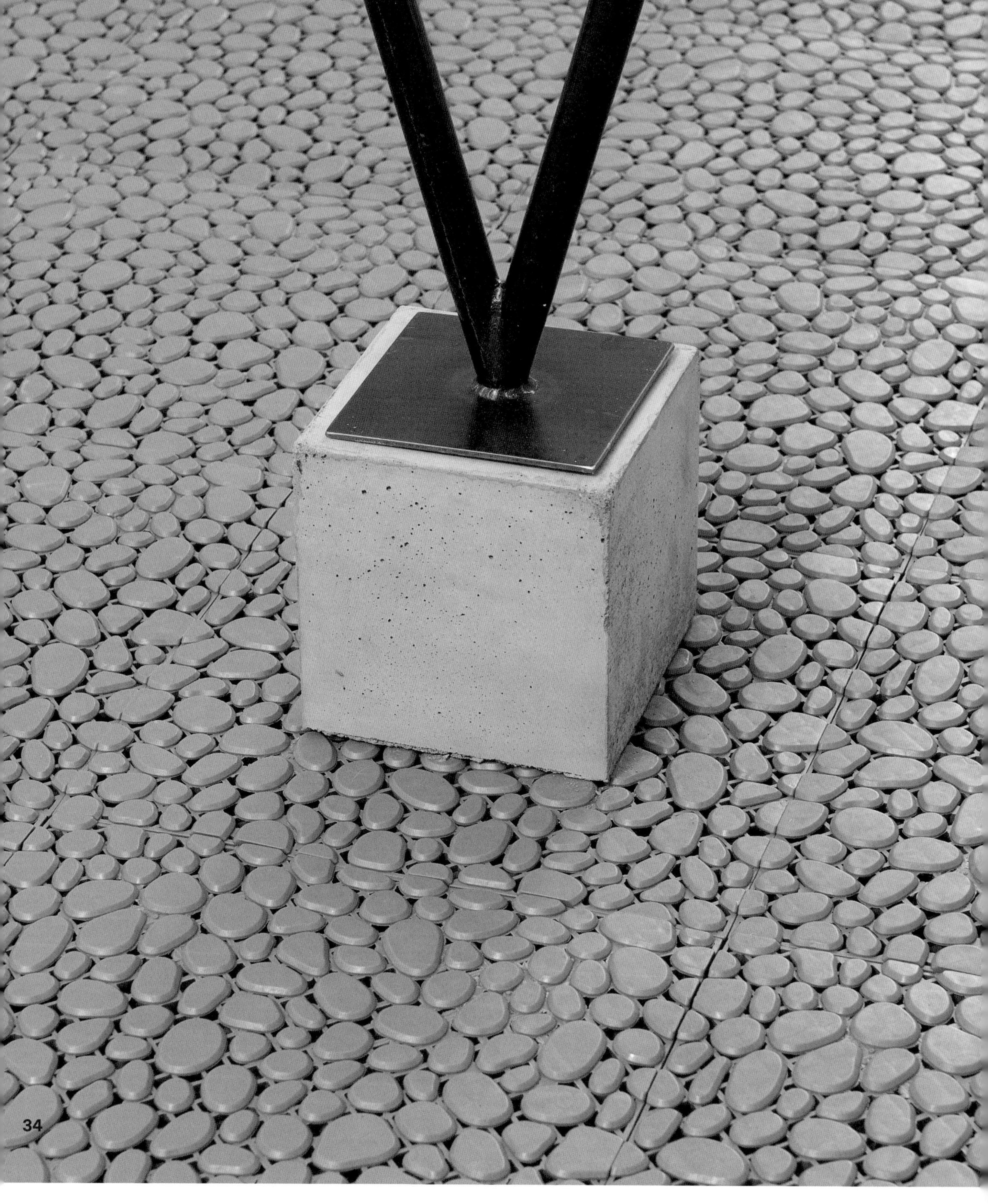

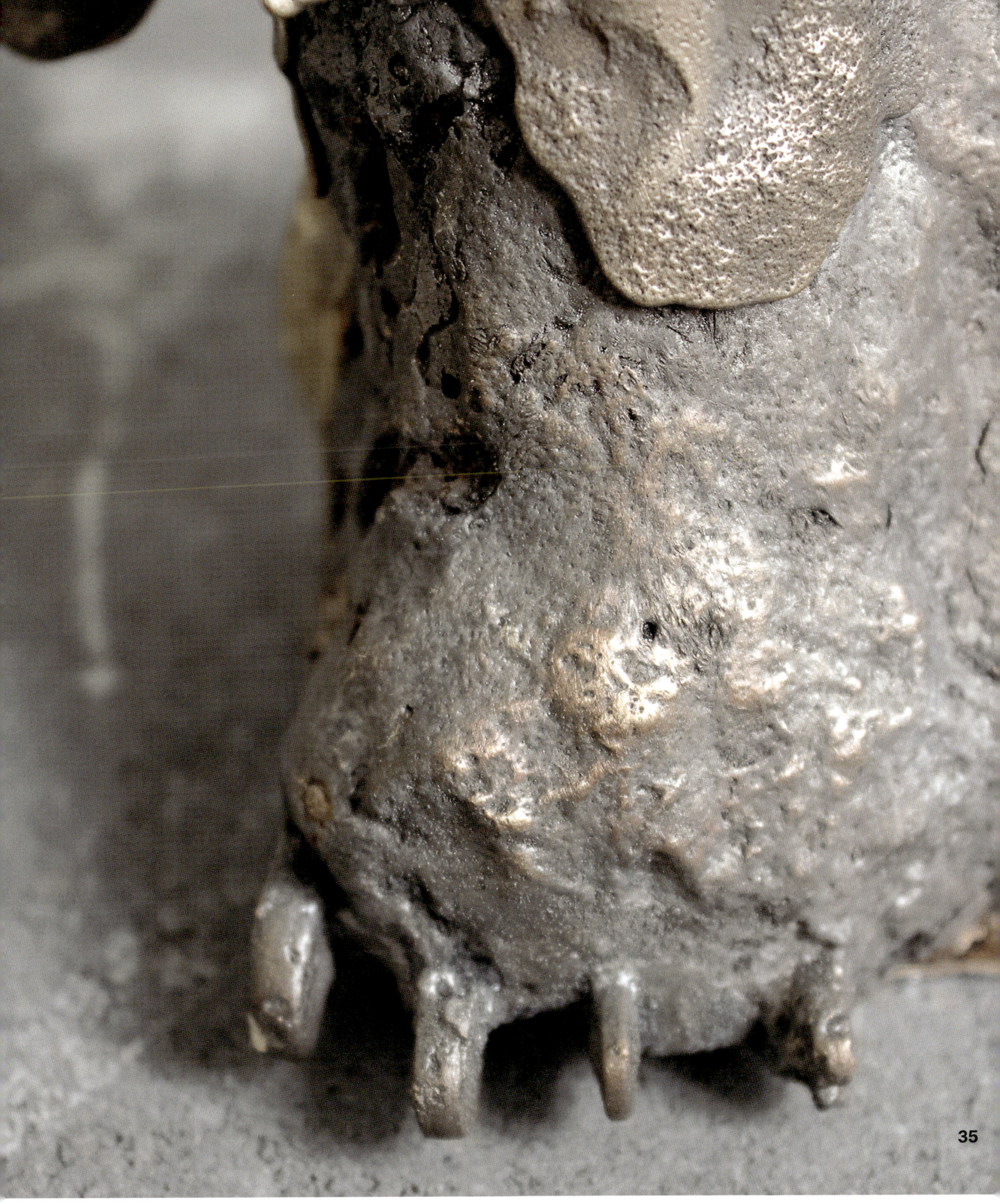

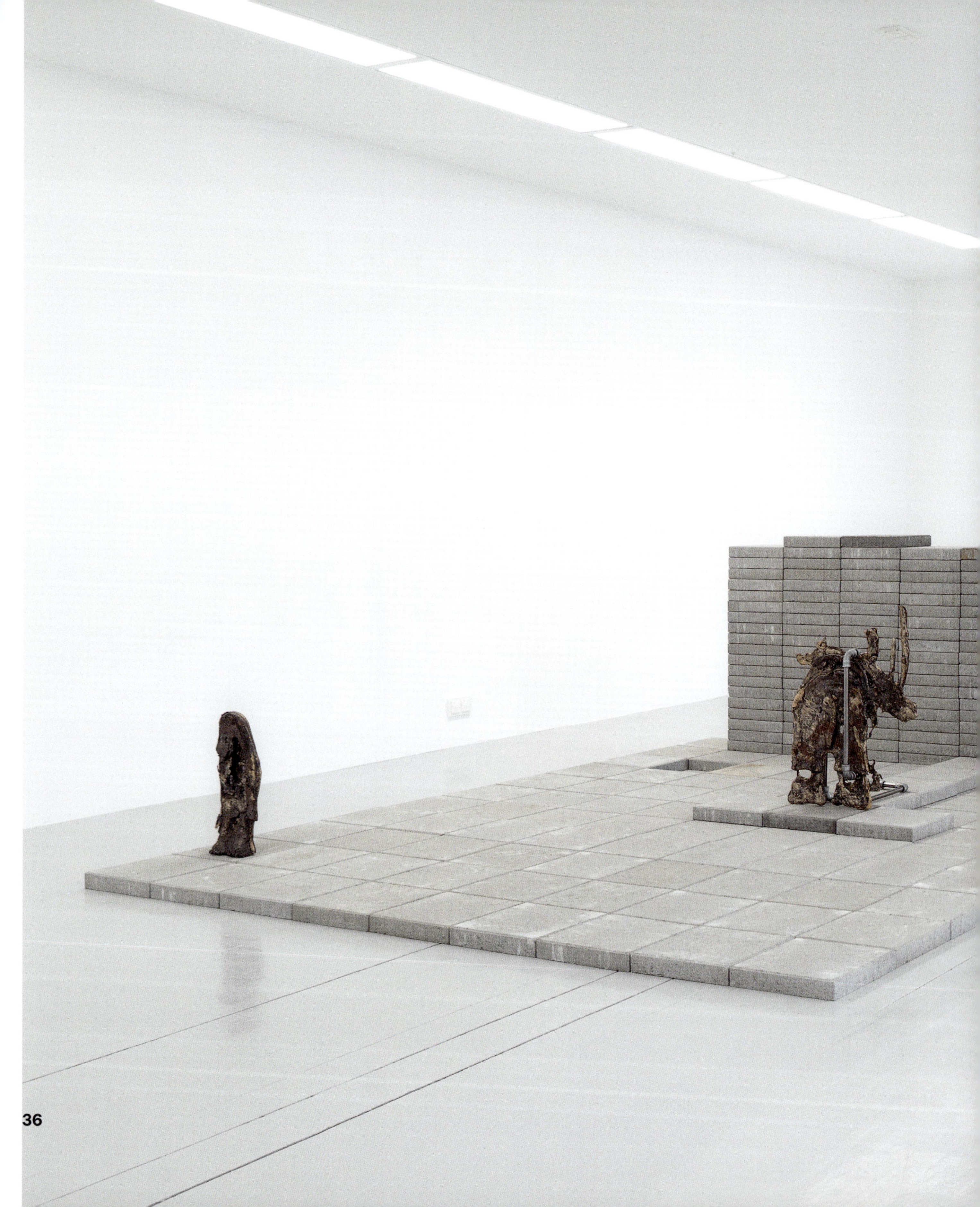

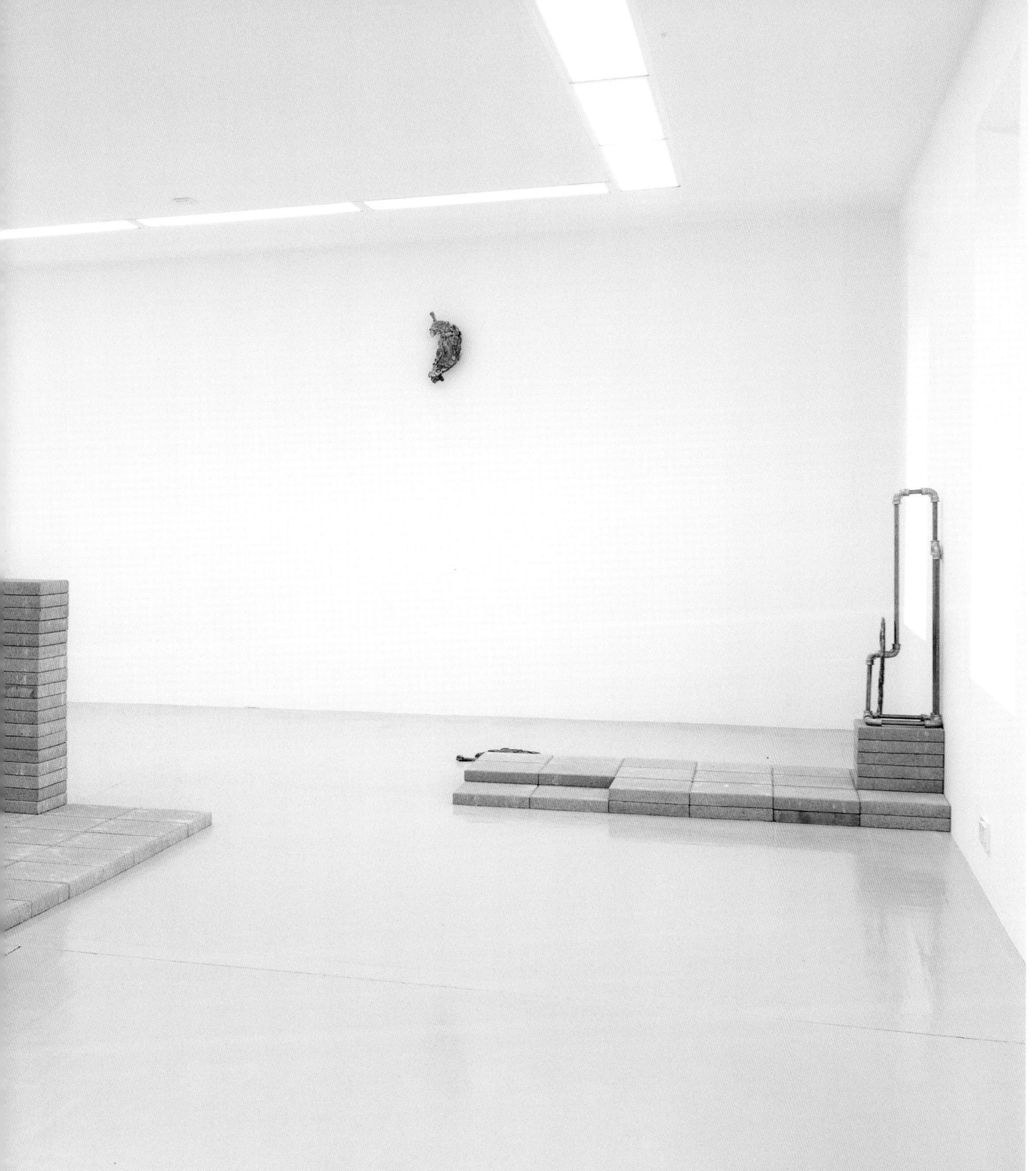

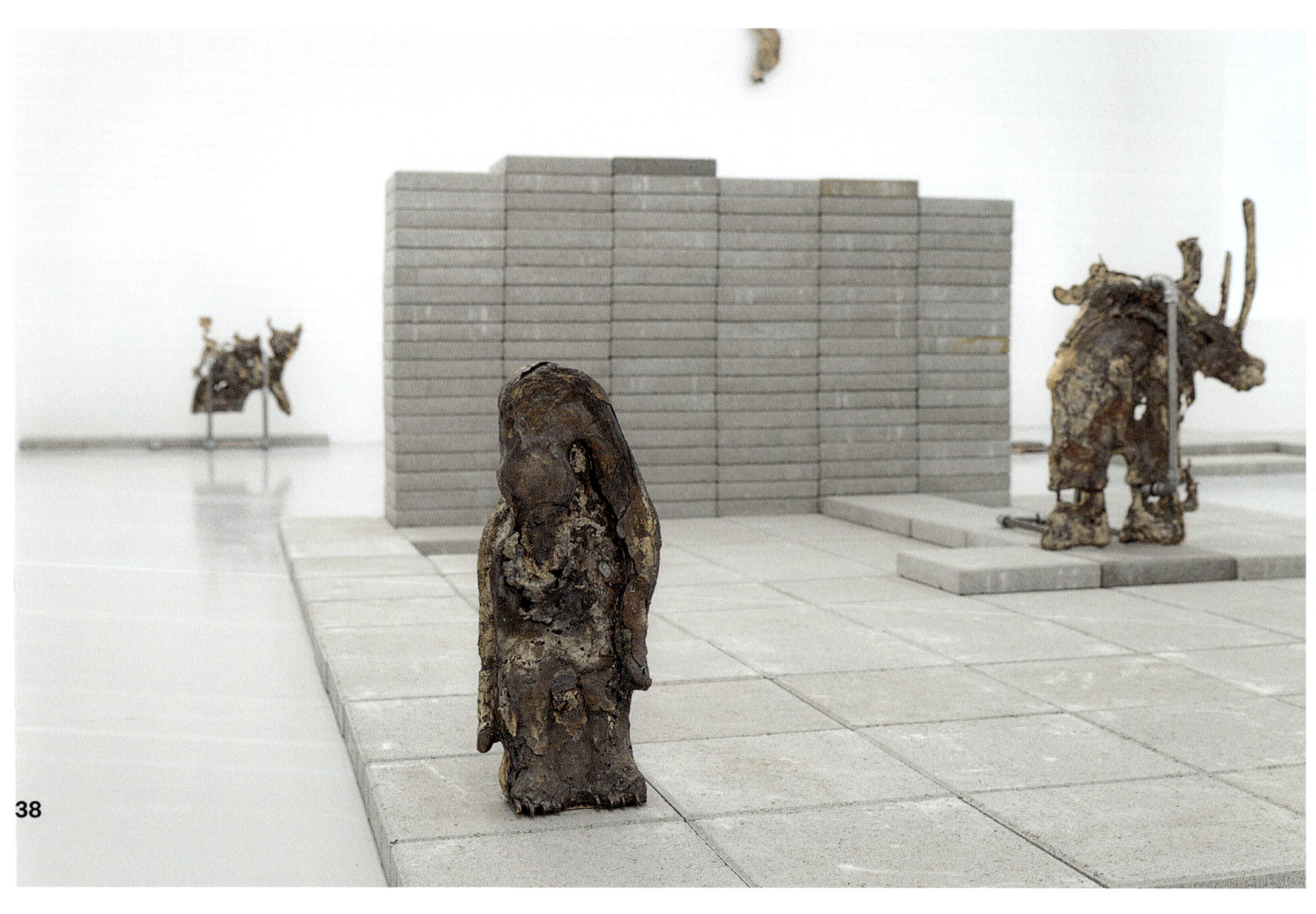

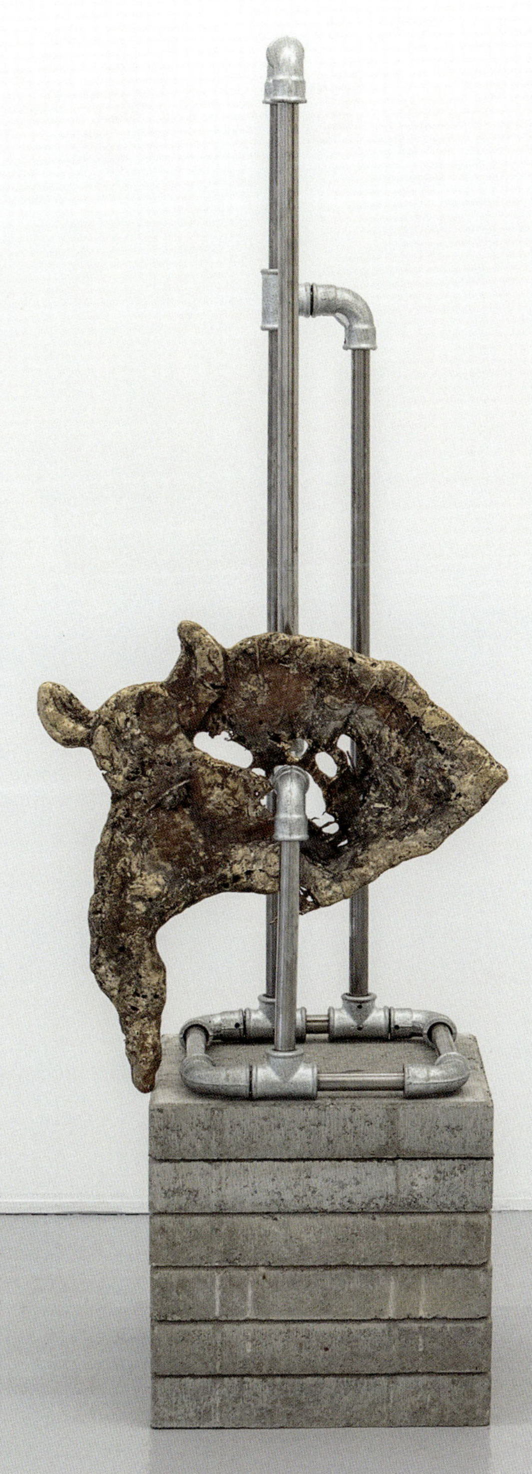

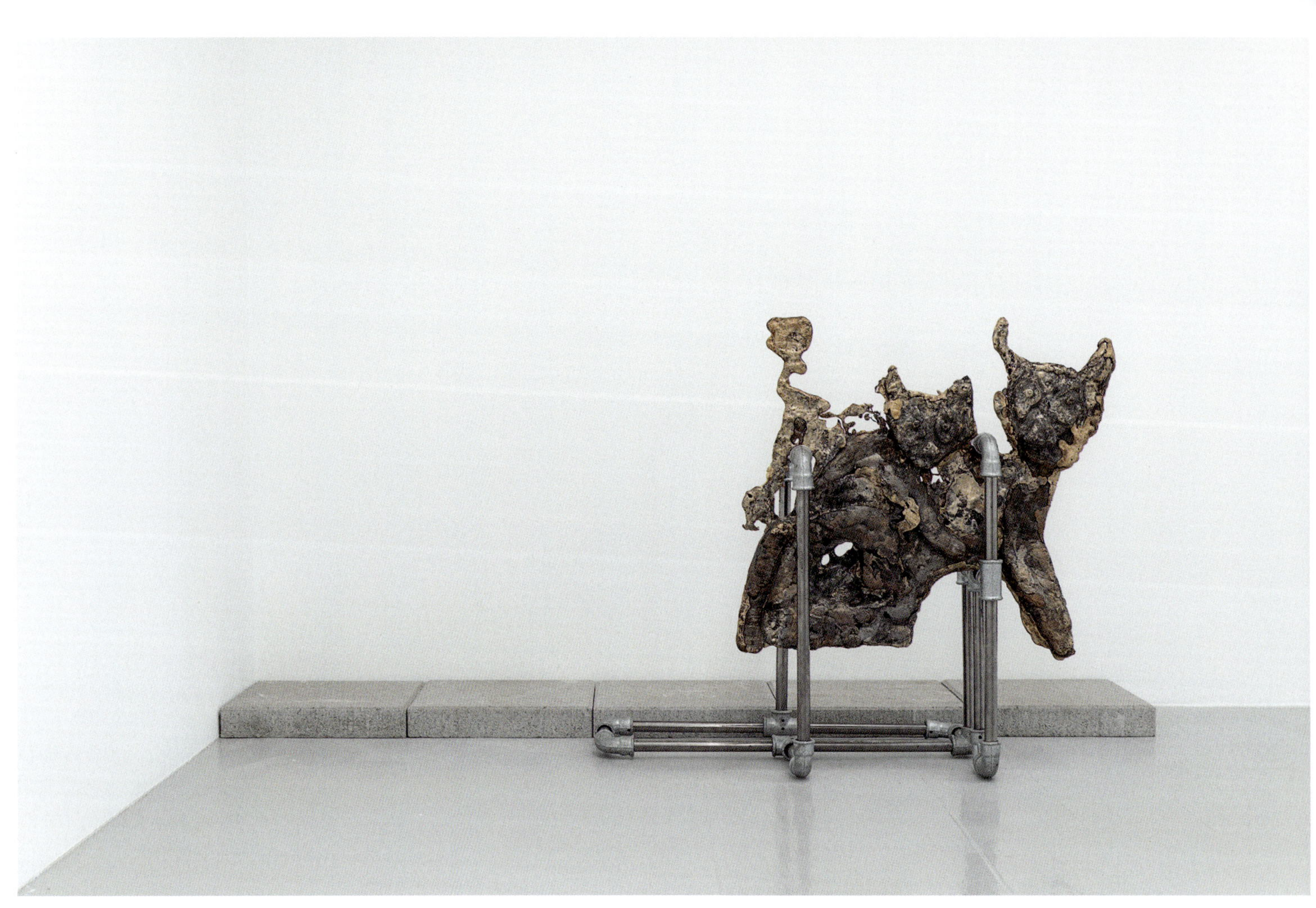

List of illustrations

FIGURE 1
Ushabti, an Egyptian funeral figurine. These figurines were placed in tombs among the grave goods and were intended to act as servants or minions for the deceased. They were called upon to do manual labor for the dead in their afterlife. This particular object depicts an Egyptian Ptolemaic sarcophagus of the prophet Ahmose, 332–30 BC.

FIGURE 2
Wilson, the volleyball, from *Cast Away*, 2000, starring Tom Hanks and directed by Robert Zemeckis.

FIGURE 3
A prop key used by Dave (Keir Dullea) to open HALs "brainroom," (Heuristically programmed ALgorithmic computer), shuts down HALs higher functions and seizes control of the ship in Stanley Kubrick's *2001: A Space Odyssey*, 1968.

FIGURE 4
One of the original prop darts from the Peruvian temple set, in the production of *Indiana Jones and the Raiders of the Lost Ark*, 1981, directed by Steven Spielberg. Used in the iconic opening sequence where we see Indiana Jones (Harrison Ford) retrieve the golden idol.

FIGURE 5
A bronze head unearthed from the seabed near Porticello, at the narrowest point of the Strait of Messina. Based on its wreckage archaeologists believe the ship sank in the fourth century BC. The two bronze heads that were found were most likely violently detached from the rest of the statues during one of the many wars between Sicilian towns (i.e., between Segesta and Selinunte) and afterwards they were shipped to be sold as scrap material. The two heads were found in 1969.

Lene: Maybe I can start by showing you how I make the sculptures. So ... I have this box here filled with earth and I dig out the forms for the pieces. Then I pour concrete into the negative space in the earth, and drip pigment directly onto the fresh concrete. After that, I cover it all with earth and let it dry for one or two days before I can dig out the sculpture and see what it looks like. I am the creator of the objects, but also its archaeologist. I can excavate the past, but also affect and change it, and make it as moldable as the future.

Jan: But there is quite a bit of waiting involved, no? What do you do in the meantime while the piece dries?

Lene: Well, there are always things to do. I can only make one sculpture per day. And preparations take time. I usually draw and draw until I find the right form. Then I start digging. It can be really hard to find the right forms, because I don't want it to have too many associations connected to it. I want them to be new forms.

Jan: New forms that still somehow might look like relics from an ancient civilization that we have not yet come in contact with ...

Lene: Yes, you sense there is some kind of reason why they were made, but you cannot really figure it out.

Jan: And these forms are buried and unburied, like relics lost and forgotten, then rediscovered. That is one aspect. But you say that for you there is something about them that allows you to create a different future.

Lene: Yes, I have the power to change the future or change the past.

Jan: So they would be museum attractions for a future civilization?

Lene: That is still to be discovered. No, seriously. I think what got the process of working on *Dear Darkling* started was an experience I had at the Neues Museum in Berlin. I found this ushabti figurine in their collection of Egyptian artifacts. The ancient Egyptians made such an effort in preparing for their afterlife. They believed the ushabti figurine would take care of manual labor in their afterlife. I find the idea of giving a sculpture a concrete task really fascinating. To put your worries in a thing and let the thing take care of it.

FIGURE 1

Jan: So the figurine is a workforce that takes care of future needs?

Lene: By virtue of their belief, yes. Their belief makes it true and somehow this is contagious. The tomb was their afterlife, so everything they placed there would acquire a particular power when the deceased were buried. They did not make art for people to see, but to make sure their afterlife would be as good as possible. I like the idea of entering an Egyptian tomb today not knowing the exact purpose of all the figurines, symbols, and paintings. You sense their importance, but at the same time you're entering a secret world you can't fully grasp. You feel the presence, but you can't decode the details. I think this is similar to what I want to create with *Dear Darkling*—to make you feel the presence of something powerful that you don't quite understand.

Jan: True! That strange sense of a mysterious power being present is totally tangible here in the studio, although, or precisely because, you don't quite grasp what your sculptures signify. So technically, by the same token, the only people who are meant to see this work would be the buried in their afterlife, not us. So, in entering the tomb, we walk in on somebody else's afterlife.

Lene: That's a nice idea.

Jan: Yes, but if the future your sculptures are working for is an unknown culture's afterlife, we should be excluded from it, no? By walking in on it, I am trespassing and I commit sacrilege. These sculptures own the place. They live here, not me.

Lene: I spend a lot of time alone in the studio with the sculptures. So at times they indeed come to life. It's like in the movie *Cast Away* with Tom Hanks. Have you seen it?

Jan: Yeah, I was just thinking of that one. What was the ball's name again?

Lene: I think it was Wilson.

Jan: I wonder what the sculptures do at night, when you are no longer in the studio?

Lene: Me too.

Jan: So now that we are sitting here facing the sculptures, are we looking at them or are they looking at us? Perhaps the fetish never lost its magic. It is there anyway. It is something that we relate to. We address art objects like people, and we talk to them. And when you live with an artwork, it watches over you. These ones here seem especially alive in a weird way. I once stayed in Armenia for a couple of weeks. My hosts took me to these very, very old Christian churches. It was the early Christians who escaped to Armenia and built their churches into mountainsides and caves. Down there in the dark you could see all kinds of strange symbols, really with a similar power

FIGURE 2

and presence as your work here. It made you feel like, Oh my god, my religion started off as a totally clandestine cult. Everything was from a time before the official language of symbols was established. I don't even remember seeing crosses, but a lot of strange animal symbols instead, doves and wolfs. And the acoustics in the caves were incredible. Our guide was singing these early chorales and each note had incredible sustain. It was there forever. It was so physical. Like the cave was one big lung out which the singing came.

Lene: Like sound waves hitting the body so it actually becomes a physical feeling.

Jan: Apparently, the choir used to even be in another cave, connected to the cave where the community assembled only via a hole in the ceiling. So you wouldn't see the singers but only hear the voices, filling the space, creating a strange presence in the dark. Dear Darkling ...

Lene: What I like about the word is that it is a mix of darkness and darling. Darkling refers to a growing dark or something characterized by darkness. And it can also refer to a creature that lives in the dark. I also think about this platform as an altar. So the sculptures are reaching out for something but they don't know what is. Does that make sense?

Jan: Yeah, it does. Talking to the creatures in the dark.

Lene: The other day I watched the *2001: A Space Odyssey*. There is this scene where David Bowman decides to let go of Frank Poole in order to get back into the spaceship and Poole just drifts really slowly away into space. We don't know if he is dead or not. I cannot imagine anything more frightening than floating away into the black encompassing universe. Gravity is great! I like being grounded on earth. Life on earth is fucked up in many ways, but at least you know where you are.

FIGURE 3

Jan: So much for being saved, yeah? Gravity saves us. It is the reason why people get buried.

Lene: Yeah. I think I want to be cremated actually.

Jan: I was thinking about that the other day .... Gravity saves us. And darkness sets us adrift. There is this fantastic text about mimetism by Roger Callois in which he talks about the pull of darkness as a force that makes you want to give in to the seduction of space.

Lene: Do you mean the space or darkness inside the mind? It is also dark inside the body.

Jan: Well, Callois at least literally speaks about the darkness of the night. He says that darkness permeates the body, it goes through your skin. And when an animal, like an insect, gives in to this pull of the dark, and surrenders to the seduction of space, it undergoes metamorphosis and takes on the shape of things in its environment, like these mimicry insects that look like the leaves they sit on. They have drifted over into the darkness of the things that surround them. Dear Darkling ...

Lene: Dear Darkling. I also used a title many years ago, called *Erasing Darkness*. I always feel like I am fumbling in the dark when I work. I sort of start blindfolded and leap into it.

Jan: You start the life of the sculpture by burying it first. You surrender it to the elements. There is something interesting about the pieces because of that, in that they don't necessarily point back to the artist, like *you* owned them. They are all we have of *their* civilization. They have an independent existence. It seems like you surrendered them to their own existence. Does that make sense?

Lene: Yes, it makes sense. In the process of making, I cannot fully control the outcome. I decide the negative form. They have the last word.

Jan: And then they are on their own. And they are actually pretty amazing in what they are. Very present. Very particular. You were saying that you think of them as projecting particular shapes into the future. So they are not random at all.

Lene: No. I spend a lot of time sketching. And when I feel the form holds something interesting, I go for it. Talking about science fiction movies, I often get inspired by the scenography. It is interesting to think in future forms.

(Walking around the sculptures)

Jan: They have a strange body, no? They do not necessarily have volume but they are not two-dimensional either.

Lene: They are somewhere in between.

Jan: They look like they could be part of an architecture, but definitely not one made of planes and surfaces.

Lene: They are like stones, more or less. Nature. They are strange forms that could have appeared naturally in mountains or rocks.

Jan: They are in between building and growing, inside a cave or hidden chamber that we are breaking into. Like some other civilization's afterlife where we shouldn't be. If this was Indiana

Jones or Tomb Raider I am pretty sure, some spikes would jut from the ceiling or arrows shoot from the walls, right now ...

Lene: The room where *Dear Darkling* is going to be exhibited at UKS has a strange resemblance to some of the grave chambers: you enter a corridor first, and there are no windows and a low ceiling.

Jan: So are we expecting any spikes and arrows?

FIGURE 4

Lene: Well, hopefully not.

Jan: In Judaic mysticism there is a figure called Golem. As far as I understand it, it is a man made of earth. You bring him to life when you write his name onto his forehead. I think it is simply the power of the name. The name brings life to matter. So as long as the sculptures are not named yet, we have nothing to fear.

(Nervous laughter)

Jan: But since we are currently starring at these guys. What is this? Life other than we know it?

Lene: It is a difficult question. I have a feeling, when I look at them that they are alive in a strange sense, that they are resurrected, whatever that means. They came back from the earth.

Jan: The strangers that came back from the earth. The Messina Strait, between Sicily and the Italian mainland, is quite narrow and rocky. Apparently, a hell of a lot of ships went down there. A couple of years ago, ancient Greek statues were found on the bottom of the sea. They'd been down there in a shipwreck for, what, more than two thousand years or something. They are now in this strange local museum, somewhat out of place, but you look at them and think, Wow ... you came back from the sea.

FIGURE 5

Lene: You sense these things.

Jan: Totally. Of course, there is no way to prove that it is not just the story that does it to you.

Lene: When someone tells you that kind of story, it is contagious.

Jan: But still, it is a material fact, you cannot deny that these objects have been surrendered to the sea and now the sea has given them back to you. So you feel like talking to them, "You guys have come back from the abyss of the sea!" Like with these ones. The earth has given them back to you. Hello, welcome back! But what is all this dust and hair sticking to the sculptures?

Lene: It's part of the earth. I use potting soil, it is the easiest one to mold. You should actually also water the concrete when it's covered.

Jan: That would really make it part of the life circle, no?

Lene: Life, love, death, and all that crap.

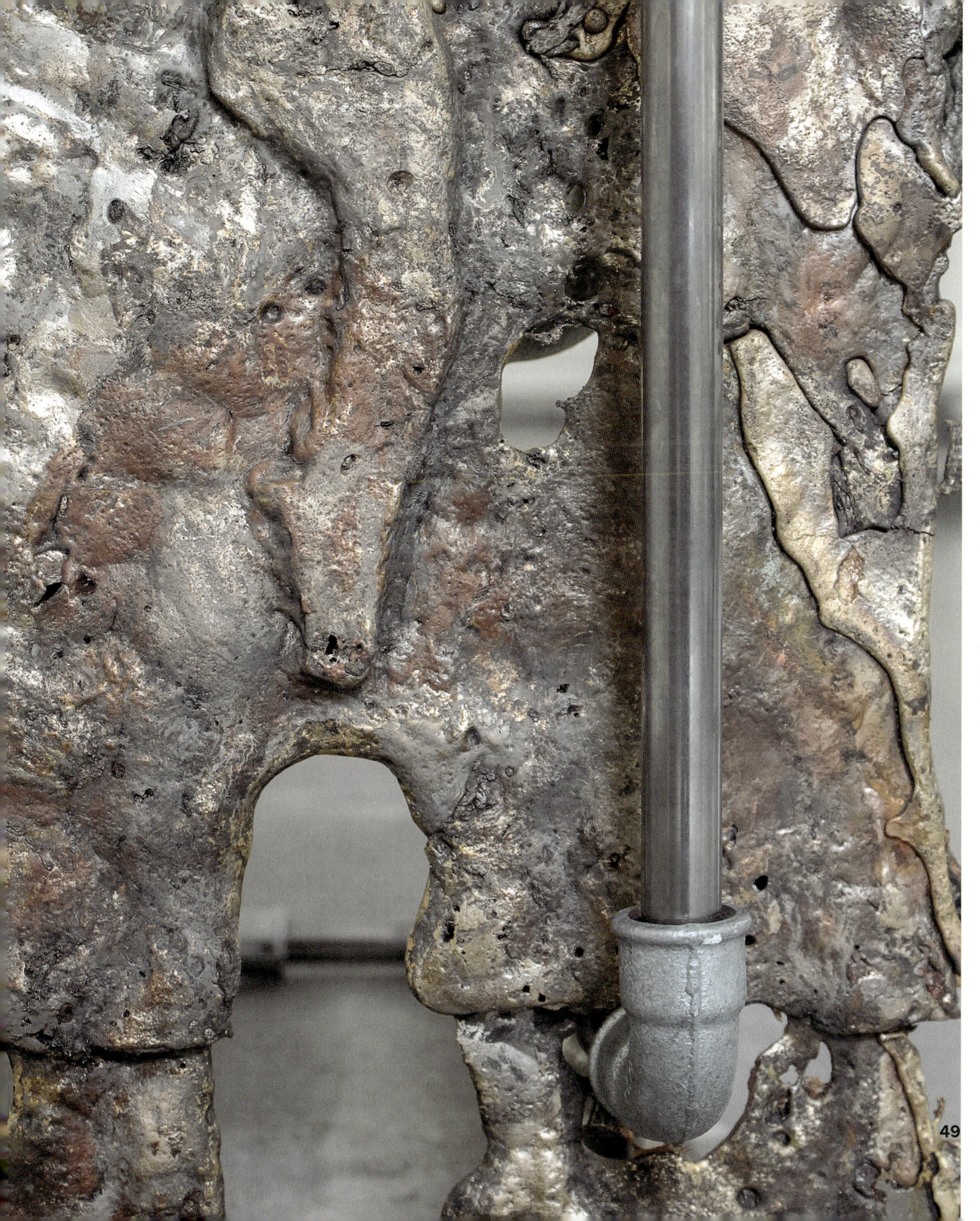

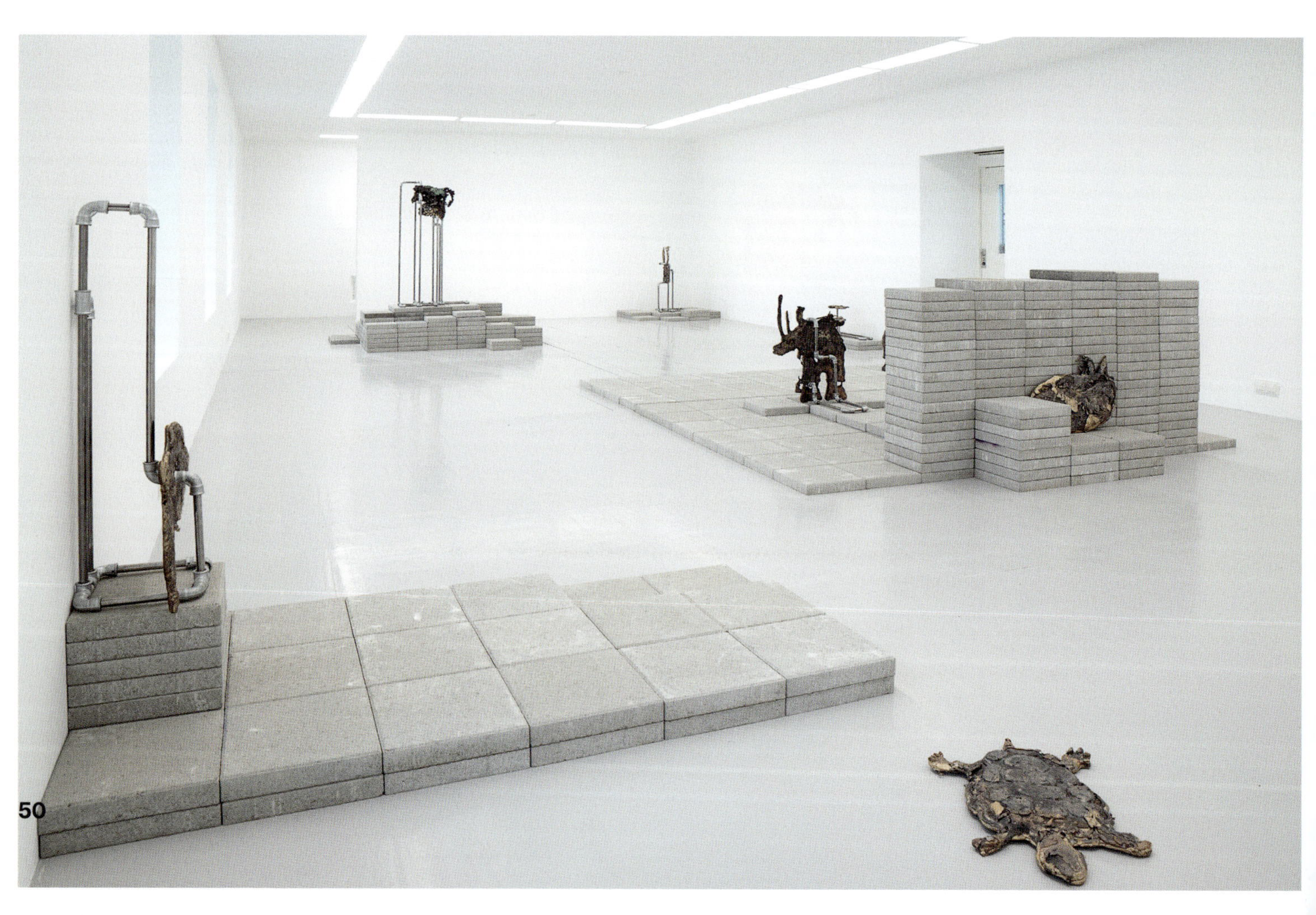

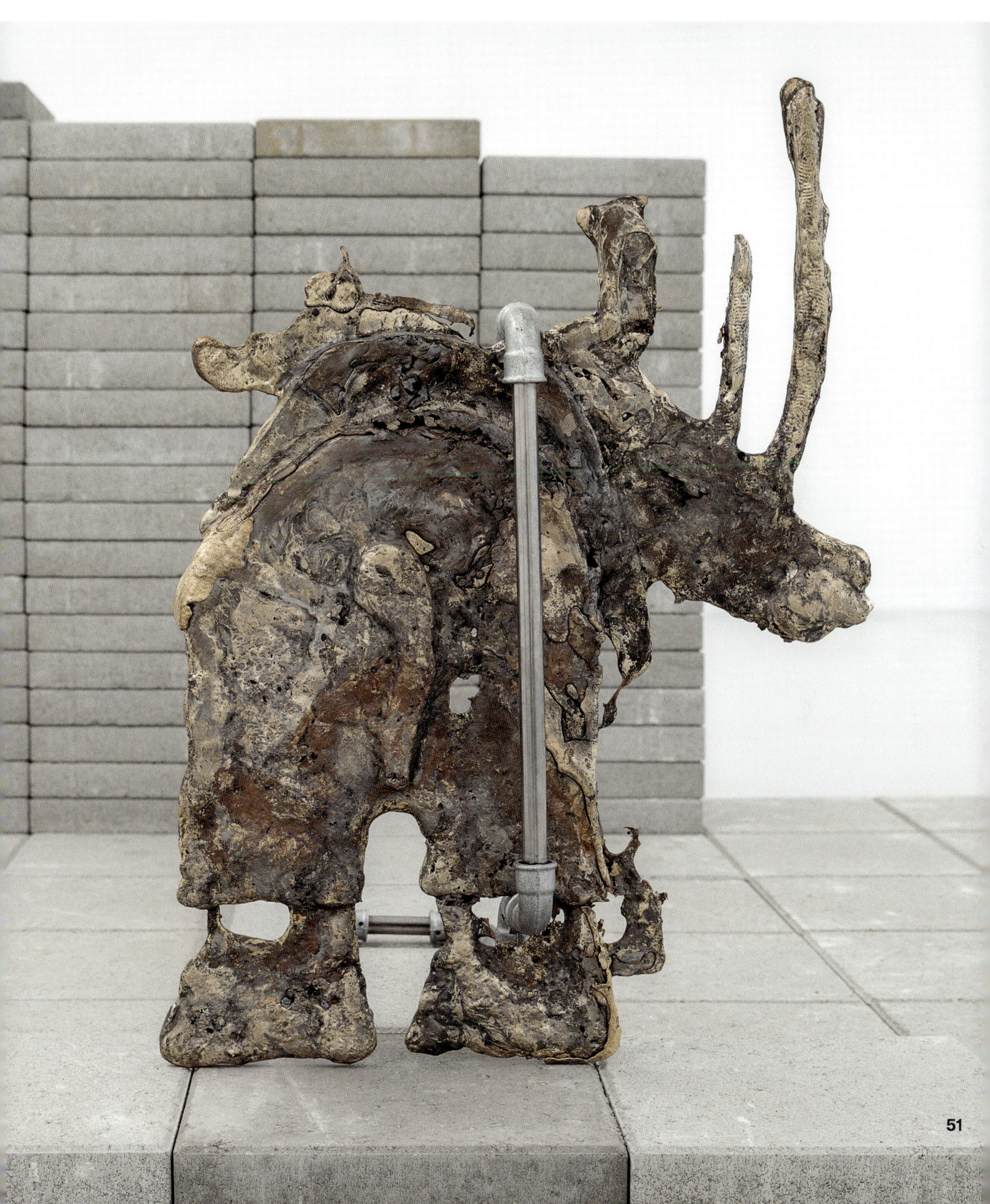

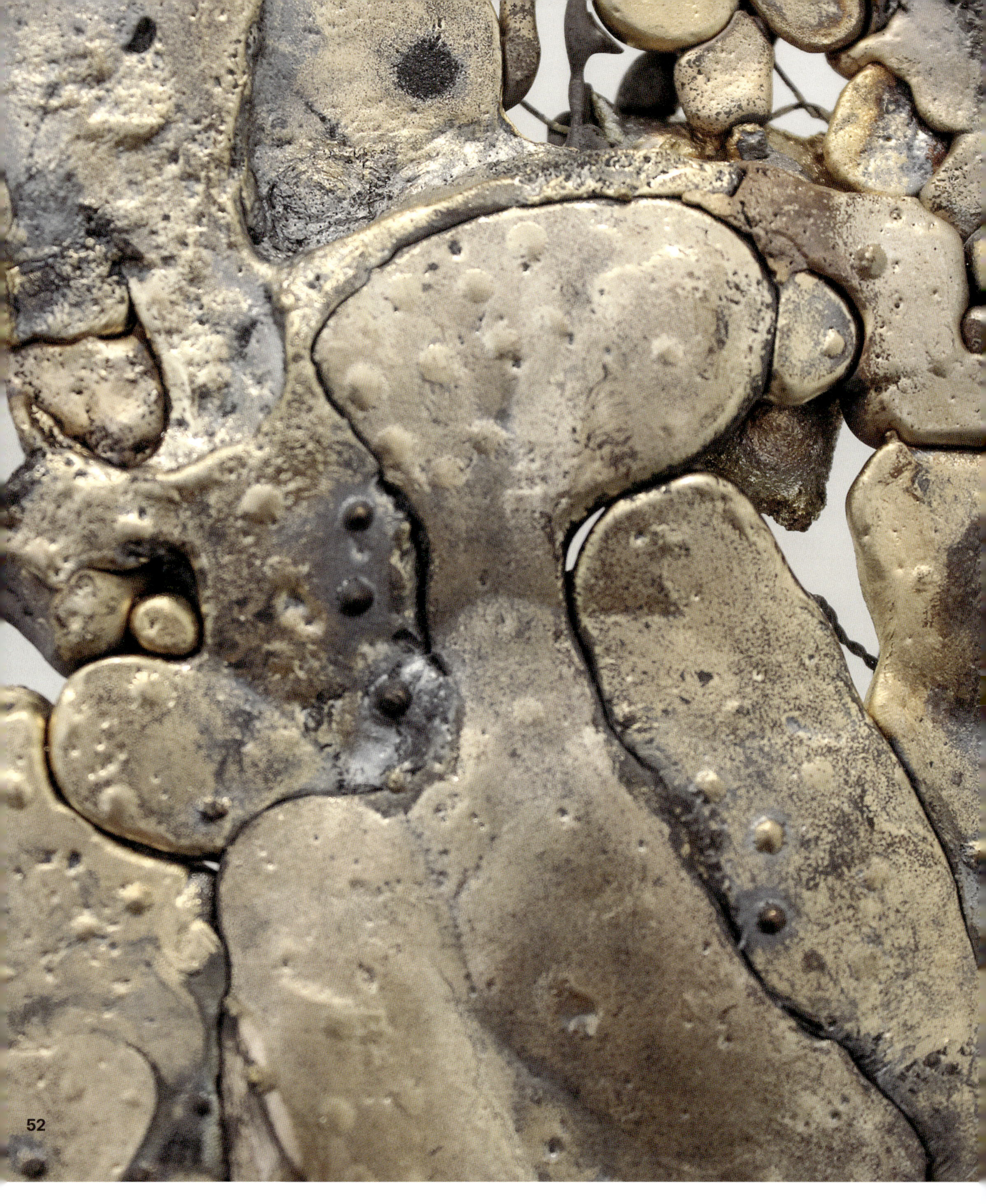

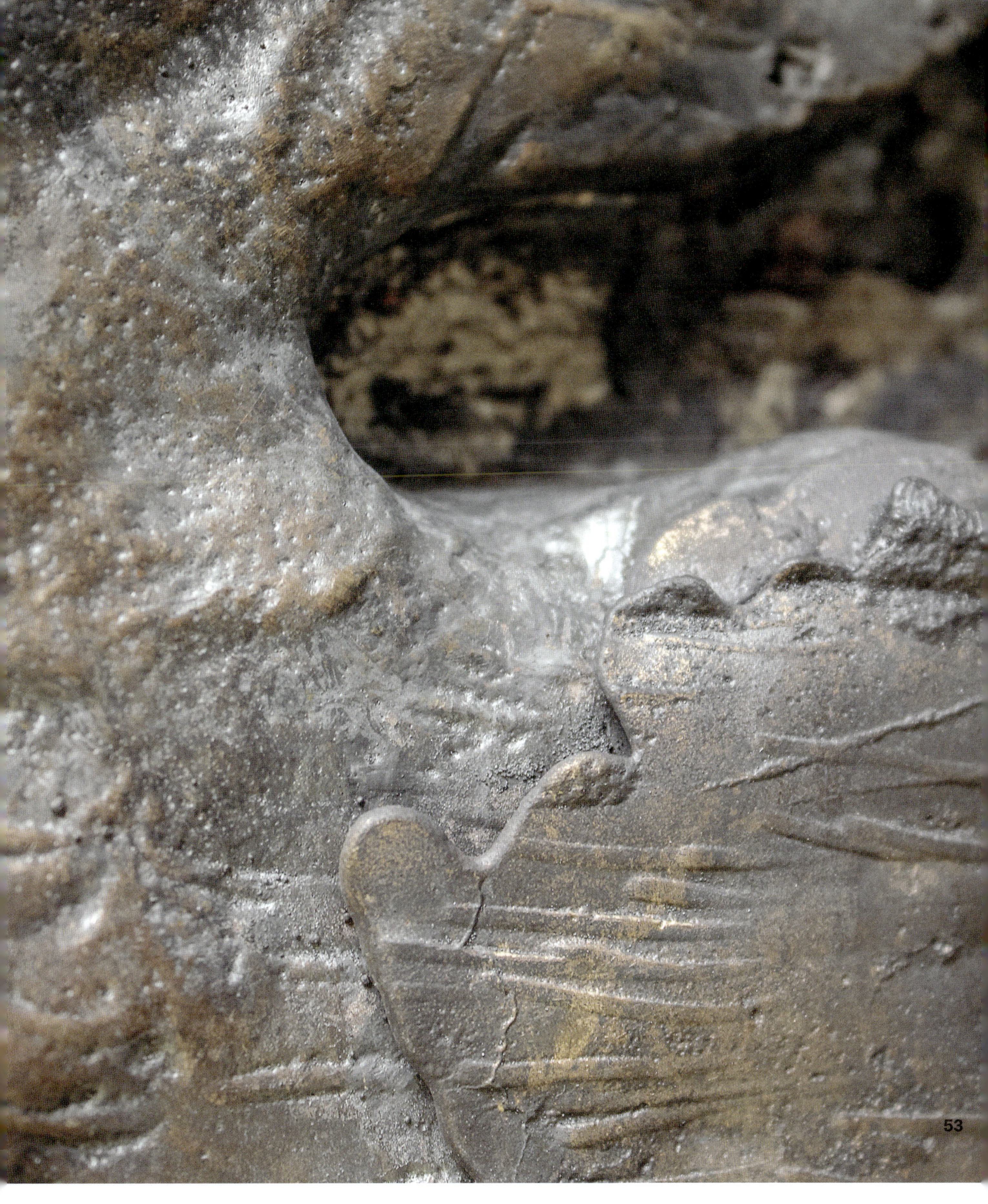

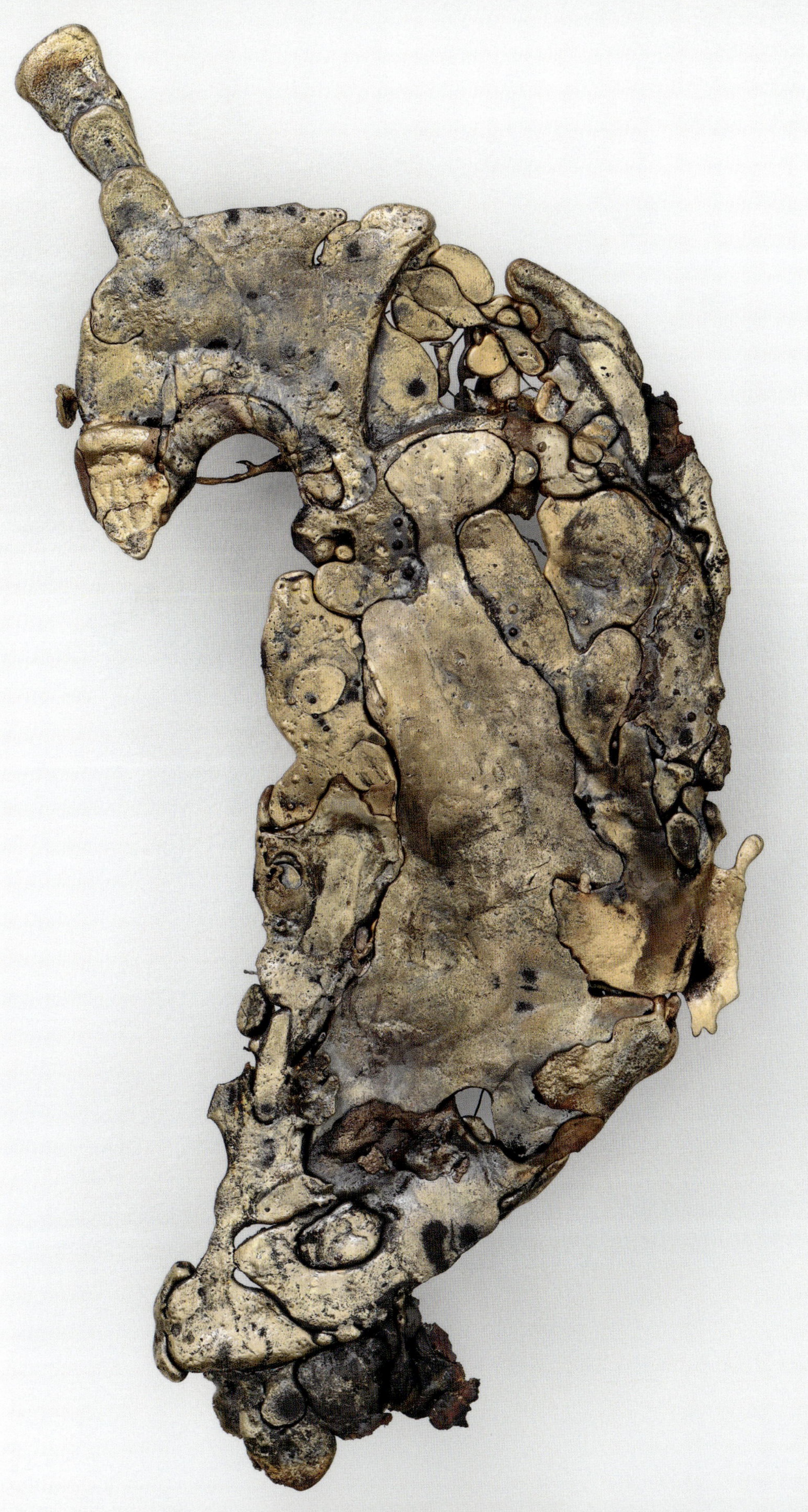

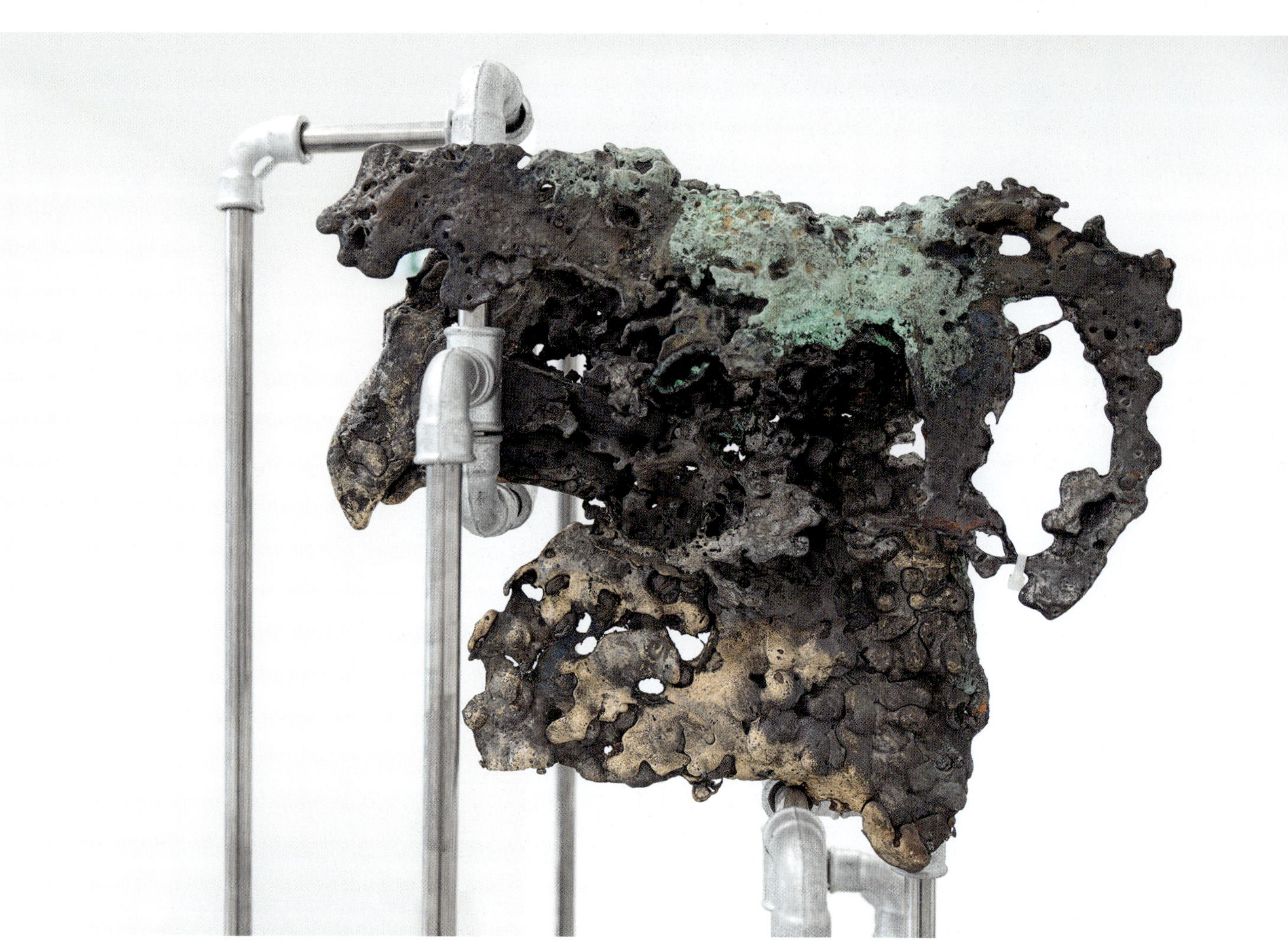

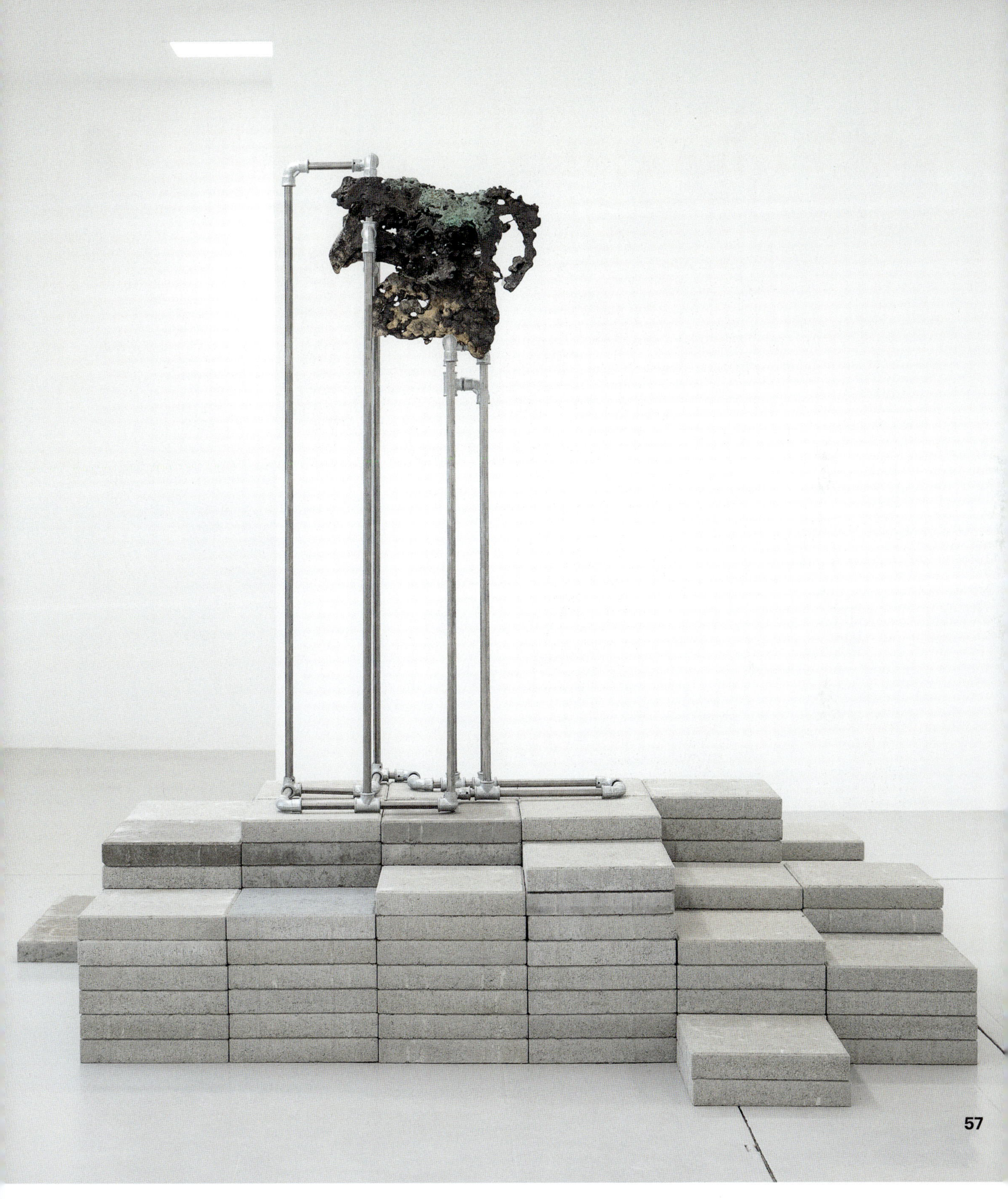

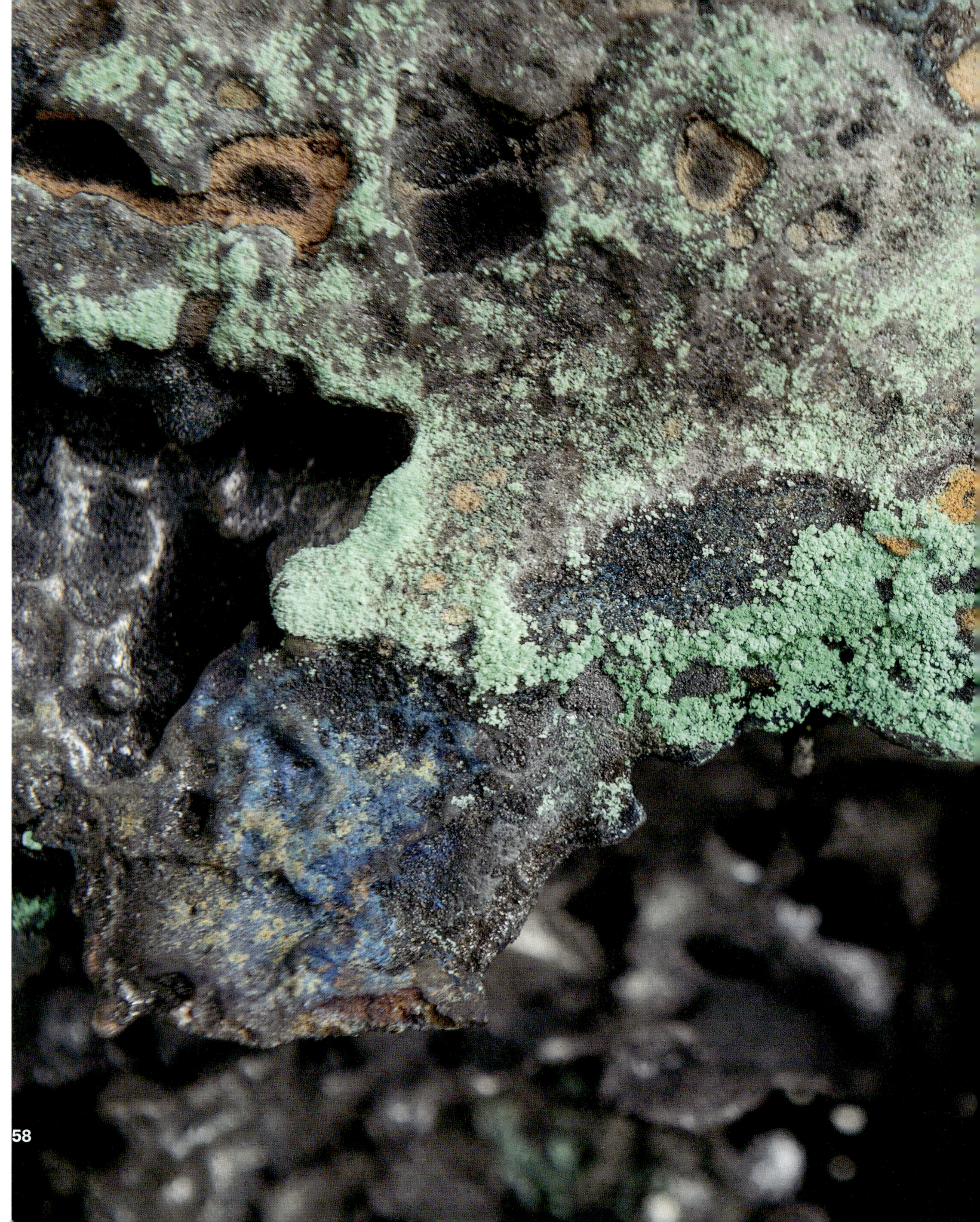

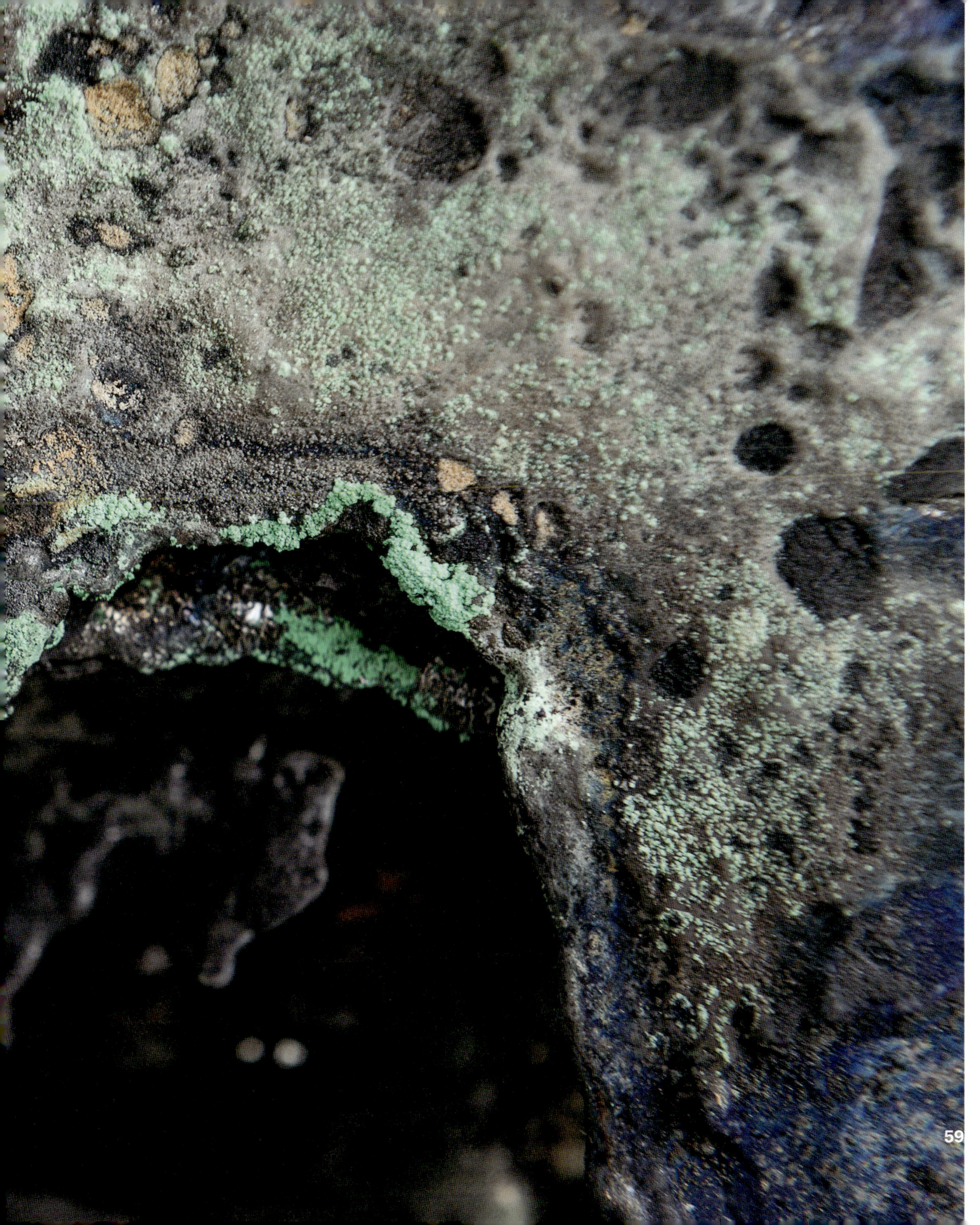

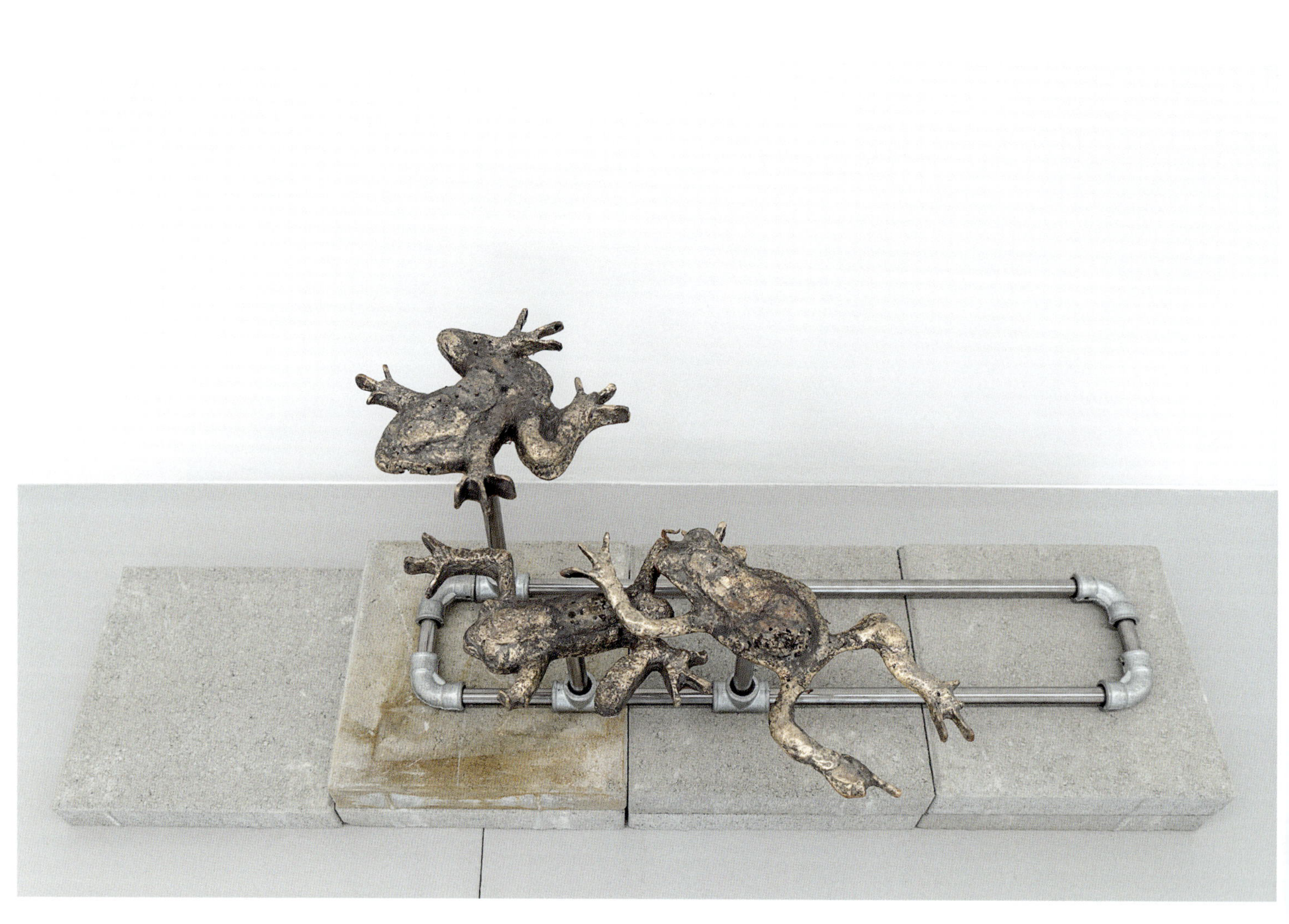

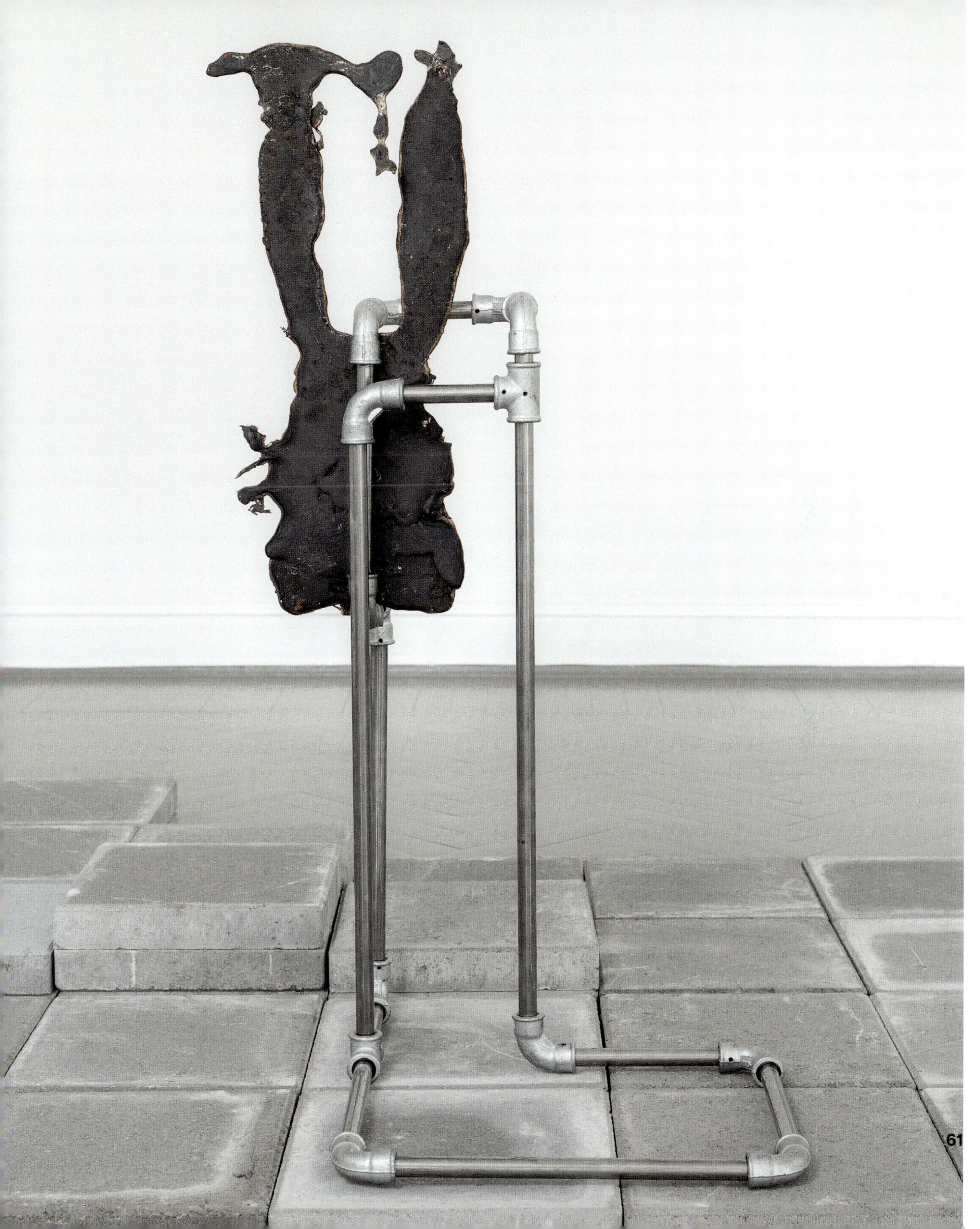

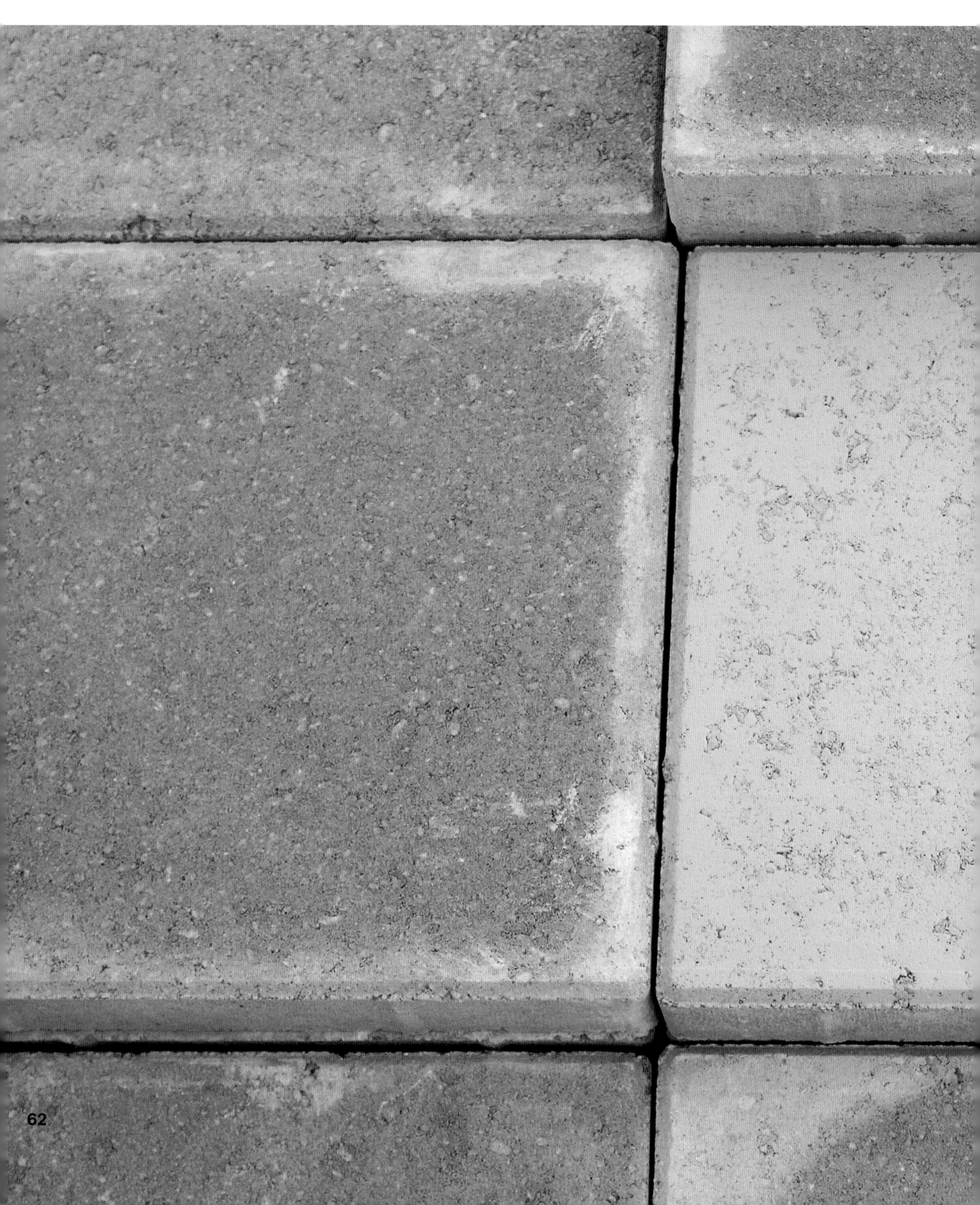

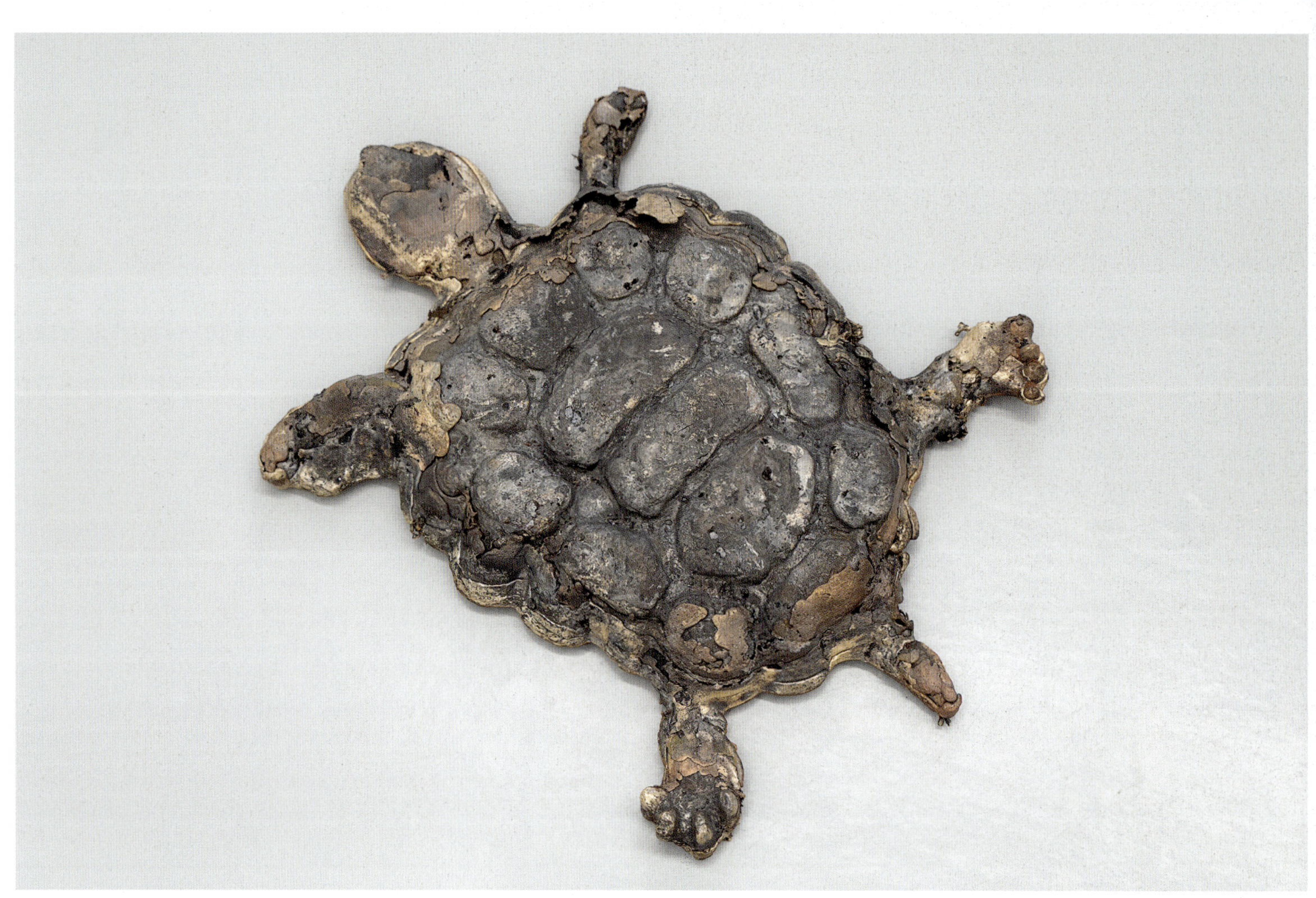

List of illustrations

FIGURE 1
Lene Baadsvig Ørmen, sculpture from *Subterranea*, 2019.

FIGURE 2
An example of chains of single cell, micro-fossils dating back approximately 3.5 billion years. Discovered in a sample of rock recovered from the Apex Chert, Western Australia. It is one of the oldest fossils ever found, also the earliest direct evidence of life on earth.

FIGURE 2
The Goshawk, a book written by T. H. White. First published in 1951 by G. P. Putnam's Sons.

FIGURE 3
Falconry is an ancient sport that has been practiced since preliterate times. This falcon's hood is originally made of tooled leather, inset with velvet panels that are embroidered with metallic yarns and metal beads, and topped by a silk tassel. Although it is difficult to pinpoint this specific hood's origin, it's believed it was made in England or France in the early seventeenth century.

Milena: I want to begin by setting the scene. Fossil-like, hard-flattened carcasses of semi-recognizable animals inhabit an artificial environment made of cement bricks laid out on the floor. Have these perhaps once-living organisms been unearthed and placed here by a human agent who has since disappeared? Many of the animal carcasses are dependent on a support structure, a set of connected steel tubes, reminiscent of plumbing pipes. In fact, this steel armature is built into the missing parts of the fragmented fossils. They can't be separated without inflicting damage. Are these elements from different worlds somehow co-dependent?

FIGURE 1

Lene: It appears to be a dysfunctional relationship. There is no desire to disentangle, and no display of gratitude. They share an acceptance of their coexistence and appear to be in a symbiotic understanding of their condition. I say this aware that I'm slipping into the trap of applying human characteristics to sculptural bodies that are intended to exist in an ambiguous space.

Milena: This symbiotic coexistence certainly has a kind of distinct agency.

Lene: The key trigger or starting point in this working process was the clustered relationship that unfolds between a human and a bird in the activity of falconry. Sort of like an analogy or metaphor I could apply to a bigger picture. I wanted to process the complexity of this peculiar relationship in more abstract terms and implement it in a larger context, such as the relationship between human and nature, and the material and the intangible. Maybe the bird's position was translated to bronze figures and the human falconer to closed circuits of industrially made water pipes. The individual parts are attached with pipe joints that for me could be translated to the glove. Of course, nothing is intended to be explicit in the work.

Milena: I really like this idea of a closed, self-sufficient circuit, trying to somehow communicate something about a human to non-human relationship. But let's expand on that later. I want to return to the way we encounter the objects and the way they appear to us as a kind of fossils ...

Lene: The flat and compressed bronze sculptures actually exist in the borderland between a screen and ancient fossils.

Milena: Yes, this tension between the three-dimensional and the two-dimensional, between the way we relate to objects of the past through a screen, is something I also detect in a lot of your past work. This tension adds to the ambiguity as to which kind of temporal reality your objects inhabit. It brings up questions for me: Where do the objects come from? Are they witnesses to the past or a future past future? What function could these objects have had? What are your own thoughts on the identity of your sculptures in terms of their status as temporal objects?

> L: I play with the established view that history is an ongoing chronological development where archaeological findings are categorized through a system of dating, partly based on assumptions and guesswork. The pieces appear to have no direct reference to any defined point in time or particular system of meaning. I think of them as fragments from fictitious civilizations; they exist within circular timelines and foster spaces between or beyond the past, present, and possible futures.

Milena: Ancient fossil are characterized by the long process of transformation they have undergone underground, involving decay of organic matter and then the copying of its imprint into natural molds. They potentially communicate vast amounts of information through their surfaces about the lived environment of the original animal and its relationships to other animals and plants. Your bronze surfaces are also ambiguous, materially layered, and in some places clearly reveal the hardening of the liquid bronze from which they are made. Casting in some sense mirrors the natural process of fossilization, but also the way that lava cools and hardens into igneous rock, for example. Is this understanding of geological time connected to your process of making?

> L: Yes, it is. I have developed a technique for sand casting in my own studio, where I dig out negative molds in the sand with my hands and fill these cavities with bronze, often in several turns. The positive outcome of the sculpture is therefore partly determined by the metal in liquid form, as it can choose how it will flow and act in the mold. This method allows choices to be made beyond my control. It is like I give each piece a will of its own. The finished bronze sculptures are excavated from the sand once the metal has settled in solid form. I follow an intuitive and process-oriented working method, where material and intellectual considerations take place simultaneously. I often experience it as two separate actions, where both actions are present in the work at the same time. Still, I think there is a silent connection between the two, as the thought affects the hand and the hand affects the thought.

FIGURE 2

Milena: And the result is, as you say, works that seem to be communicating outside a specific system of meaning. This makes me think of your work *Dear Darkling* (2015), where your worked with earthy, rough pigmented forms cast from dirt and presented on a lacquered platform. Here I felt more confronted with a type of unfamiliar, crude, and slightly clunky artifacts, perhaps signs of a forgotten language or an alphabet which I did not have access to. There is almost a frustration built in, because we cannot contextualize them or decipher the codes that are perhaps inscribed in their surfaces. *Subterranea* (2019) on the other hand is made up of bronze fossils resembling animals I can identify: a tortoise, a kind of rodent, frogs, a bull. But if you look closely, the scale is off, and they are accompanied by other more mythical looking creatures.

> Lene: I dealt with the term “animal” as a whole—as “natural objects,” such as growing, living, and sensory beings in nature—rather than specifically depicted forms. I try to draw the reference objects in the sand, exactly as I remember them. Since this is practically impossible with regard to the technique, a necessary displacement or distortion of the reference occurs in the finished results.

Milena: I think this displacement you mention is mirrored in the much larger displacement happening as a result of our connectedness to the land, the sea, and to other species inhabiting Earth. Indeed, I think a lot in our time calls for a return to an understanding of these deeper layers of contact, something which, from my perspective, requires consciousness raising that can only occur if the heart is switched on. Also implied is the eco-feminist thinking of Vanessa Watt, for example, where agency is by no means exclusive to humans but is something that extends to all natural elements. This thinking draws on an Indigenous worldview of humans as an extension of the land.

> Lene: When digging in the sand with my bare hands, I see it as somewhat of a reductionist working method. I understate the traditional focus on perfection within regular casting techniques. By leaving each step in the process unattended and treating the bronze as a collaborator, I might get closer to the crux of the material. I would find it interesting to search both ways though, to follow the latest technological development or to simplify the method and go back to the beginning of it. I am drawn to things that are peculiarly basic in ancient concepts, which I often think relate to a more direct and authentic relationship with nature, other beings, and with ourselves—outside the realm of ego development.

Milena: Last night, I woke up at 3 a.m. and couldn’t sleep. For some reason I kept thinking about your notion of the closed-circuit relationship between the bronze animals and their support structures, inspired by the framework of the falconer’s relationship to her falcon. A falcon is let free to hunt, only for it to then return to the falconer’s gloved hand. At the same time, it is not a straight ownership, where the human tames the wild animal, but a much more complex relationship, because the falconer knows that the falcon might on any outing take off and not return.

In *H for Hawk*, which I read some years ago, Helen MacDonald describes the process of building a relationship to her goshawk as one involving in some ways withdrawing your human qualities, so as to condition the hawk to consider the falconer as food-provider and to establish trust. You point to the falconer in your work *Beat* (2019), which was exhibited together with your *Subterranea* sculptures at the Norwegian Sculptors Society. Beat is an elegant steel structure that hovers and zigzags out from the wall, down into a concrete vase on the floor, and up again, ending in a large falconer's glove. There's a strong sense of movement in the work, like in a graph.

Lene: Fear and excitement resemble similar emotions, on different sides of the scale. The graphic representation of a kind of pulse or heart rate can play with this concept and relate to the co-dependency that unfolds in the relationship between the falconer and the falcon. There are huge ethical questions concerning falconry, but still this utopian relationship represents a beautiful idea. MacDonald is in some ways withdrawing her human qualities inwards, but the book also describes how she is projecting human qualities onto the bird. In T. H. White's book *The Goshawk* we can follow a complex relationship between the author himself and a hawk he set out to train, where power, control, and mutual dependence unfold with a lesser degree of empathy involved. White's growing desperation intensifies after a number of defeats in the taming process, and his distinction between fantasy and reality is gradually blurred as the hawk appears more and more human in White's subjective reality.

FIGURE 3

MacDonald's fascination for the birds seems to derive from a more respectful and compassionate outlook, yet she obviously deprives the bird its natural environment and keeps it trapped by force to benefit her own obsession. To regain a necessary balance on earth, and maybe prevent this unsustainable attitude we find among humans, we need to reinvent our perspectives. I am reading a book now called *Animal Internet* by Alexander Pschera. He tries to redefine the relationship between humans and nature and has a quite positive outlook on the future. He thinks the internet is creating a historic opportunity for a new dialogue. The data gathered and studied by major scientific institutes about animal behavior can, for instance, warn us about tsunamis, earthquakes, and volcanic eruptions.

Milena: I hadn't thought specifically of the cardiogram, but now that you've pointed it out, it makes sense. The work has a pulse, and the same unresolvedness when it comes to the presence or moreover absence of a human protagonist. I haven't read Pschera, but it makes me think of how falconry, however problematic, is actually also used in conservation and rehabilitation of birds of prey.

FIGURE 4

Lene: I mentioned earlier that my intention was to give the pieces a will of their own. Thank you for sharing Vanessa Watts's article "Indigenous Place-Thought and Agency Amongst Humans and Non-Humans (First Woman and Sky Woman Go On a European World Tour!)." Her idea of dirt having an agency really resonated. If we follow an Indigenous perspective and the premise that we are in fact made of soil, then our principles of governance are reflected in nature. If we think of agency as being tied to spirit, and spirit exists in all things, then all things possess agency.

This returns us again to my sand casting, in which I try to surrender to the process so that the sculptures can emerge somehow independently of my control. I recently attended a funeral, and before the coffin was lowered down to the ground the priest said: "av jord er du kommet, til jord skal du bli, av jorden skal du igjen oppstå" (loosely and literally translated as "earth you came, earth you shall become, from earth you will return"). It just dawned on me that I grew up with this ritual, I just never took it literally. Following Watts's ideas of agency, now I sort of can.

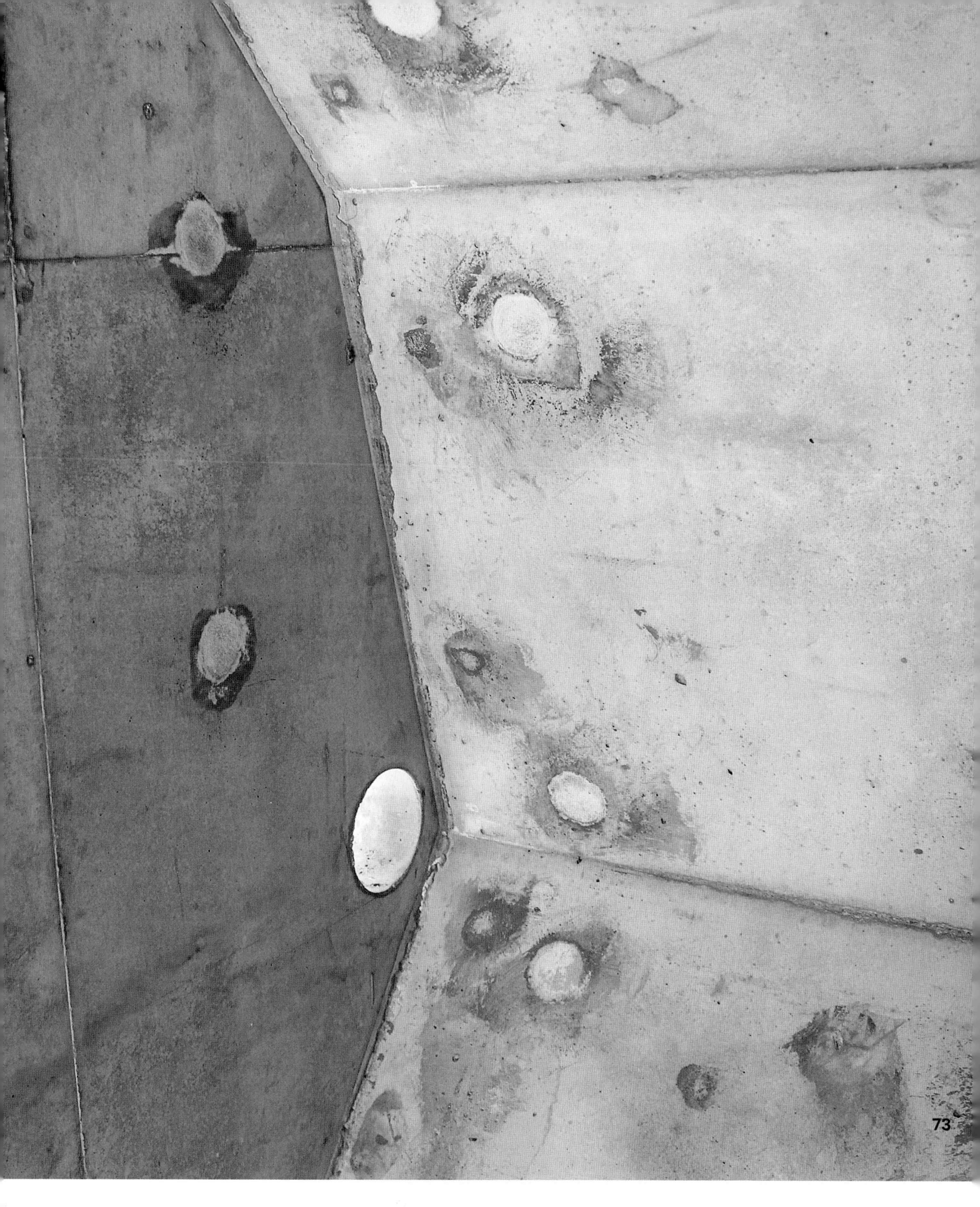

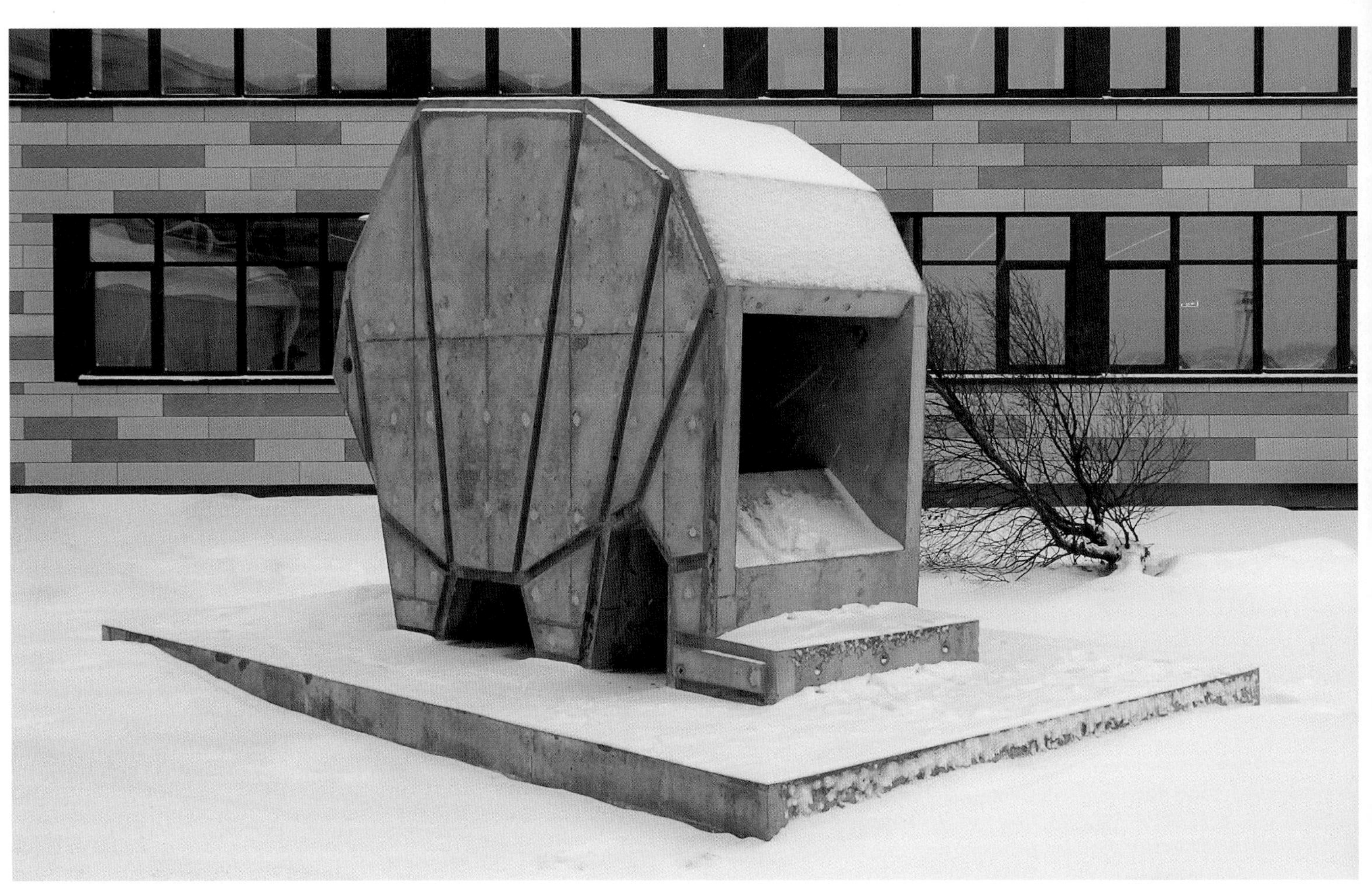

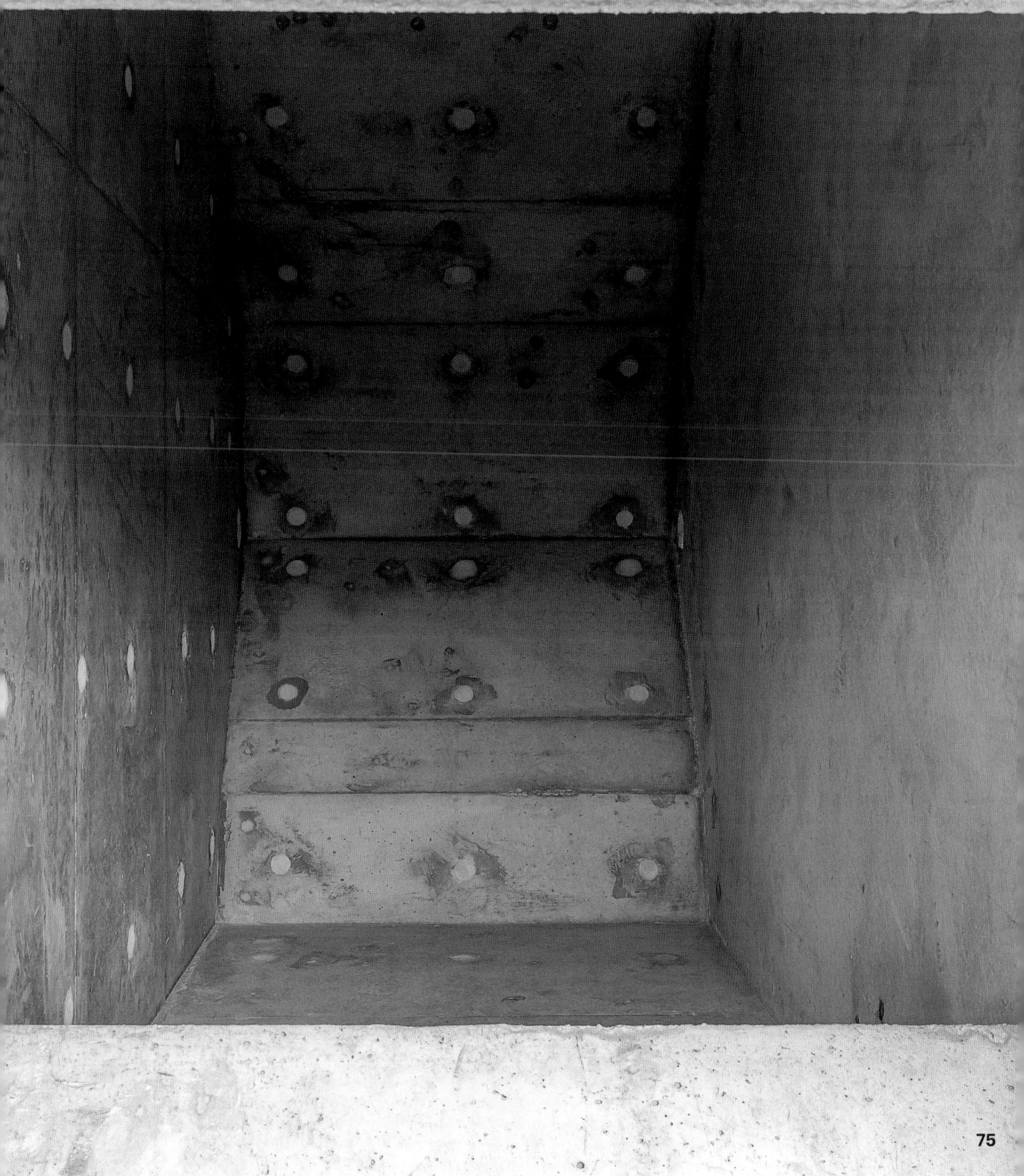

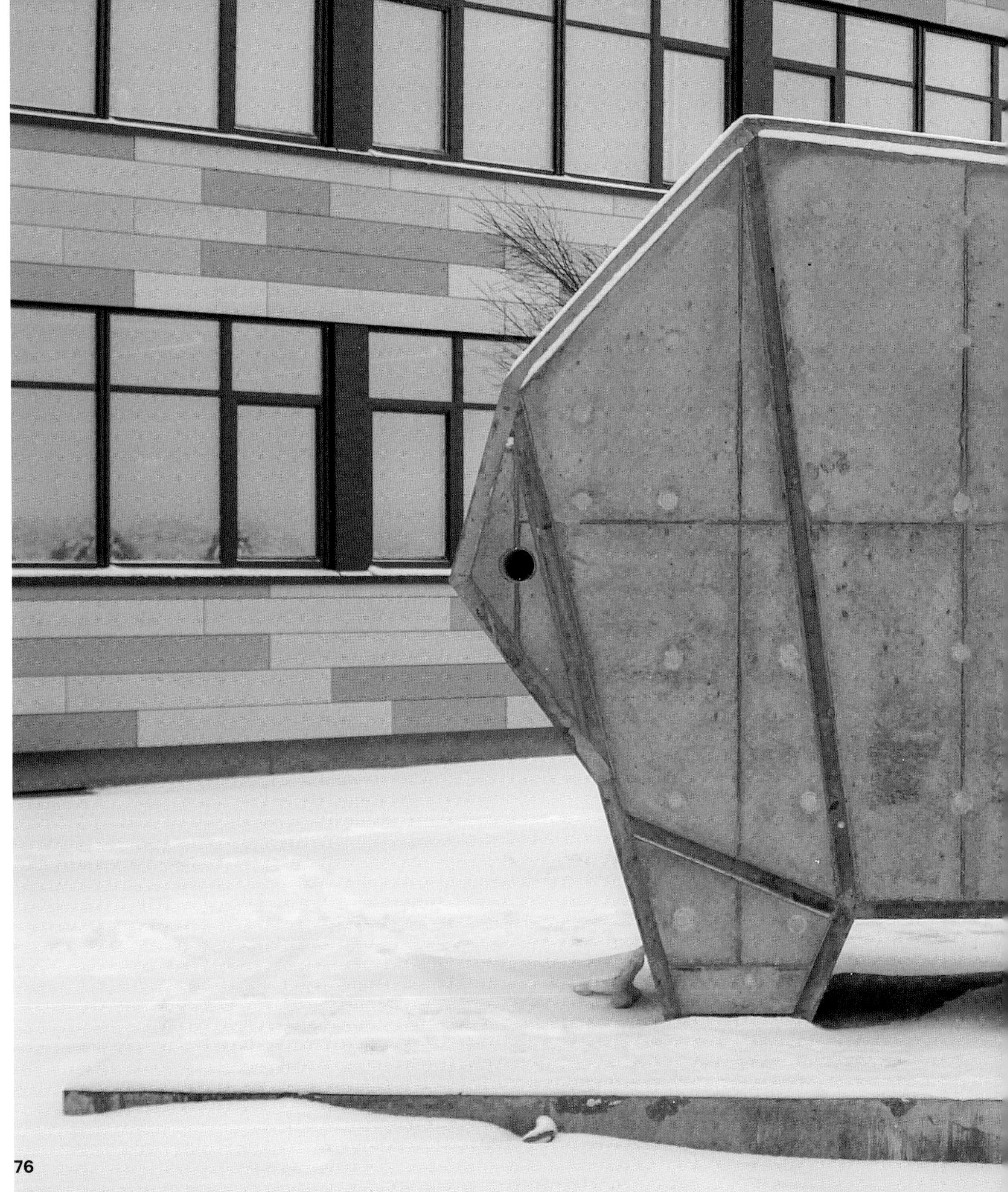

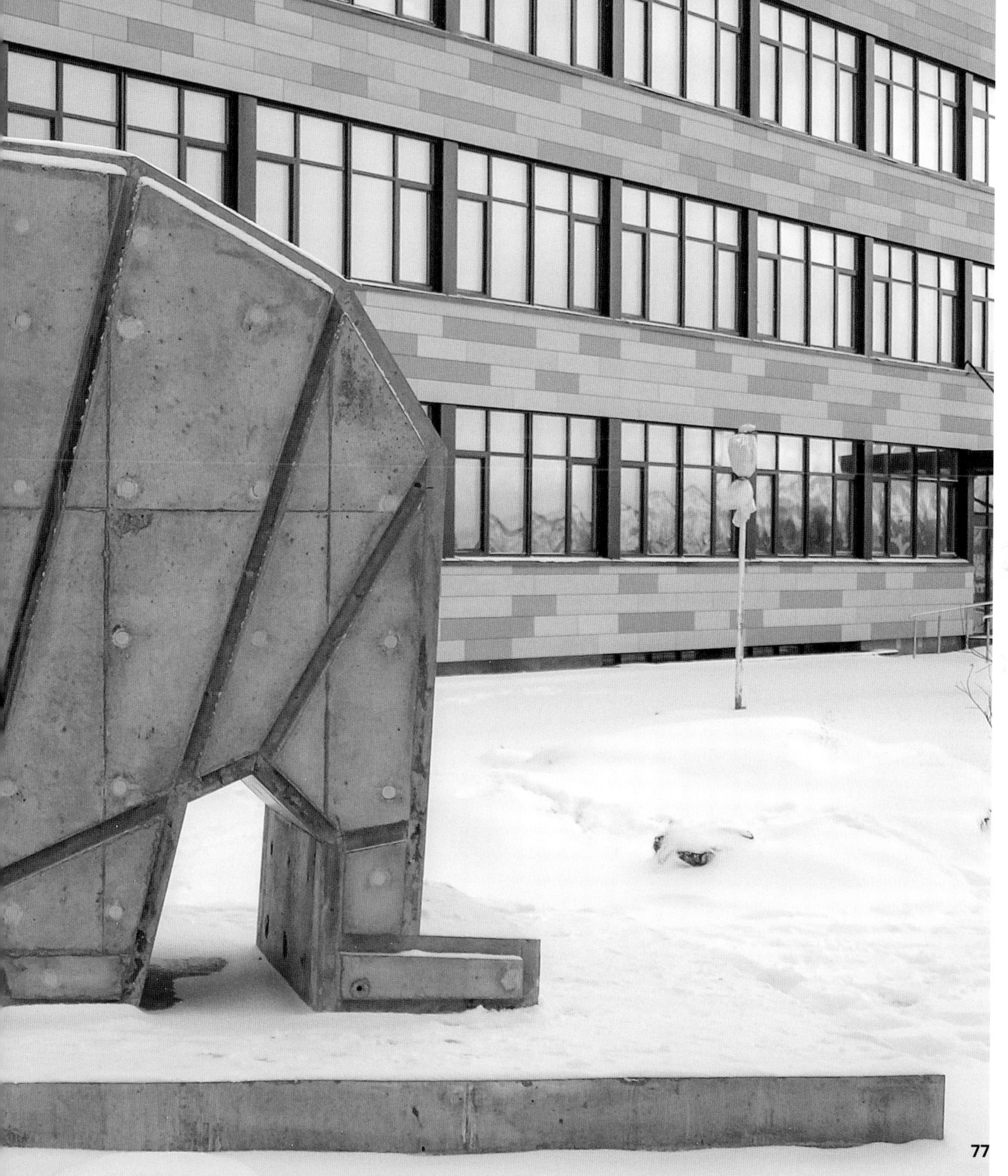

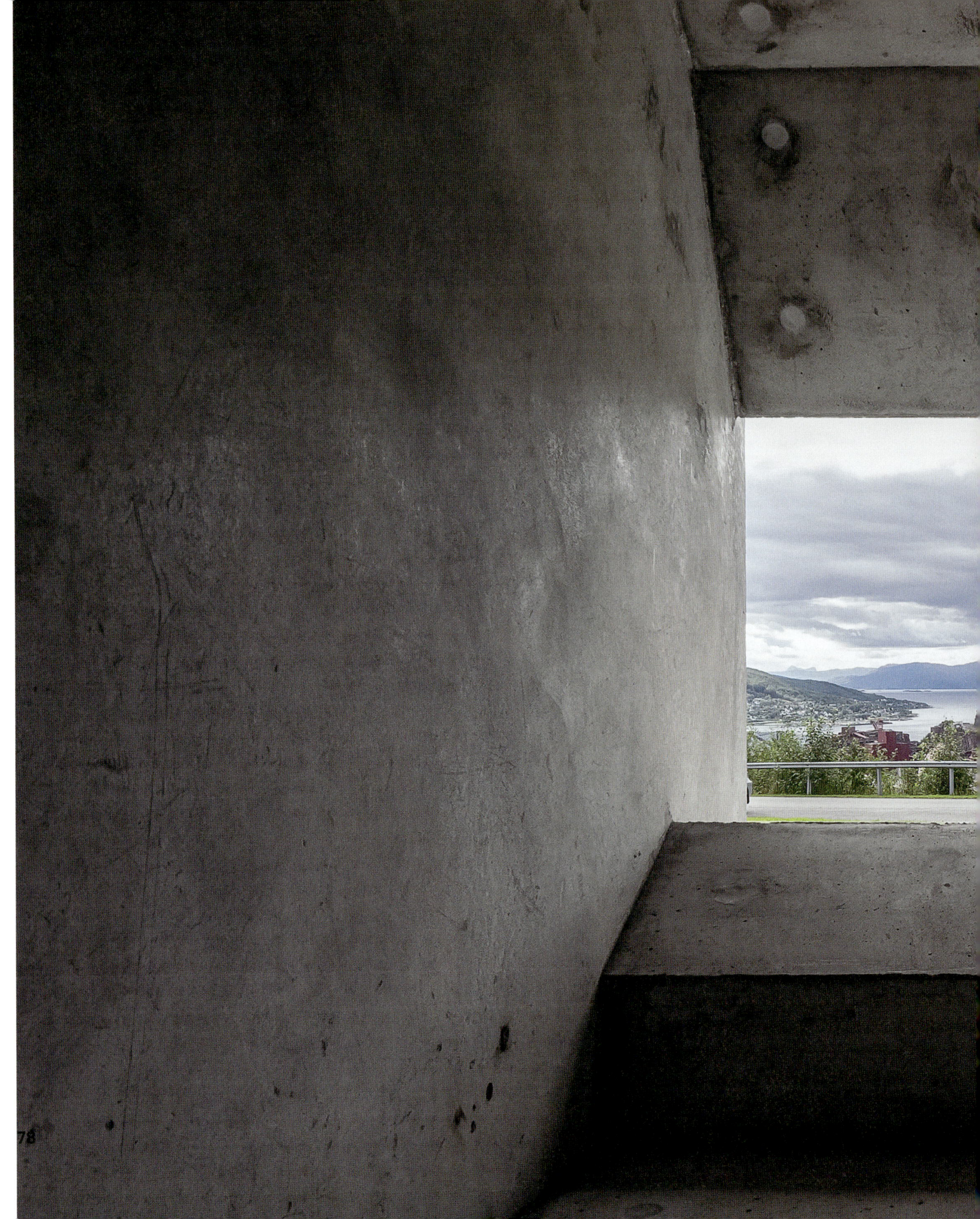

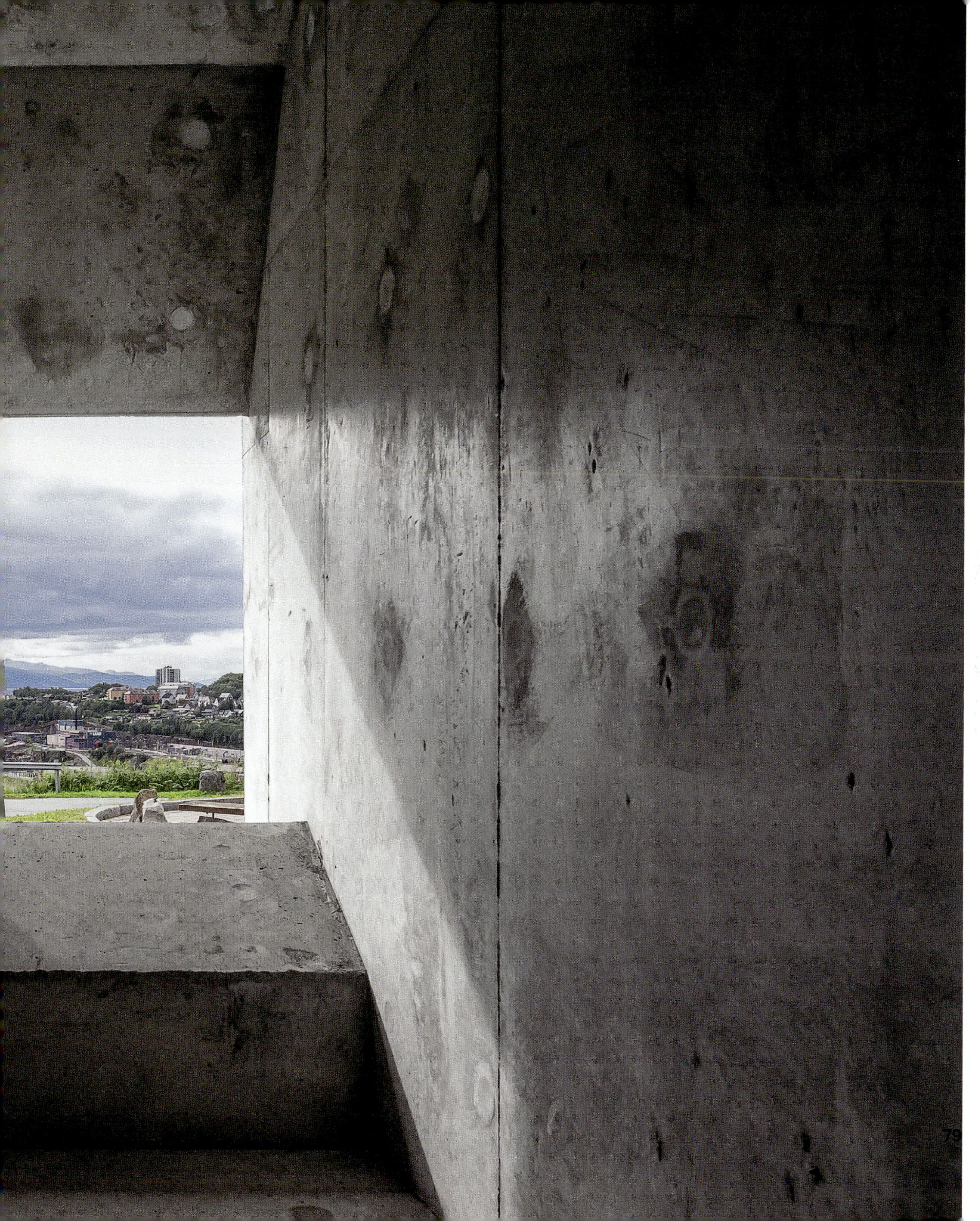

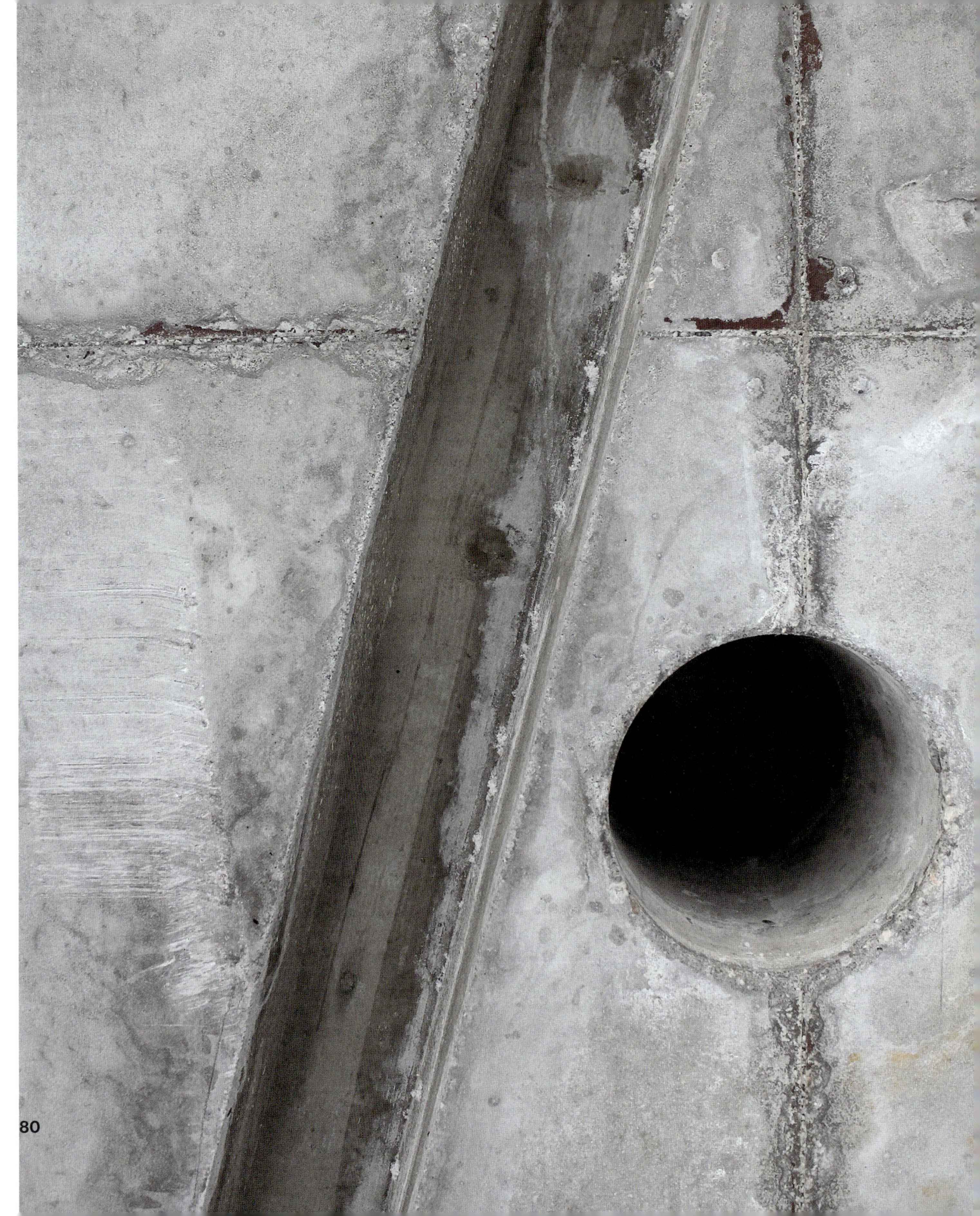

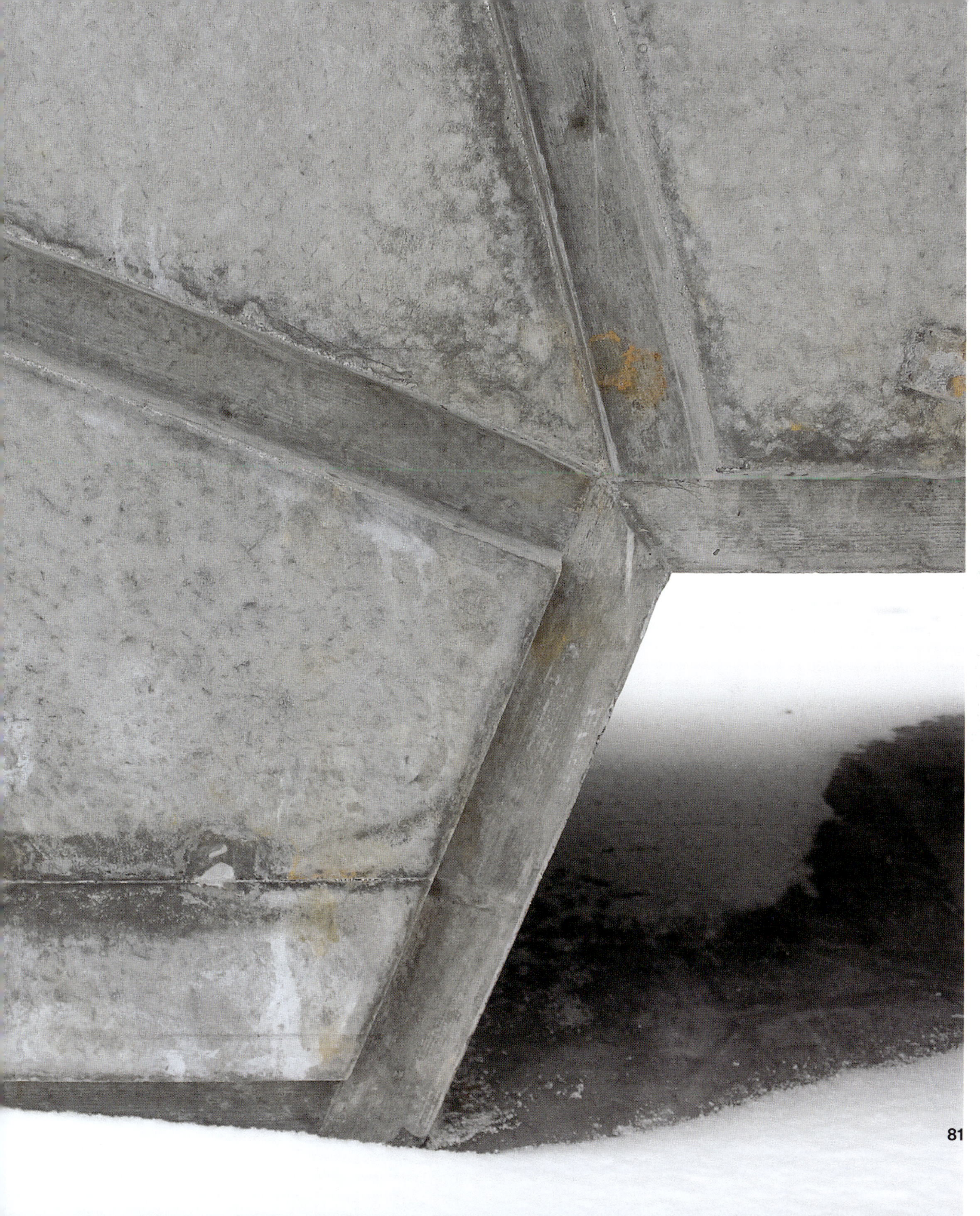

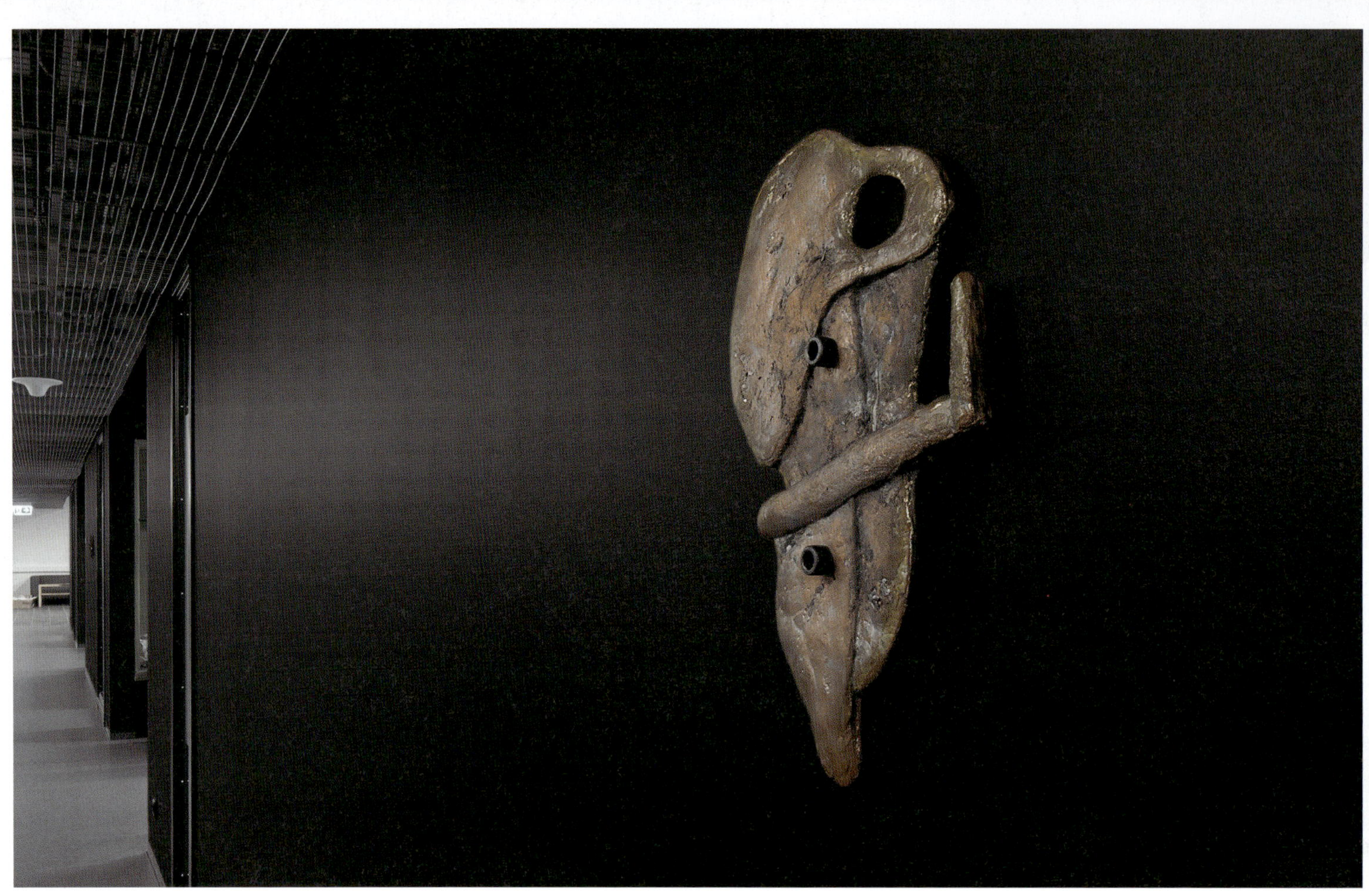

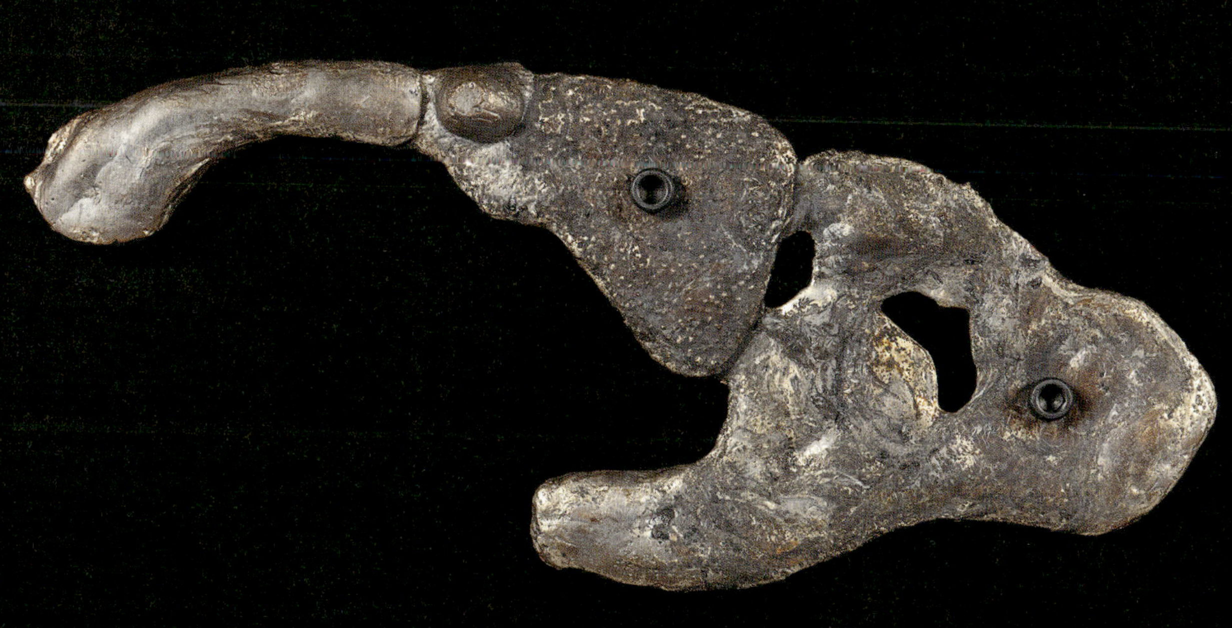

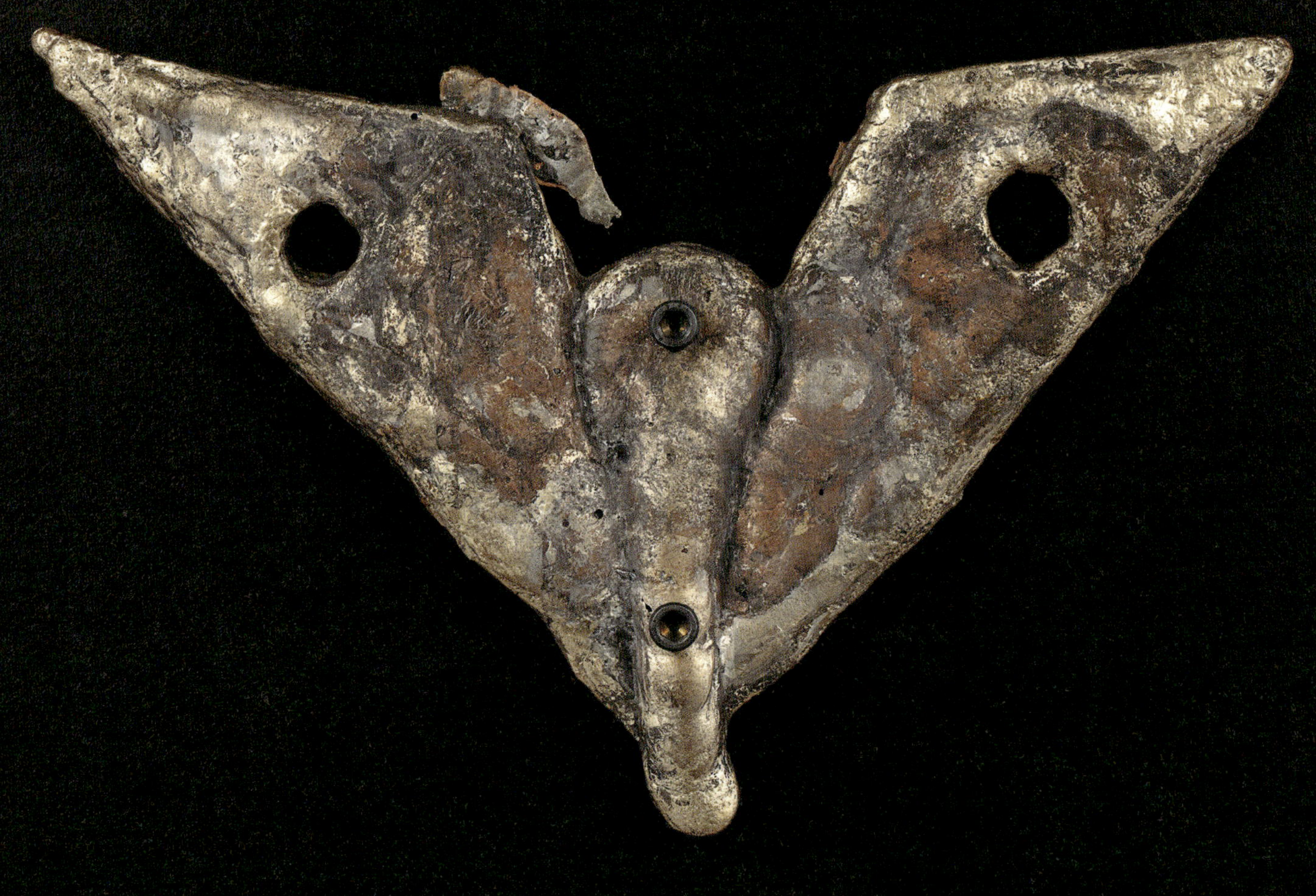

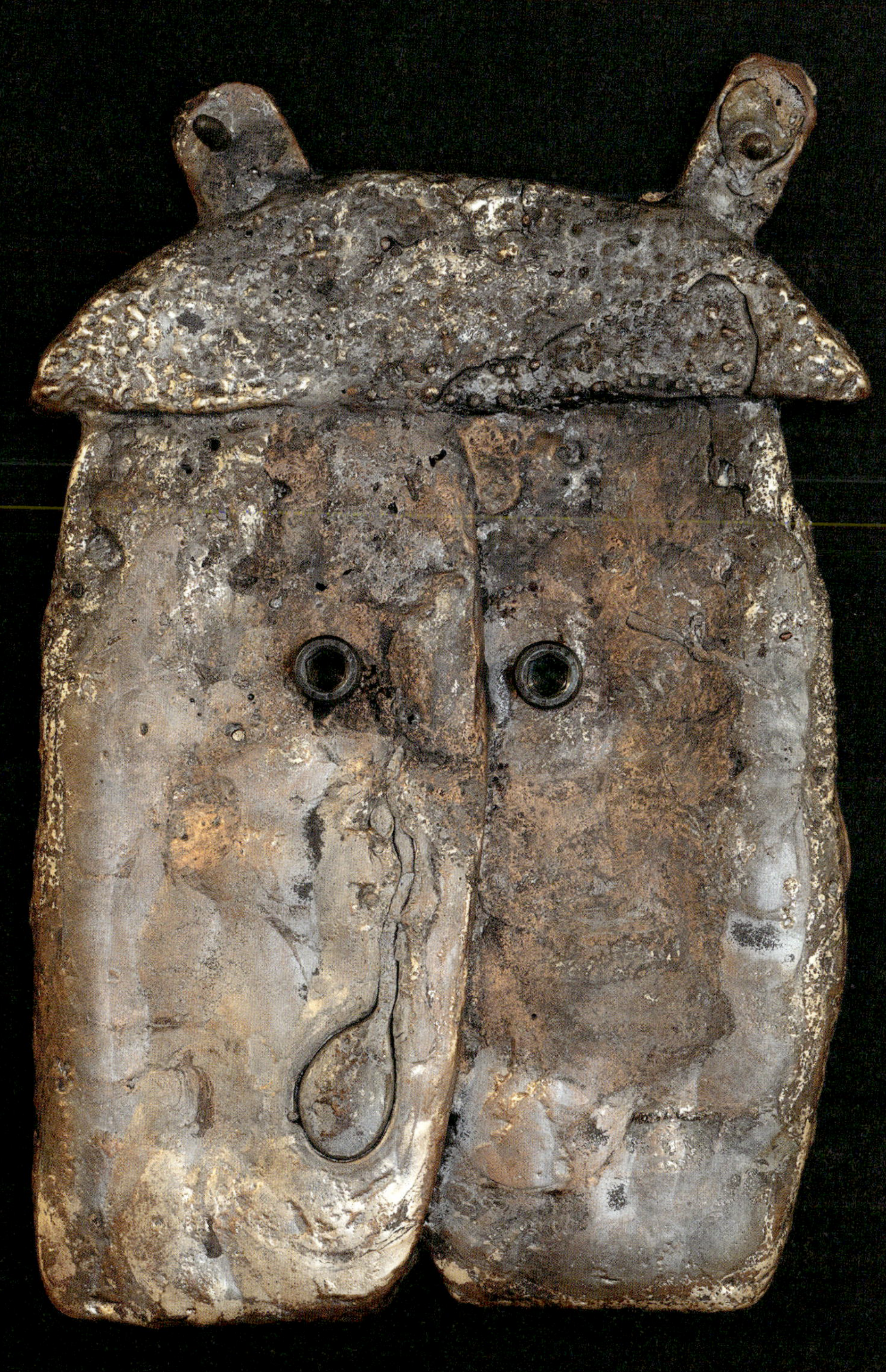

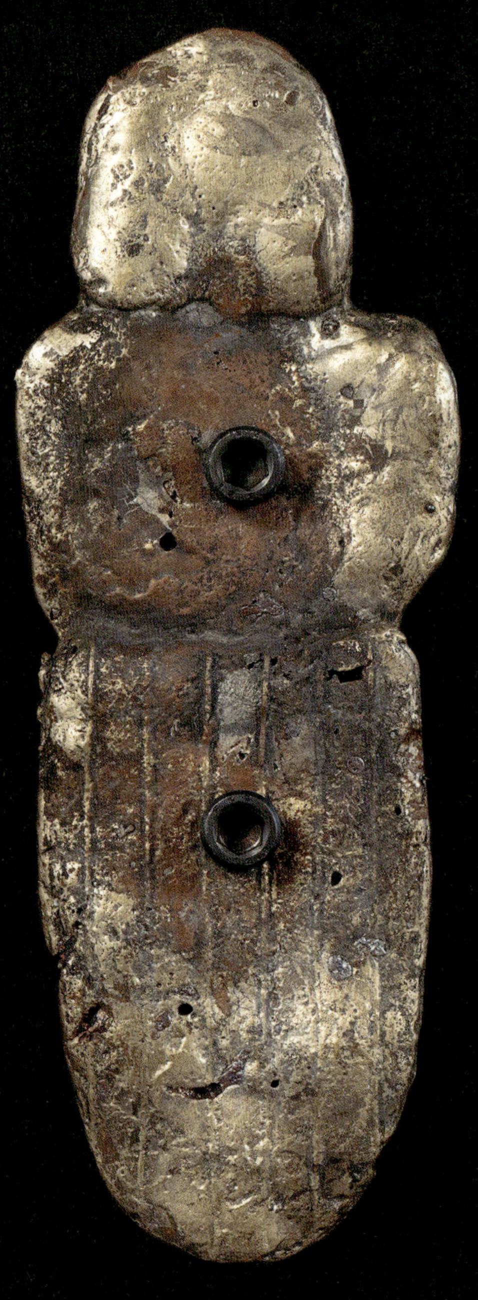

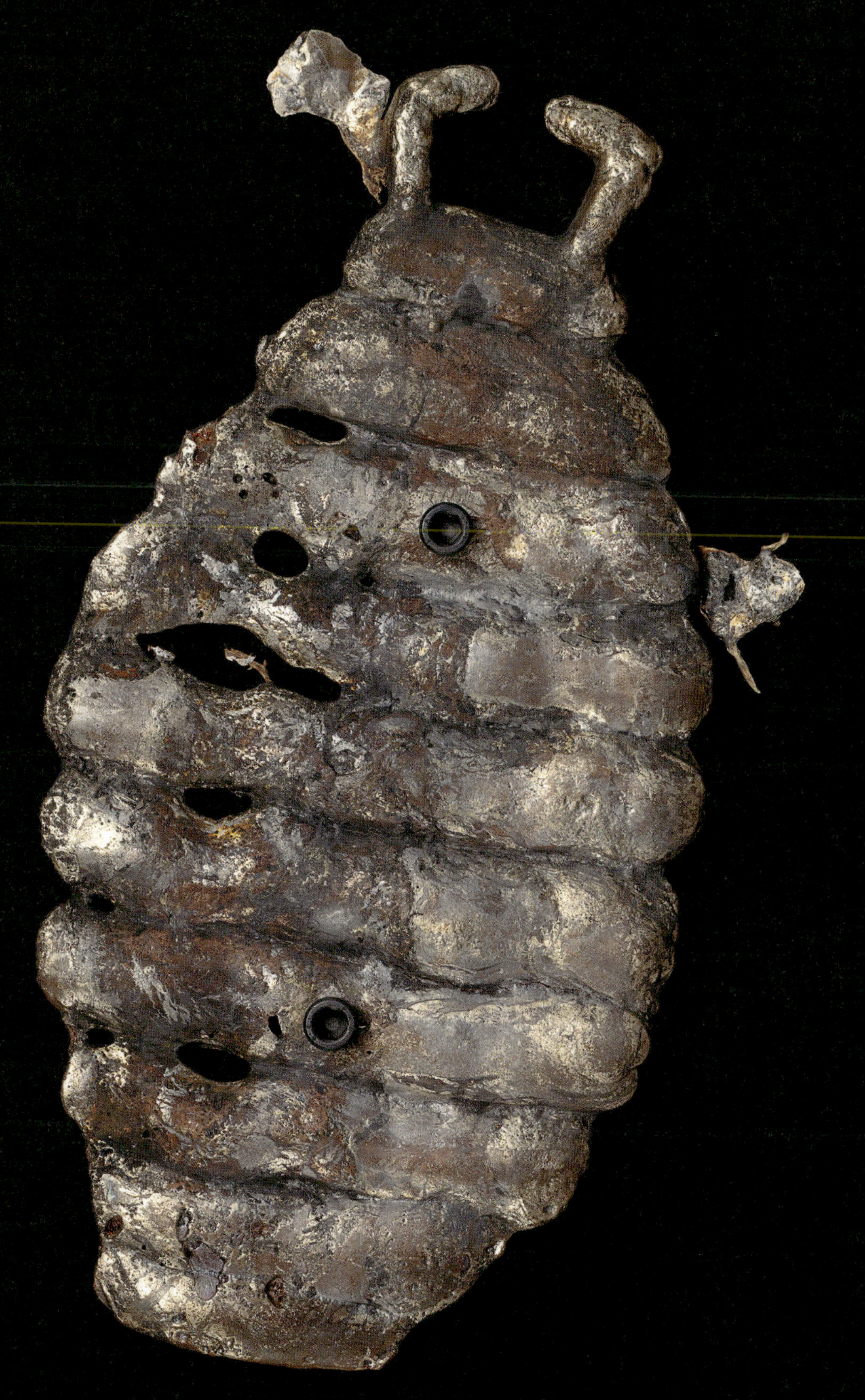

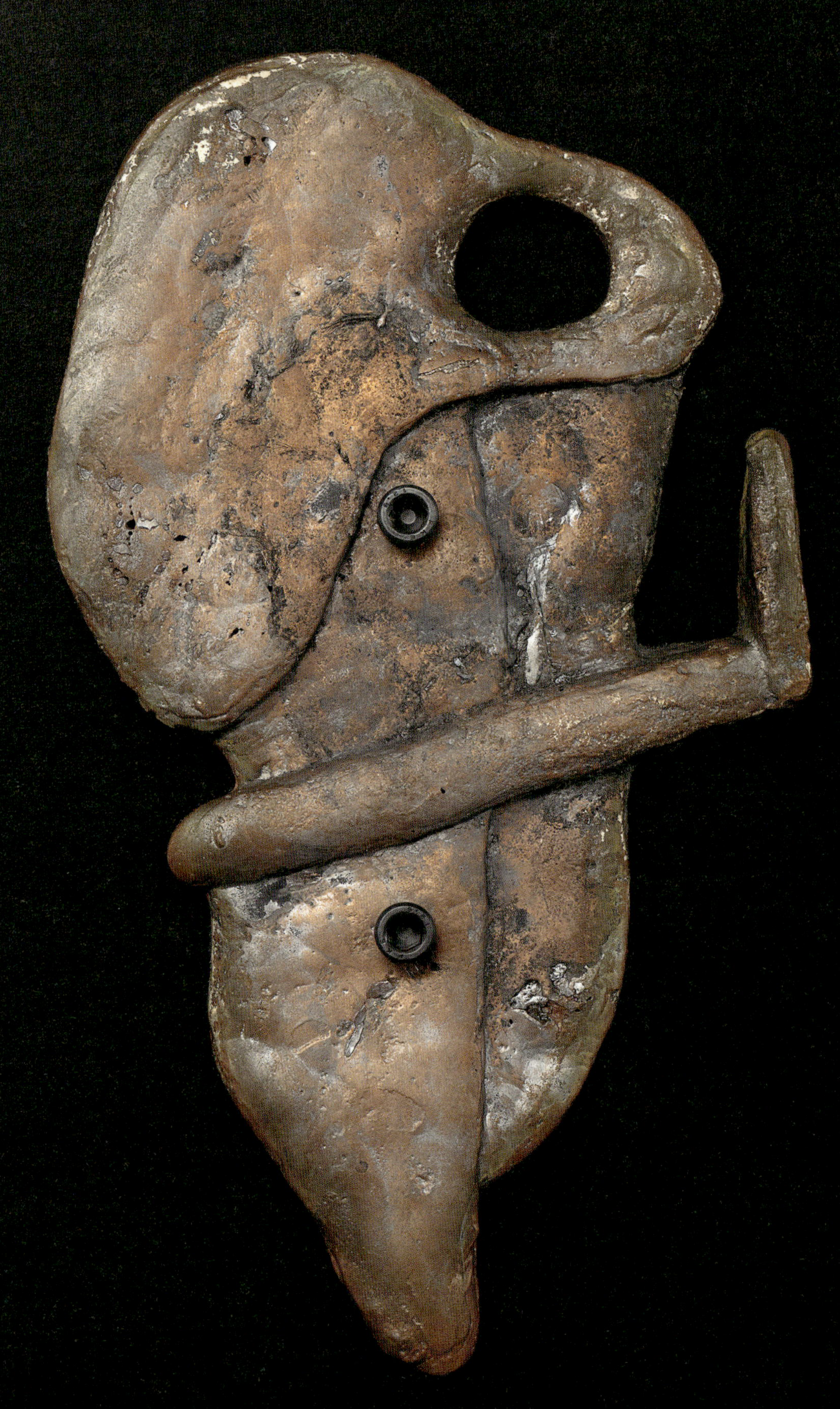

List of illustrations

FIGURE 1
Schrödinger's cat: a cat, a flask of poison, and a radioactive source are placed in a sealed box. If an internal monitor (i.e., Geiger counter) detects radioactivity (i.e., a single atom decaying), the flask is shattered, releasing the poison, which kills the cat. The Copenhagen interpretation of quantum mechanics implies that after a while, the cat is simultaneously alive and dead. Yet, when one looks in the box, one sees the cat either alive or dead, not both alive and dead. This poses the question of when exactly quantum superposition ends and reality resolves into one possibility or the other. This thought experiment was devised by physicist Erwin Schrödinger in a discussion with Albert Einstein, in 1935.

FIGURES 2
Lene Baadsvig Ørmen, detail from the sculpture *(w)hole*, 2018.

FIGURE 3
Gemini is associated with the myth of Castor and Pollux, collectively known as the Dioscuri. Pollux asked Zeus to let him share his own immortality with his twin to keep them together, and they were transformed into the star constellation Gemini. The sculpture was made by Robert Fagan, a painter, diplomat, and archaeologist, between the years 1761 and 1816.

Leah: Let's start by talking about quantum physics, a topic that excites both of us. I'd say that one of the main reasons we are both drawn to quantum physics is because of its dual nature. It's a scientific framework which seeks to describe the world, but it then presents a version of the world that is really murky and strange, unfamiliar to the world that we see. Inevitably, this murkiness creates a lot of space for thought—about perception, spirituality, aesthetics, measurement, imagination, etc.—as we try to make sense of it. I love that something can be so "scientific" and so abstract—ungraspable and open to interpretation at the same time. I've been trying to understand that paradox for years, and it's had a huge impact on my work. It's made me really curious about everything that goes on in the world at scales that we *can't* see.

Lene: Yes! One of the most familiar aspects in quantum physics is that there need not be only yes or no. An electron can be both a particle and a wave, even though that's difficult for us to imagine. As I understand it, in terms of quantum physics, everything exists as waves until we try to start measuring or defining them, and that's when they become particles. Quantum physics is full of paradoxical, complementary relationships between waves and particles, position and momentum, probability and certainty. Similarly, it is the tension between dichotomies such as the rational and irrational, abstract and figurative, organic and industrial that often spark the formal essence of my work.

I am thinking about a book we both read last summer, *Deciphering the Cosmic Number: The Strange Friendship Of Wolfgang Pauli and Carl Jung*, by Arthur I. Miller. Pauli being a physicist and Jung a psychologist, they shared ideas and found a mutual and complementary understanding in the abstract land of quantum physics. Pauli and Jung made several attempts to combine theories of neurophysiology with physics, which was quite radical in their time. I was drawn to their peculiar relationship, a profound intersection of modern science and mysticism. And to the fact that their ideas could meet midway. That there could be in-betweens, as well as ambiguities, when we try to make sense of the world. Miller emphasizes the puzzle of how we reason, how we think, how we create knowledge from already existing knowledge, and how we draw conclusions that go beyond the premises. It's a puzzle that cannot be solved by logic alone.

Leah: That also was striking to me, the in-betweens and ambiguities in how we make sense of the world. That, perhaps, everything *isn't* or *can't* be rational. I liked how Miller explored bridging the ambiguous mind (and psychology) with quantum physics and math, suggesting that each could be a mirror to help understand the other. When I was just getting interested in quantum physics, around 2011, I realized that because quantum activity is not something that we can directly observe, the only way we can make sense of it is by framing it in context of what we *can* see or experience. For me, that means looking at the natural world. And that's similar to thinking about quantum activity in the context of our dreams or our psychological experiences, like Jung and Pauli did.

I just started reading a book about math and found a passage today that fits right in to this discussion:

> "We have the ability to construct 'conceptual metaphors,' where we understand an idea or conceptual domain by employing the language and patterns of thought that were first developed in some other domain."

For a long time I really believed that science was something that could be separate from us. Maybe this was naive. But in time, through learning about quantum physics, I came to many realizations about our selective, or limited, perceptual relationship with the world. Now I see science as just one system of describing—a critical, crucial system, but a system of description nonetheless. I can totally see why Jung and Pauli got along so well and had so much to talk about.

But let's talk about material! Quantum physics is so "immaterial." After all, atoms are 99.999 percent empty space, yet they add up to construct the material world. Your work is so material—in process, in concept, and in form.

> Lene: I sort of have two separate processes going on simultaneously. My mind constantly deals with information and ideas while working, but when I develop the physical work I tend to let intuition or my hands be in charge. I feel like I am *on to* something when my gut feeling is calm but my thoughts are spinning. My mindset favors the idea of constant change between hats and embarking on paths expanding from several perspectives rather than searching for the right one. The choices that make sense for my thoughts do not always make sense logically for my hands and vice versa.

FIGURE 1

Leah: I heard an interesting thing on a podcast the other day. An Indigenous woman from present-day Guatemala, and a descendent of the Mayans, spoke about quantum physics being the closest modern-day science has ever come to their understanding of the world. She mentioned this same fact about the atom being 99.999 percent empty space—"pure energy," as she put it. But then she said that while Western science focuses on the 0.0001 percent of the atom which is matter, her people focus on the 99.999 percent which is energy, immaterial, invisible. I was really struck by that and thought of you immediately.

Lene: It makes sense that the woman from the podcast talks about this. I am drawn to ancient cultures, because they had a closer and more intuitive relationship with nature and existence. I keep returning to this technique that I have developed, where I dig out the molds or negative space for the sculptures in sand. I pour whatever material I am using into a mold in a liquid state, and then I excavate the sculpture when it is fully solidified. In some weird sense and totally constructed scenario inside my studio, I feel closer to nature when doing this. I stopped using photography as a medium because I wanted to work more embedded in the three-dimensional world and not only as an observer. It is kind of a paradox that my sculptures tend to be so flat though, existing somewhere in between the two- and the three-dimensional. The process is similar to developing analog photography in a darkroom: I want the positive outcome to be somewhat of a surprise.

Leah: I'm always curious about individual artists' processes. How does an artist get from an initial inspiration—or an observation or idea—to an artwork? What are the processes of translation that happen from an idea to an image or object? Obviously, it's completely different for everyone, and that's what I love. In my work, too, there's a big difference between some of the things in the world that capture my attention and the pieces I make. Since 2011 or so I've been fixated on the quantum physics concept that pure emptiness isn't empty and is in fact quite dense and turbulent. It struck me that "emptiness" and "density" are formal terms, too, and I decided I was going to spend some time making images that explore those ideas conceptually, *through* form and landscape, without making them appear overly scientific. It's almost like the scientific inspiration, which is crucial, is covertly hiding in the background. I wanted the images to suggest structure and logic, motion and attraction, but not "science"—it felt too specific.

Lene: The interesting part is that the more confusing it is for me to try to understand how other artists' minds operate, the more interested I become in their work.

Leah: I agree! There was an outdoor sculpture in the exhibition *Subterranea*, at the Norwegian Sculptors Society, called *(w)hole* (2019). Can you talk about that piece a little bit?

Lene: The sculpture *(w)hole* is a two-and-a-half-meter-tall steel frame. The aluminum sculptures on top are attached to the metal structure with ball bearings, which allow them to spin 360 degrees. When the wind is strong enough, they will stir. "0" can represent the idea of *nothing*, be a physical entity in our experience and frame a hole at the same time. The wind takes part in the piece *(w)hole* as an invisible force, yet equally important as the aluminum, the zero and the whole construction. The work deals with macro and micro perspectives, referring to measurements of size, linking relativity (the study of the very large, the universe) and quantum theory (the study of the very small, the atom). I've been drawn to quantum physics-inspired ideas that are mostly intertwined with concepts related to spirituality or cosmology. I enjoy that the fundamental premise of quantum physics is that uncertainty is a part of it, and we must accept that. Since I (or we) have been raised within a Western culture, it is hard to follow beliefs that are not "intellectually" reasoned. As you put it, it deals with invisible or abstract ideas explained through hard science. It is interesting, yet confusing, to follow the idea that everything in the universe is basically movements of energy—your thoughts, air, the electron, equally as the coffee cup in front of you.

Leah: I love that sculpture, and the way it interacts with the wind: some wind hits the object, some goes right through it. I have often thought about wind as both empty and dense, as both positive and negative space. But I hadn't considered that for this piece, the wind could be seen as a stand-in for spirituality or invisible energies or abstract ideas. That's great, a really direct way of putting something concrete and material together with something invisible. And making invisible energies more tangible! The "0" really gets to be something and nothing, and it gets you to think about the wind that way as well. Last year I started to think about how we have our own understanding of wind (and weather, more generally) on earth, but that "wind" is something that exists in other forms on other planets and in outer space. There are so many varieties of wind.

One of my favorite facts is that the fastest wind ever measured was in relation to a black hole called IGRJ17091-3624: 32,000 km/h, or 20,000,000 mph, or three percent the speed of light! There's something so unimaginable about all of that: the sheer speed of the wind, of course, but also the strange numerical identifier for the black hole. And then there's solar wind, which is not "wind" as we understand it. Solar wind is plasma—a stream of charged particles—and leaves the sun's atmosphere at speeds of 400 km/sec or 890,000 mph. Neptune has the strongest winds in the solar system, despite being the farthest planet from the sun. Its winds blow at speeds up to 600 m/s, 2200 km/h, or 1300 mph—approaching the speed of sound!—and are powered by Neptune's immense internal energy. It's so nice to think about the wind as a universal phenomenon that can bring all these disparate locations together, and to arrive in Oslo to interact with your sculpture.

Lene: I love that idea! When you say this, I realize that I have never really thought about wind on other planets before. The other element, besides the zero, on *(w)hole* bears resemblance to a pair of glasses. The "glasses" are inspired by a piece of timeless technology made by the ancient Inuit. They carved pieces of wood/bone that fit tightly against the face, blocking light from above, below, and the sides. The goggles were meant to protect from snow blindness, with the help of narrow lines of holes in them. Like a permanent squint, the snow goggles kept light to a minimum. What they discovered was that the glasses also helped to focus images at a distance! Apparently, they use this logic when making lenses to correct crooked cornea today. It made sense to me to connect the Inuit glasses and the "0." The initial purpose and actual outcome reflects a contrary movement. An attempt to narrow something down to a minimum, but when doing so, creating an unexpected or opposite expansion.

Saying this, I should maybe also explain the beginning of the process of *(w)hole*. I have been drawn to sculptures and artifacts connected to religious or spiritual activity for many years. And I knew I wanted to make a piece relating to the wind for the outdoor space. I started digging into archives of ancient sculptures from cultures with tendencies leaning towards more holistic or pantheistic cosmologies. After appropriating elements of already existing sculptures for a while, I figured it is more interesting to try to develop a piece that reflects my own ideas around cosmology. Let's say a more contemporary one. It ended up being a potential body-like structure, with clumsy concrete feet. Maybe a prop you could find in a corny *Mad Max* film, or a retro futuristic character inspired by brutalist architecture. Go figure.

FIGURE 2

Leah: Ha ha, go figure. I guess that makes me wonder what it all says about your personal cosmology. In context of our conversation about material and immaterial, I like the contrast between these clumsy brutalist or bulky futurist forms—which very much exist *in* time—and the wind, which is obviously timeless and immaterial, at least in the way we're talking about it. Do you feel like a contemporary cosmology has to deal with a different set of conditions than a cosmology we might idealize? Going back to the Mayan woman's comment about 99.999 percent energy versus 0.001 percent empty space or energy ... do you think the contemporary cosmology that you're describing reflects Western culture's fascination with matter? I would say that your choice of materials suggests these associations of immateriality, energy, or spirituality.

Lene: I think it reflects upon my subjective experience of the world. And I grew up in a Western culture, so maybe implicitly, yes? But I would not impose anything on behalf of the general crowd, except perhaps those with crooked corneas. I like to use solid materials that I can manipulate in a liquid condition, that can be transformed or shaped by an outside force. At the same time, I use materials as a kind of language. If metal is one alphabet, maybe aluminum can be one of the letters and bronze another one. Contemporary cosmology might sound a bit pretentious, but I love how it tastes. It is not as concrete as a belief structure, and it does not have an ultimate framework. I can obsess with a theory or mindset for a period of time, and then jump to a new one when I get bored of it. My mind always switches back and forth between perspectives. I remember ordering a calculation and interpretation of my astrological chart online at the age of 17. Ever since, I have kept track of people's zodiac signs. I like to play with astrology, but certainly not as an ultimate predictive structure. It triggers questions rather than giving answers. To me zodiac signs work in a kind of synesthetic term. It is similar to recognizing people at a distance in the way they walk, how they move and hold their body. Not on the specific characteristics of their appearance.

FIGURE 3

Leah: I love that you said it's like synesthesia. Like seeing someone whose general vibe appeals to you, and then discovering how your astrological signs line up. I totally know what you mean.

Lene: I guess the fascination for religious sculptures or artifacts is located within the attempt to materialize abstract ideas (or worries) into something concrete. As a coping mechanism or a way to out-distance oneself from the "problem." It can be easier to direct attention to it, if it is manifested in a physical object in front of you. Maybe *(w)hole* is an attempt to demonstrate how I relate to the search rather than what I am searching for. And that the point of it all is to ask questions, and not worship answers.

I grew up in a small municipality and was surrounded by friends who participated in activities organized by the congregation. Therefore, I often tagged along. The ones who fully embraced the concept of Christianity seemed to be so convinced.
I remember being at camps and feeling totally lost. I felt like a fraud when joining the evening meetings. So often, I stayed in my tent and felt confused instead. Ha ha, I guess I have been searching for something else to give me a sense of peace ever since.

Leah: I grew up in an atheist and culturally Jewish family. We didn't really do anything religious aside from celebrating a few holidays, and more in a cultural way. Once a month, though, we did go to a congregation and Sunday school that was called "humanistic." The name referred to the idea that humans could (and should) solve the problems that we usually ask a god to solve. This upbringing might have led me to think about a kind of spirituality within the material world, or it might have made me curious about a spirituality that's outside of (but completely connected to) the material world. Or both! Certainly I feel like my ideas about and feelings towards spirituality have changed over the years, largely thanks to conversations with friends. It's funny how spirituality without a "god" figure—like mysticism,

I guess—has a particular connotation that's sort of negative. It bristles against "hard science" even though it's still generally acceptable to believe in a god. But maybe that view is changing?

Lene: Hmm, yes. I have a kind of ambiguous relation with the term spirituality myself. It pushes me away and pulls me in at the same time. Spirituality is definitely problematic when there are economic interests, prevailing techniques, or exercises of power involved. And I often associate it with people I don't want to relate to. At the same time there are too many unanswered questions and interesting ideas out there. I think that is why these topics often return in my work. In these dystopian times, it can at least alleviate anxiety symptoms, keep my brain occupied, and suggest new perspectives.

Leah: I really like to think about your title *(w)hole*. It could almost describe a philosophy or outlook that recognizes its own inability to answer any questions firmly yet is still "whole" because it is built out of strong questions and with a strong curiosity that it *is* a kind of whole. A whole made of questions. Does that make any sense?

Lene: Yes!

Leah: Like an artwork that never resolves, that doesn't answer the questions it poses, but still poses them in a really engaging way.

Going back to something we were talking about earlier, I wouldn't actually ask you to draw out or describe a "contemporary cosmology"; I agree that it does sound pretentious. A cosmology is something that I'd personally like to leave vague, something I can abstractly picture, something I can get a sense of, but not something I would ever map out. That kind of vagueness is important to me.

Lene: It is an interesting term though, "contemporary cosmology." What is that? I definitely have the same attitude towards this as you—I prefer an abstractly painted picture.

Leah: Maybe it's just something that is better left as a feeling or an approximation rather than anything meant for language. It's nice to let language drop off sometimes, and to sit in this space of abstraction or vagueness or questions or whatever you want to call it. Maybe that's a model of what this contemporary cosmology should feel like? A very non-specific model.

Lene: Yes, that makes sense. A very non-specific model.

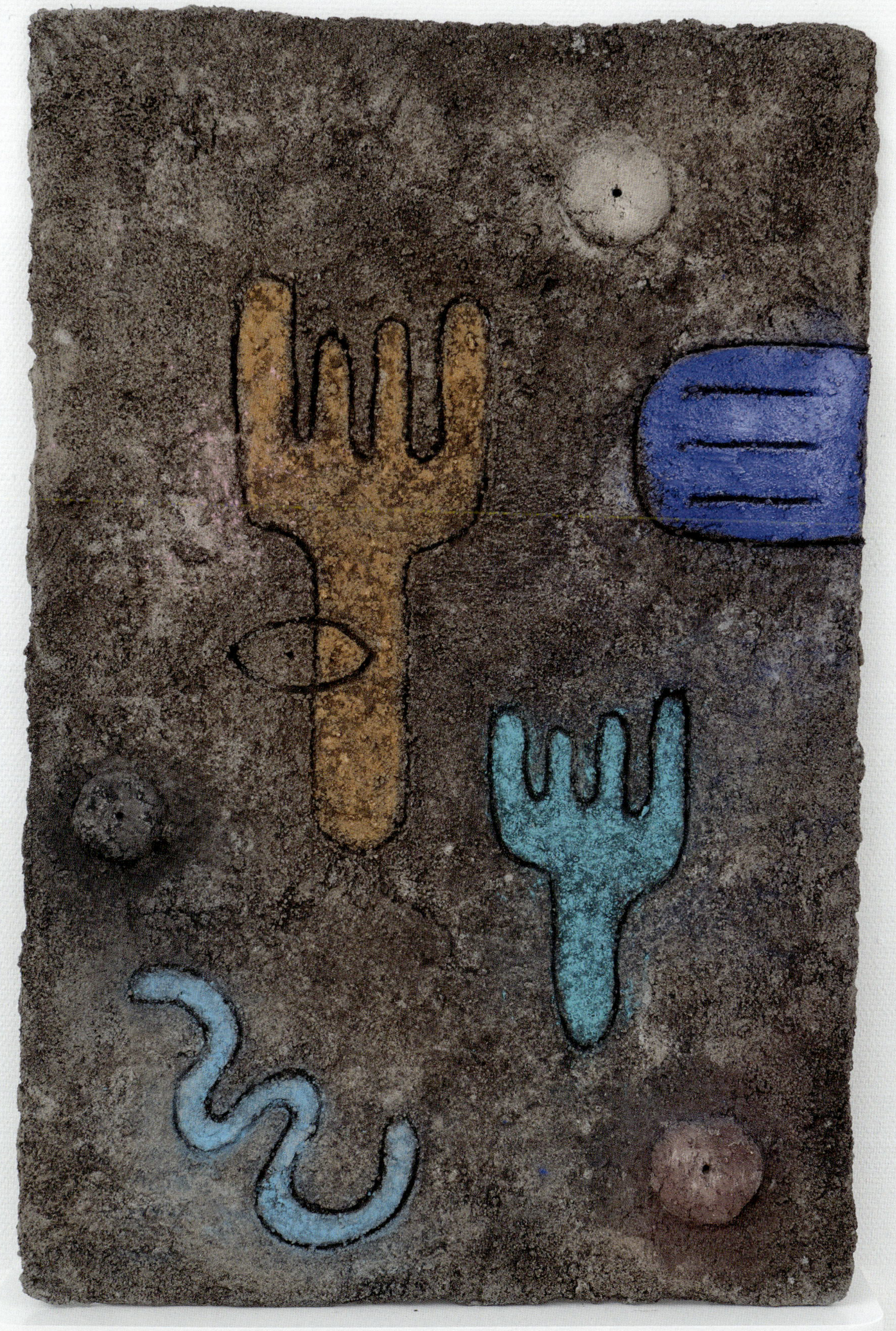

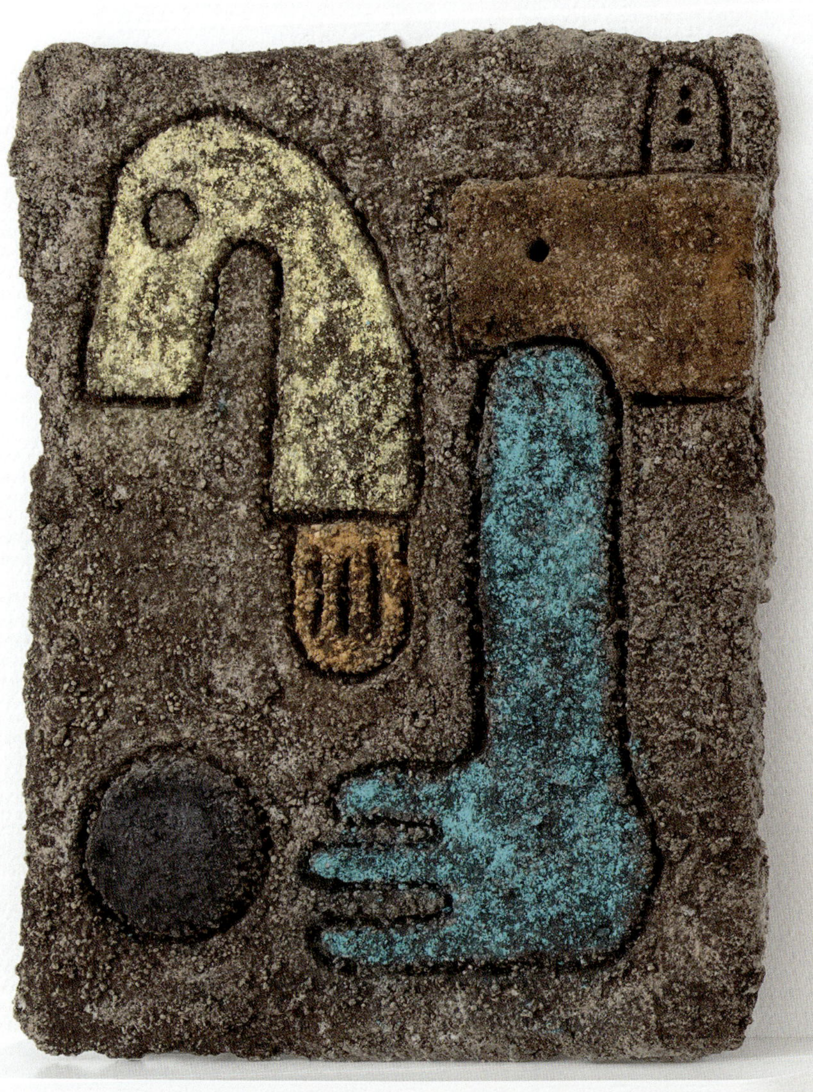

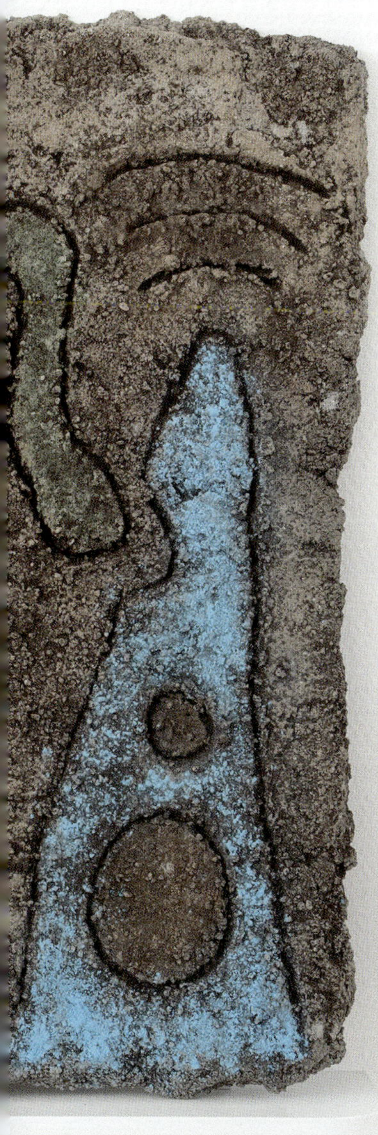

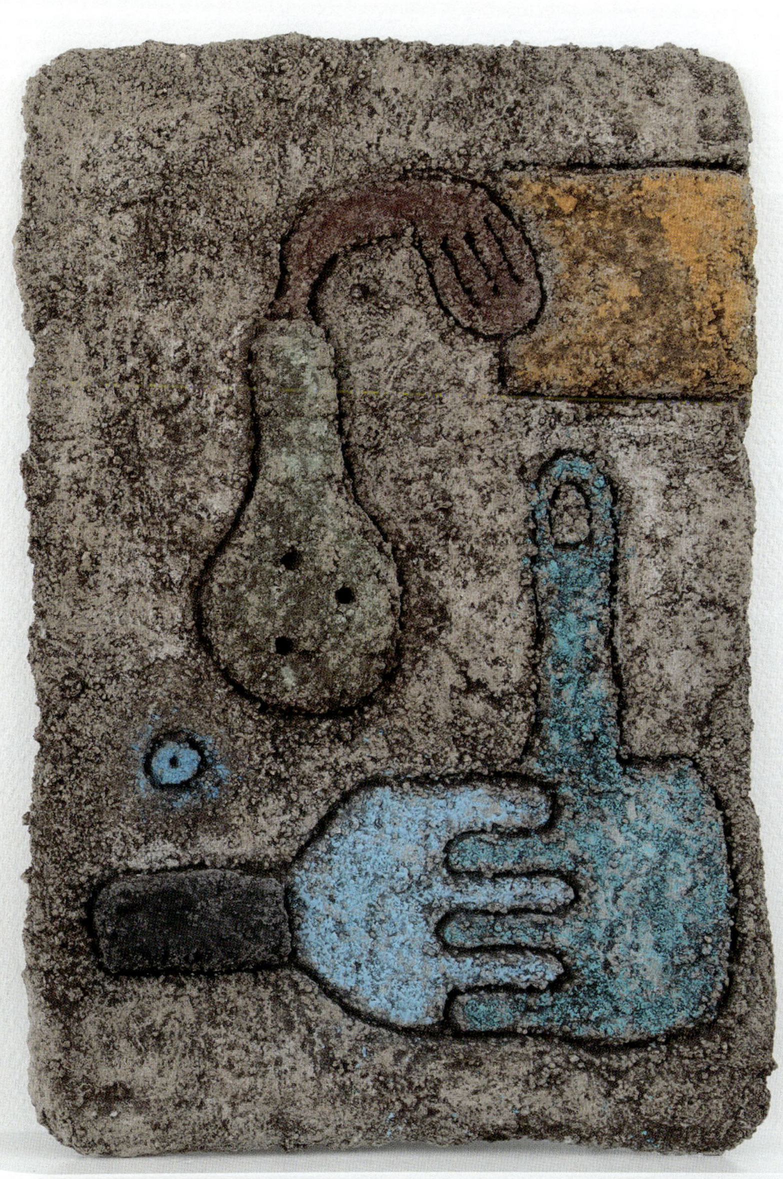

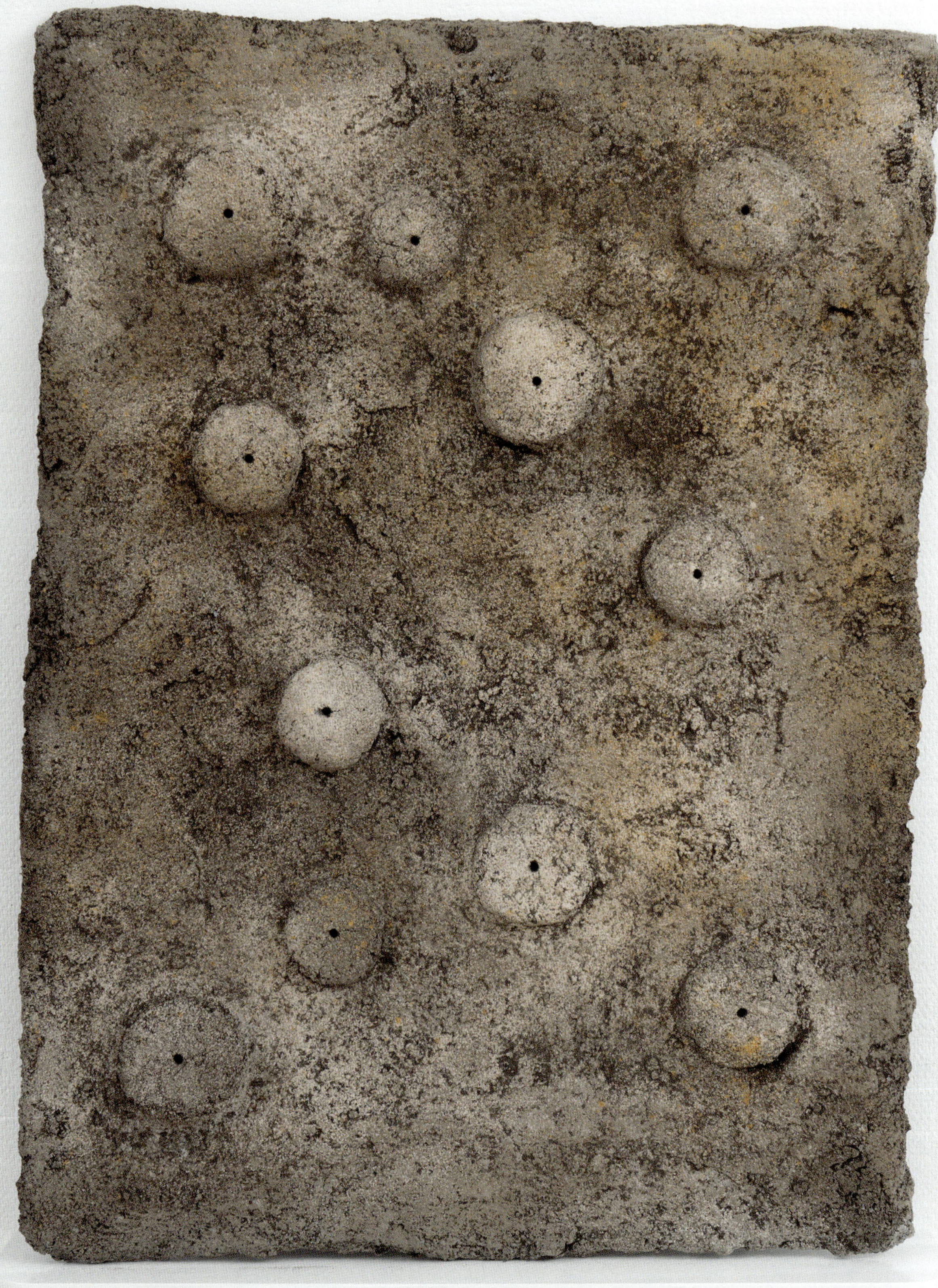

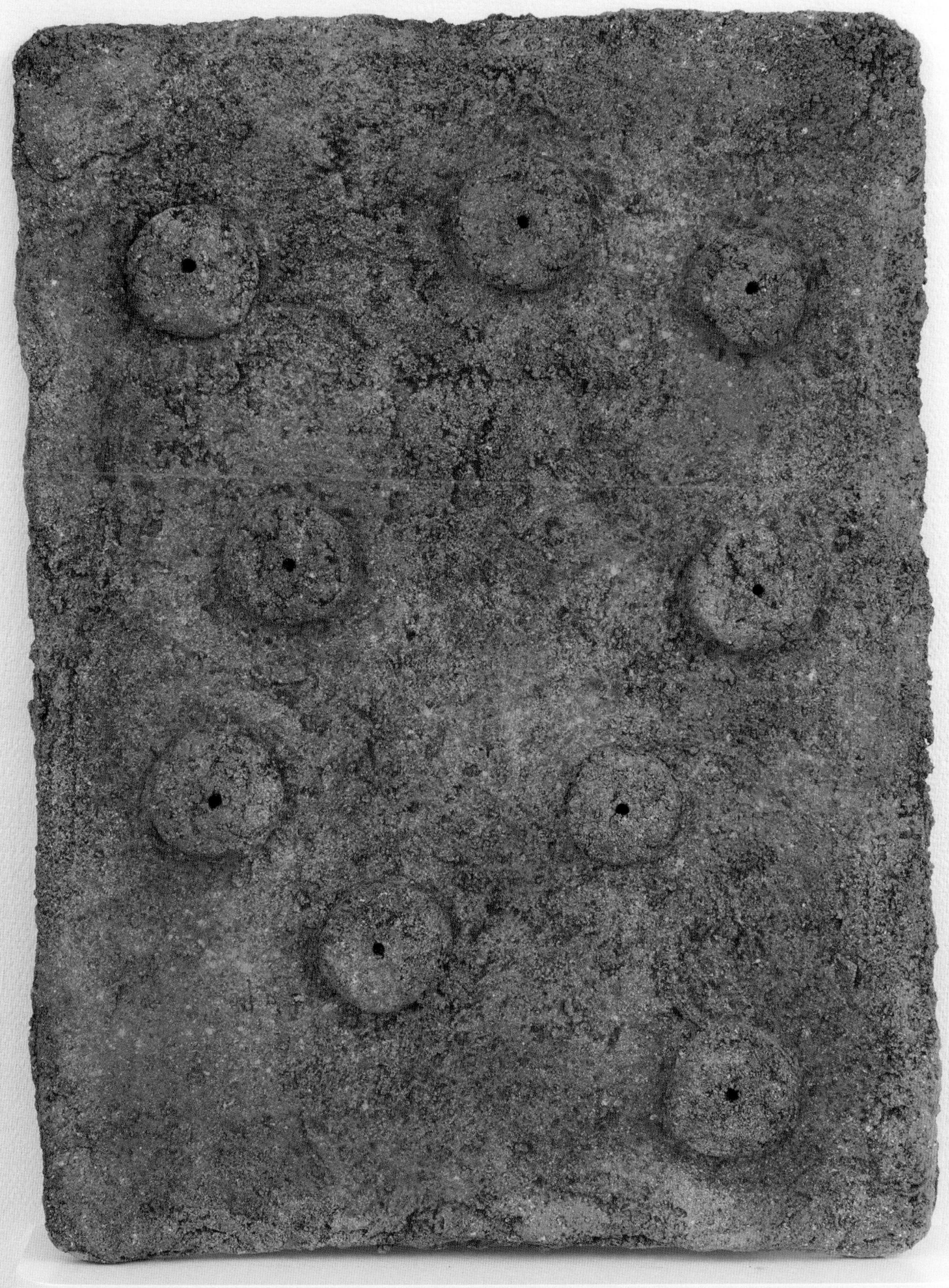

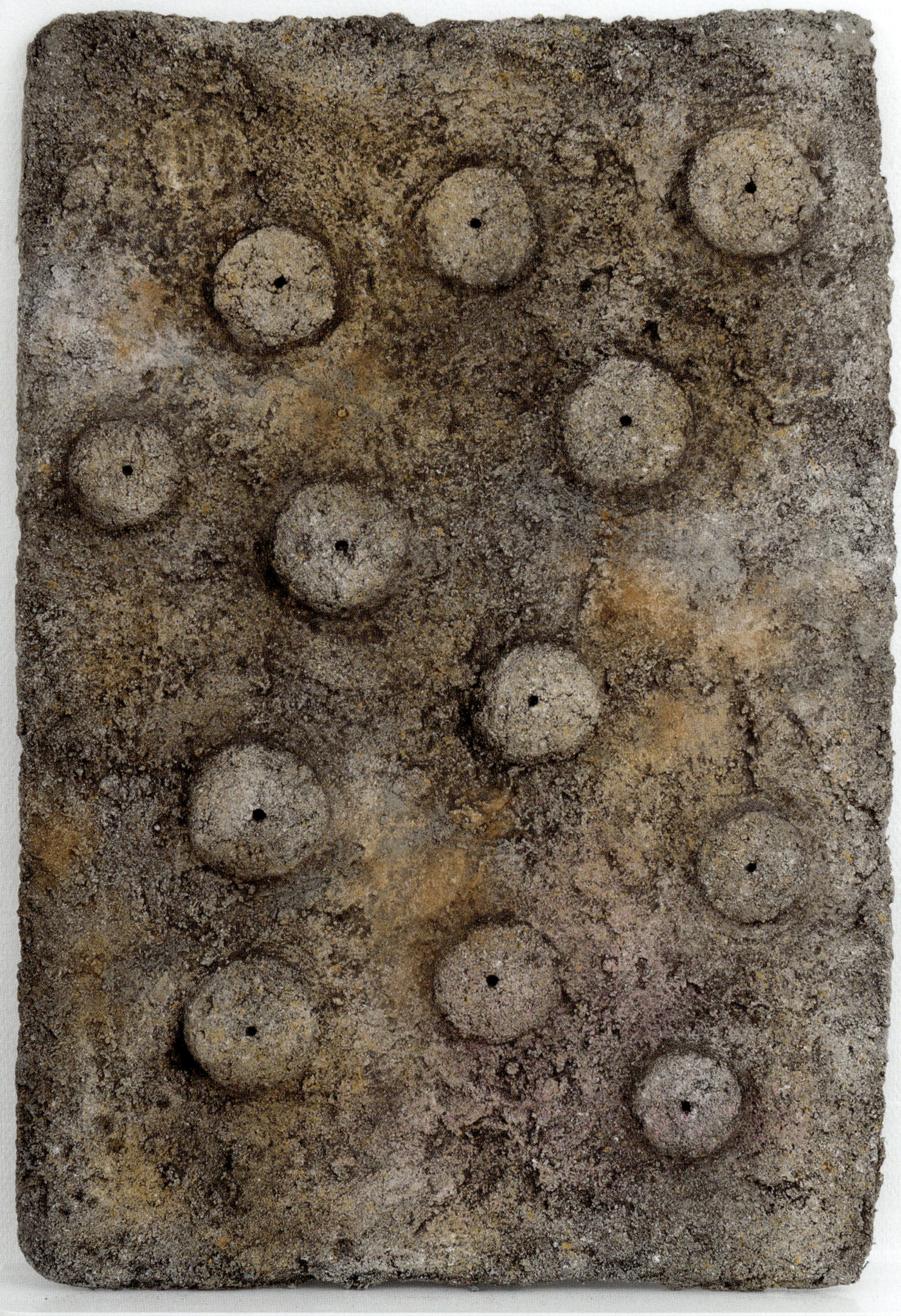

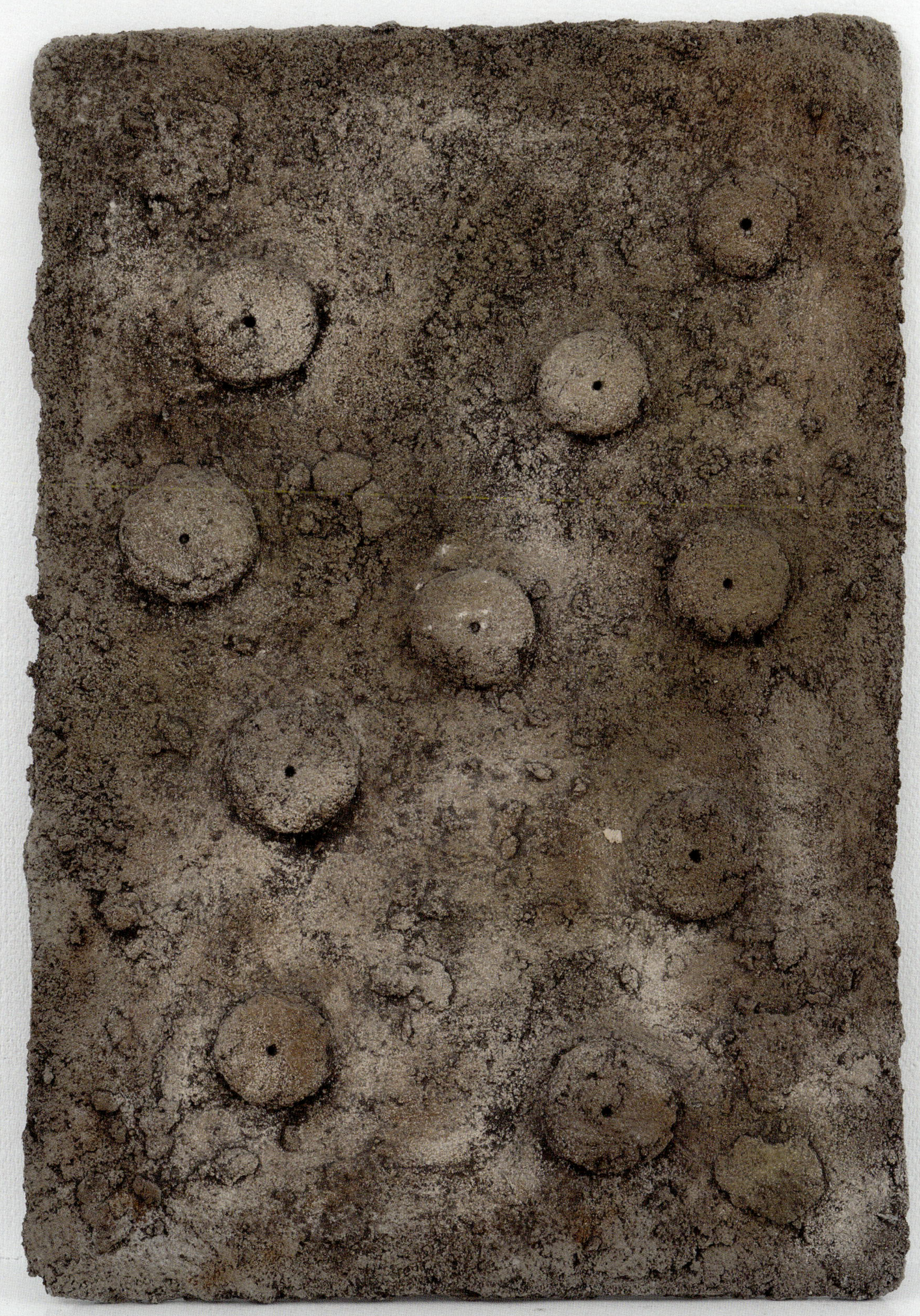

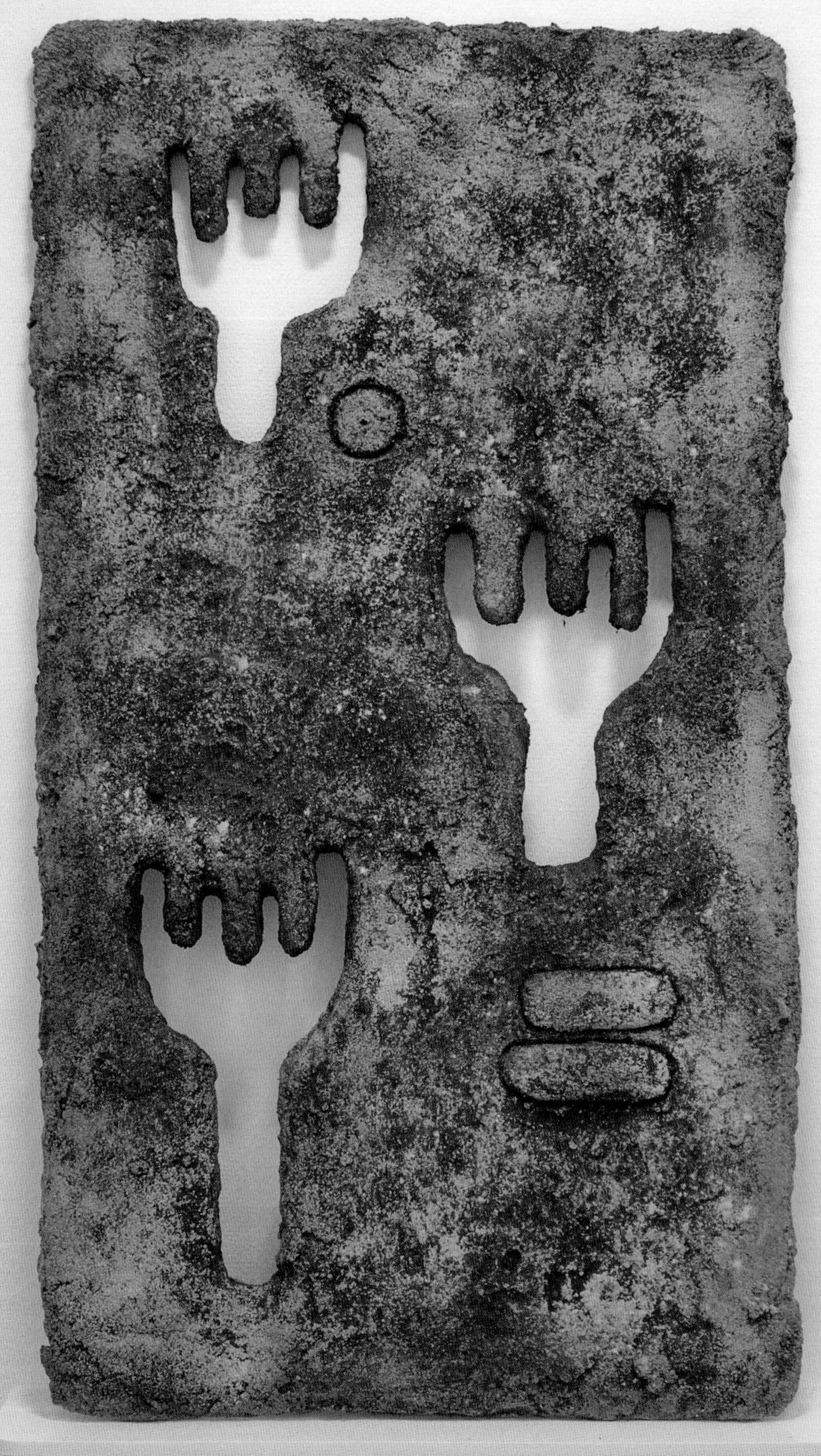

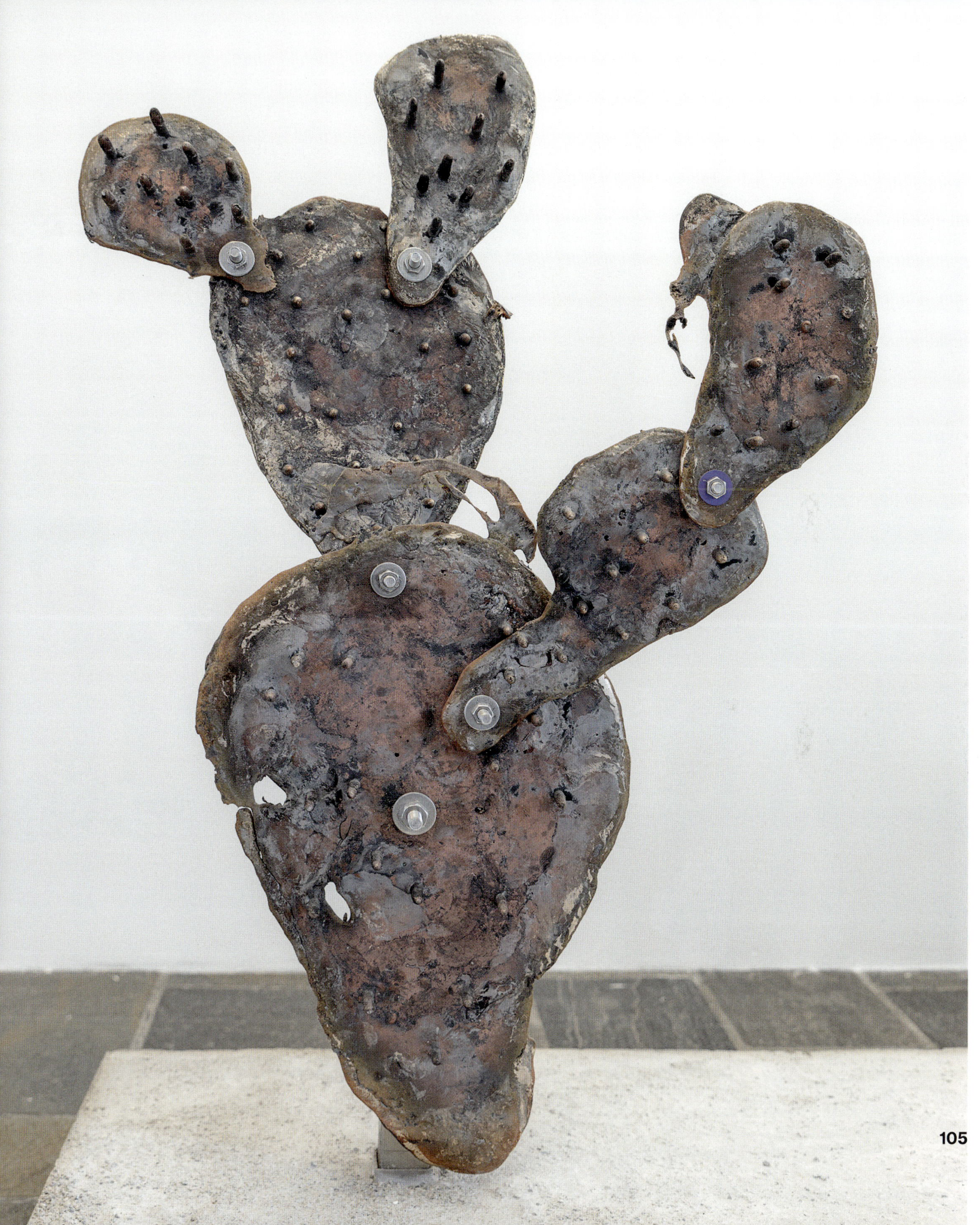

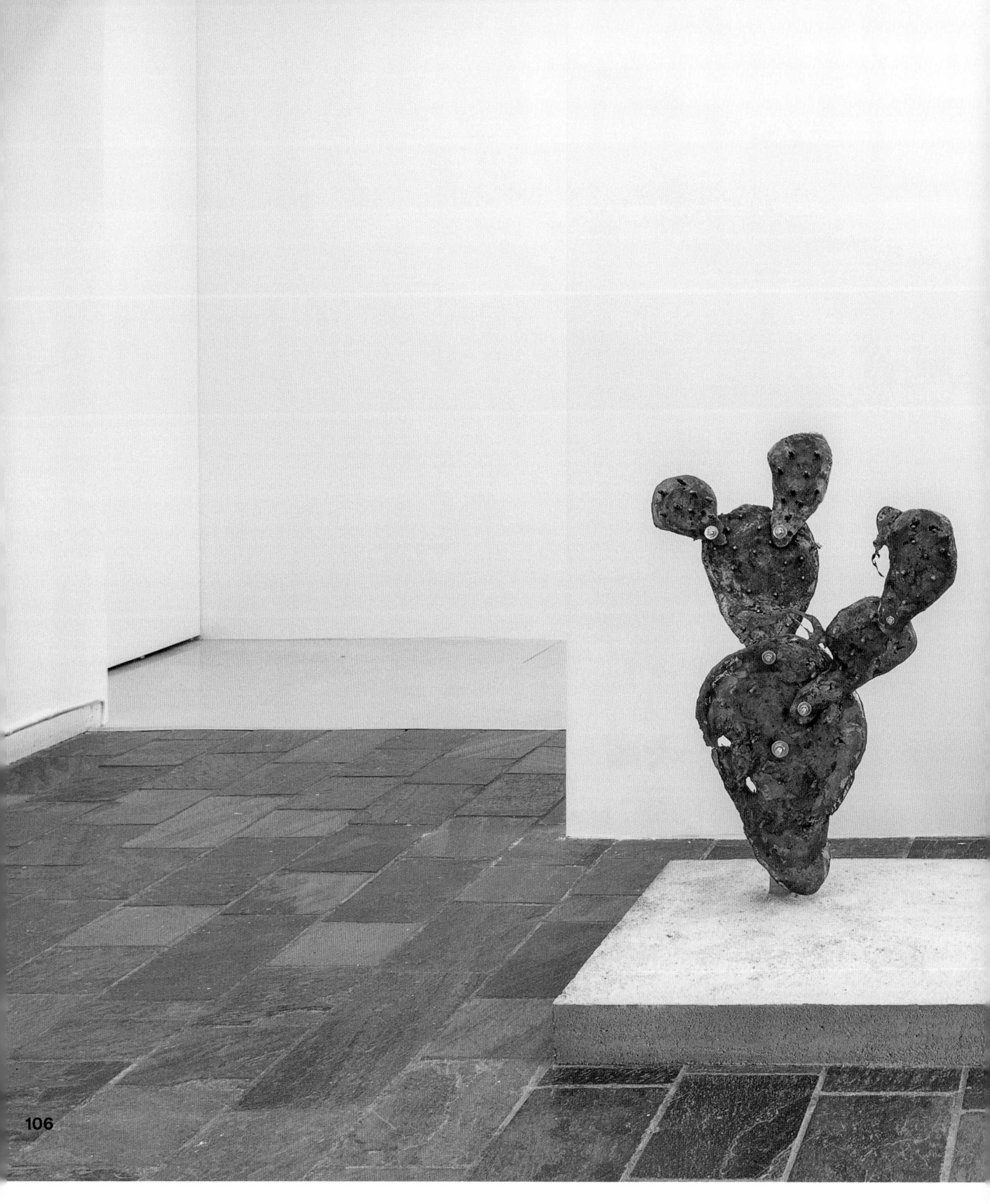

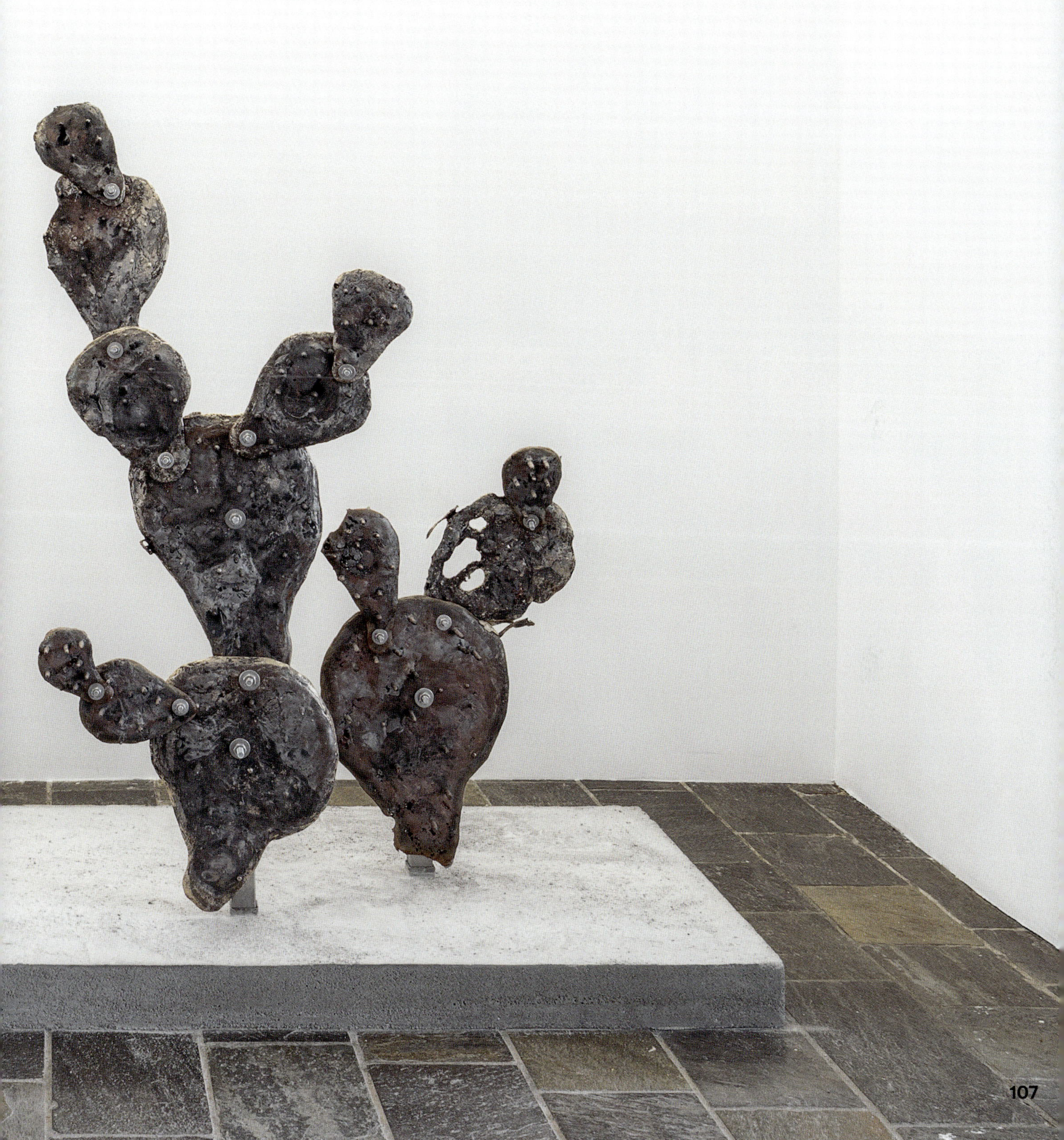

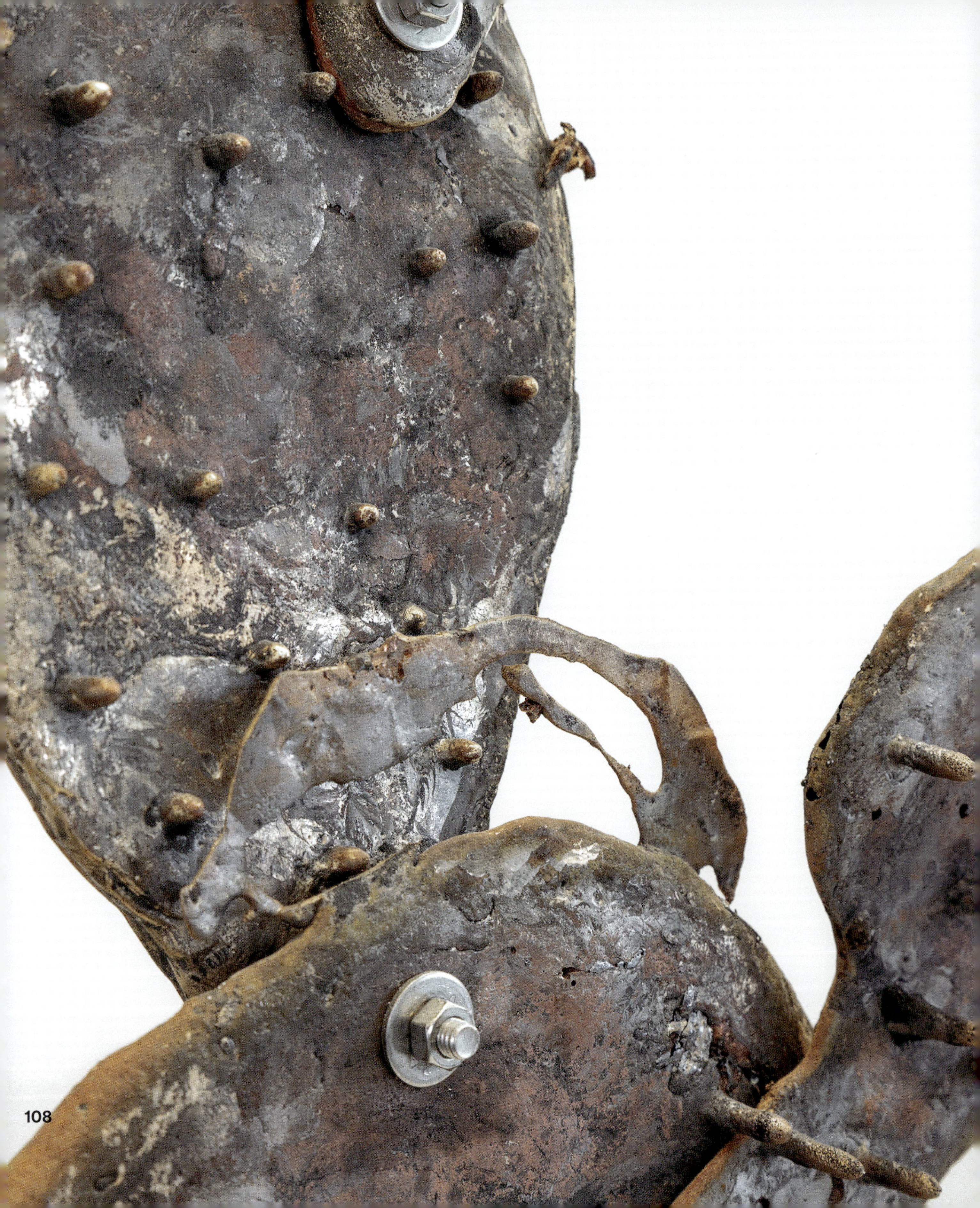

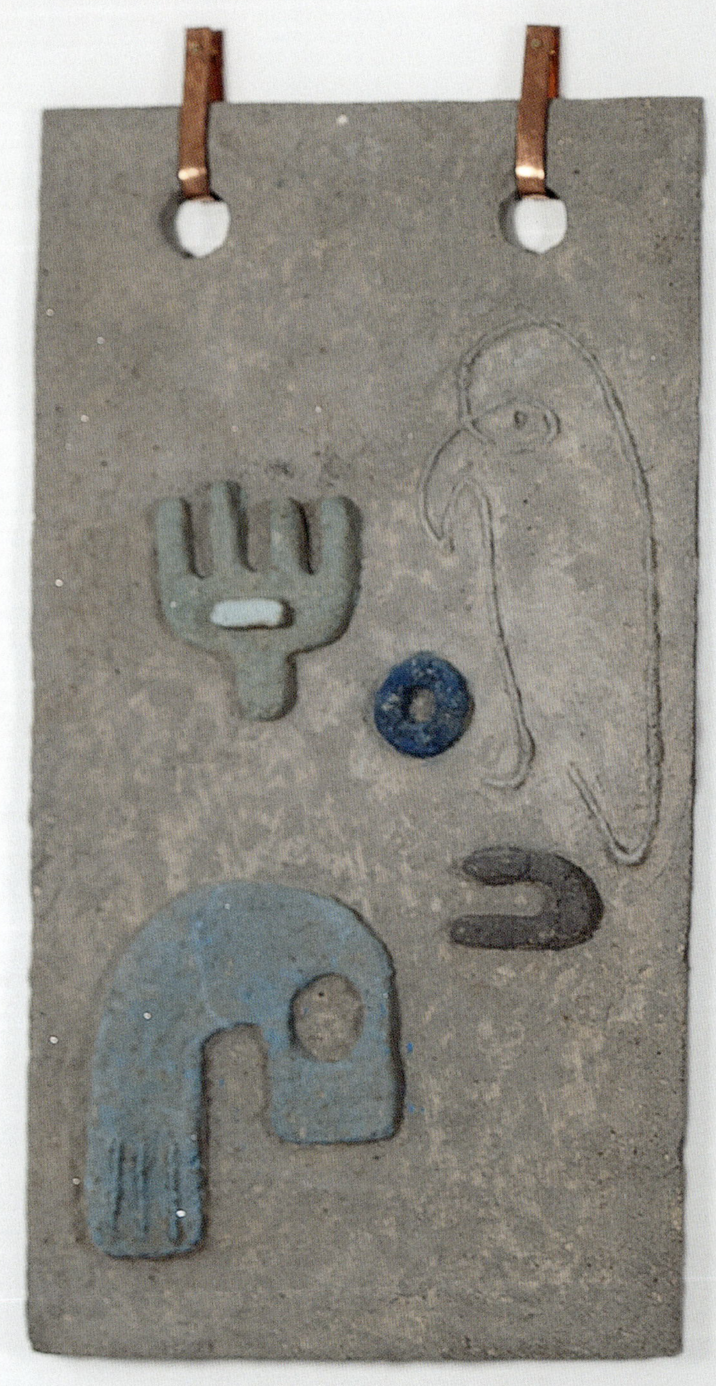
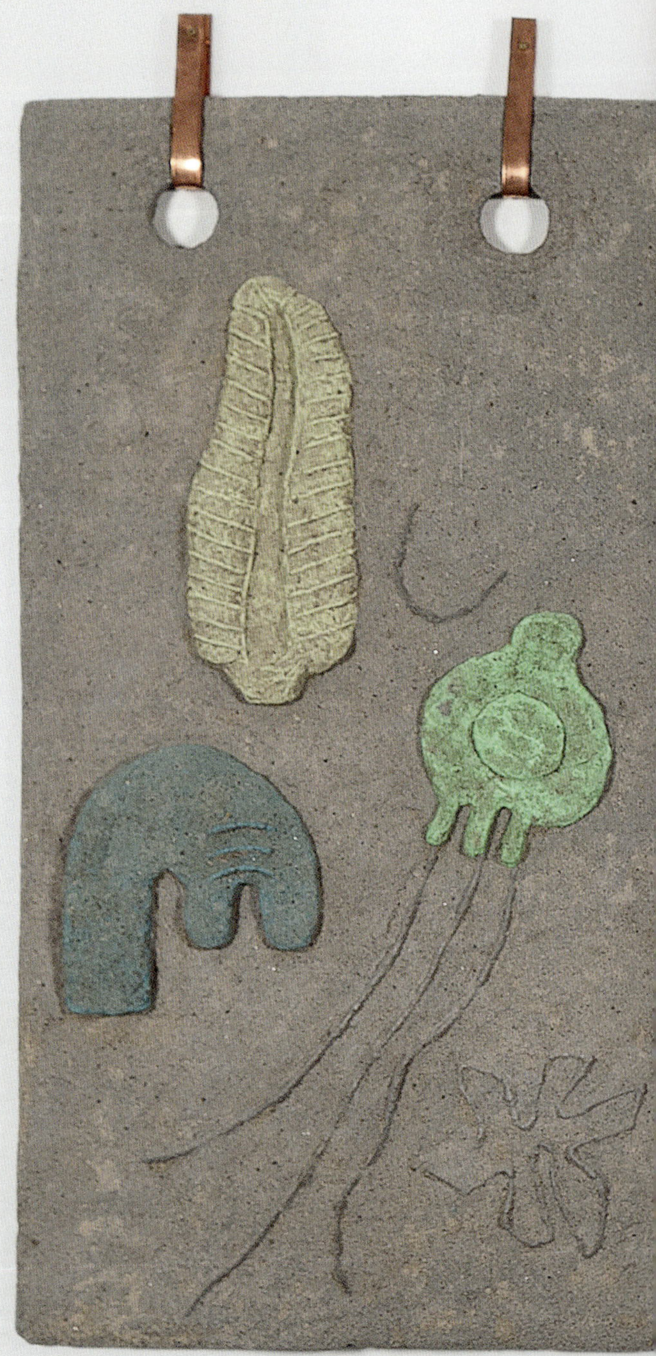

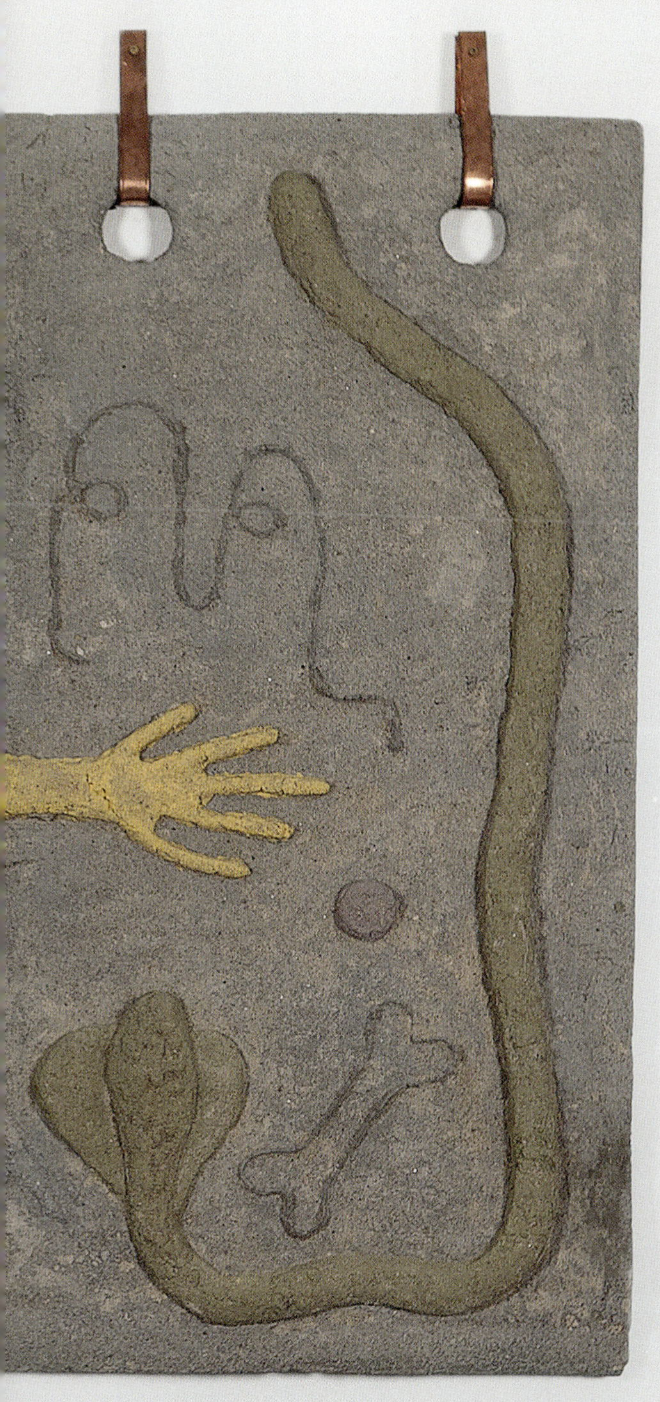

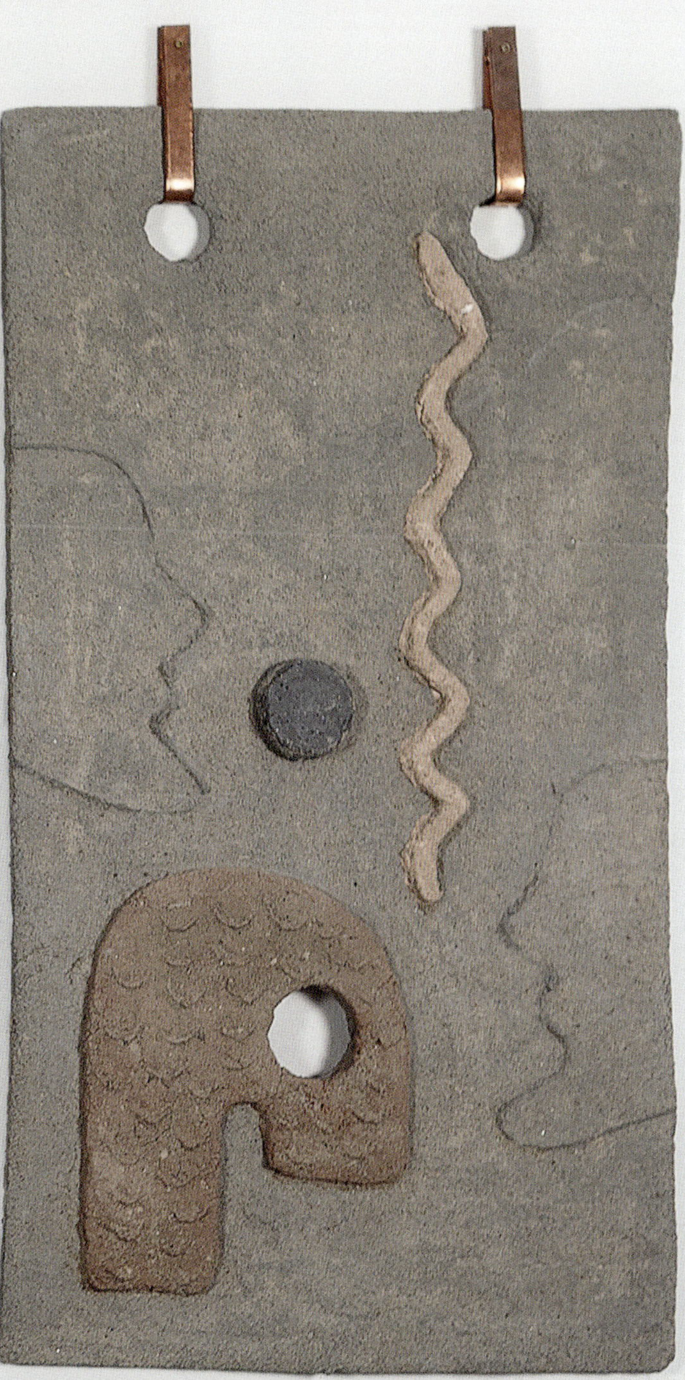

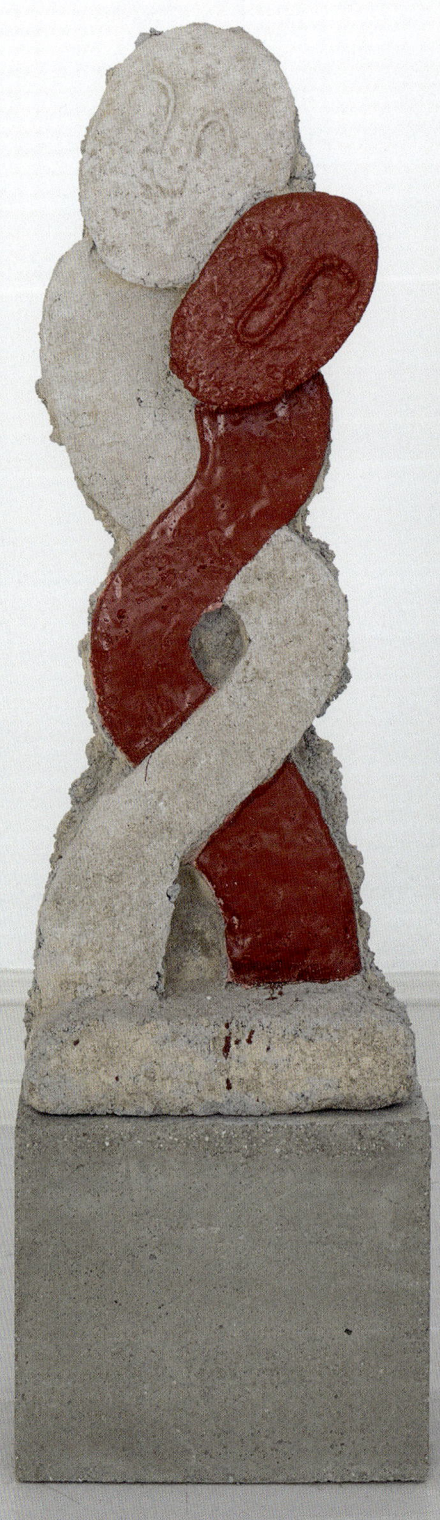

List of illustrations

FIGURE 1
The reverse (tails side) of a Norwegian 1-krone coin, designed by Ingrid Austlid Rise. Original size: 21 mm in diameter.

FIGURE 2
Lene Baadsvig Ørmen, one of the sculptures from the series *hôtel* (part three), 2021, at the Arctic University of Norway, dep. Narvik.

An encounter with Lene Baadsvig Ørmen's sculptures might just jolt one off their perceived timeline. Being in the presence of Lene's sculptural installations always tends to confuse my own sense of the here and now. It feels like time suddenly warping around me, allowing my imagination to drift to myriad possible histories and futures.

These experiences of temporal distortions have to do with how Lene, through her sculptural language, interrogates the idea of history as an ongoing chronological development. In her sculptures, the fascination with cyclical time takes forms that simultaneously hint to the past, the present, and possible futures. They feel like echoes of cultures that have first thrived and then perished, leaving behind signs and symbols that present-day earthlings cannot easily decipher. Or perhaps I am looking at traces of worlds that still exist, but in another corner of the multiverse. In Lene's oeuvre, the linear and cyclical conceptions of time seem to intersect and complement each other.

Lene's artworks do not seem to be from this time, nor from any other defined point in time. They do not point to any particular system of meaning and thus resist clear-cut categorizations. However, there is integrity and an internal logic to each body of work. They are based upon, in Milena Høgsberg's words, "an alphabet I do not have access to." The syntax of Lene's sculptures only begins to unfurl when one takes time to attune to the particular language of each of the materials used and the multiplicity of meanings the materials make when combined. In the artist's own words: "In an alphabet formed by metals, aluminum is one of the letters and bronze is another one."

Lene is sensitive towards how linguistic and descriptive systems evolve in an intimate relationship with the material stuff of the world. The feminist theorist and theoretical physicist Karen Barad has argued that matter and meaning evolve in relations that can best be described as intra-actions.[1] The best response I can utter to Barad's brilliant theorizations is that everything happens in a kind of material-discursive dance. It is quite challenging to attune to the languages used by philosophers and scientists, and therefore artistic attempts to investigate the materiality of language, and the language of materiality, deserve our attention. In this book, Lene, in conversation with artist Leah Beeferman, discusses the language of science and how much the underlying assumptions about the world dictate what kinds of questions scientists are able to pose, how these inquiries limit the range of the possible. What is an artist to do then? To develop engaging questions and to widen the scope of the possible.

Language is always a matter of approximation, and Lene feels an especially strong pull towards the realms of the ineffable. She is often finding ways to tackle phenomena that escape current scientific attention or methods. She is curious about the traces that cultures leave behind for the generations and other cultures to come, and the attempts at translation happening in the encounters between different systems of description. Something will always be lost in the translation process, something always gained. What is certain is that meanings will be morphed, the dancing goes on.

THE PUSH AND PULL BETWEEN MATTER AND MEANING

In Lene's artistic practice, matter and meaning are inseparable. When she works, the material and intellectual processes are entangled. Even if she often experiences these as separate actions, she has described to me how her thoughts affect her hands, and the hands shape her thoughts. Lene seems to be always experimenting with materials and techniques, formulating novel questions and fostering transdisciplinary collaborations. She is constantly steering her attention and artistic practice into uncharted waters.

At the root of Lene's art is an immense curiosity towards how materials such as aluminum, bronze, concrete, sand, soil, and steel behave when exposed to changing circumstances. Lene began her artistic career working with photography, until she came to a realization that working with sculpture might allow her to feel more embedded in her environment, its material flows and cycles, compared with making observations mediated by the camera's lens.

Over the years, Lene has developed her own casting techniques that require letting go of the idea of absolute artistic control and mastery over the materials. Understating the strive for perfection within typical casting techniques, Lene is not interested in trying to impose strict pre-dictated forms upon the materials that she works with. Instead, she tries to strike a balance between holding space for material agencies and cultivating the nuances of her sculptural language.

Through a lengthy process of sketching and drawing, trying to find forms that hold something intriguing for her, she invites new forms into being. She in a way makes and holds space for them to emerge from inside the dark layers of soil or sand. When working with bronze, for instance, she first digs out with her hands the negative molds in sand and then fills these cavities with liquid bronze. The exact ways the metal flows in the mold are beyond Lene's control, and this opens up an opportunity for a dialogue between the artist, the metal, and the mold. Once the metal has found its solid form, the finished bronze sculptures are resurfaced from the sand.

Lene is creating new forms, but she also feels, listens to, and goes with the materials, collaborates with them, acknowledges their agencies. Agency here is understood, as suggested by Vanessa Watts—a scholar on Indigenous material knowledge among the Anishinaabe and Haudenosaunee—not as something belonging exclusively to humans but extending to all natural elements.[2] In one of their dialogues, Lene and Milena discuss Watt's article and what its propositions entail to the so-called Euro-Western ways of knowing.

Among other things, embracing this kind of approach to agency requires dissolving the dualistic divides between humans and other animals. Within the web of life, agency always happens in coexistence, but not always in harmony. Deboleena Roy, a scholar in neuroscience, behavioral biology, and women's, gender, and sexuality studies, notes that instead of using a term such as agency, we could perhaps discuss "the push and pull of things" to highlight how nothing exercises agency on its own.[3] With this approach, one has to accept that things are permanently transforming through processes of mixing and mutating. I find myself thinking how the truly fascinating stuff is always happening in the spaces between the polar opposites.

PATIENCE—ON THE CURVATURE OF TIME

In her conversation with Jan Verwoert, included in this book, Lene mentions that being patient was an important part of the process when making the sculptural series *Dear Darkling* (2015). It takes time for the concrete to dry and to develop cocooned in the darkness. Lene takes the credit for being the creator of the artworks but adds that her role also resembles that of an archeologist. The sculptural pieces are born in the embrace of the earth, while Lene waits for their transformation from liquid to solid state to become complete.

When Lene gently excavates the solidified forms, what emerges are sculptures that are curiously compressed. Some are perforated or otherwise signal how the spaces that appear empty are brimming with potentiality and meaning. Due to their wilful flatness, they seem to be hovering between a two-and three-dimensional existence. To Milena, Lene's pieces bring to mind fossils shaped over eons by the earth's weight.

One might sense a prehistoric as well as a futuristic feel to these artworks, but Lene stresses that they are not intended to represent particular phenomena nor convey pre-determined messages. They might equally well hint at ruins of an ancient culture or belong to the imaginary landscapes of a science fiction novel set out in a distant galaxy.

I find myself pondering, what would it entail to inhabit a cyclical space-time, in which the cosmos, the biosphere, and societies are periodically regenerated? I am reminded of these words by philosopher-magician David Abram:

> The curvature of time in oral cultures is very difficult to articulate on the page .... Yet to fully engage, sensorially, with one's surroundings is to find oneself in a world of cycles within cycles within cycles.[4]

The natural cycles dictate the ebb and flow of earthly phenomena, regardless of whether we take notice or not.

OSCILLATING WAVES BETWEEN REALITY SYSTEMS

Instead of relying on the logic of binary oppositions, Lene's sculptures seem to be undulating between different dimensions. They negotiate various types of tensions: between different cosmologies, between the spiritual and the scientific worldview, between organically occurring and strictly pre-dictated forms. They are signaling yes, no, and maybe, all at the same time.

The thematic red thread running through Lene's oeuvre is the fusing together of varied systems for assigning meaning to the world. Lene subtly and skillfully highlights the tensions that form when incompatible worldviews collide. This can happen, for instance, through juxtaposing rigorously geometrical and polished support structures with the raw and textured surfaces and organically curving forms of the casted sculptural objects.

Platforms, pedestals, steel tubes, wires, and other supportive structures always play an important part in perfecting the tension of each sculpture and installation. In the body of work *Subterranea* (2019), stacked concrete slabs and interconnected steel plumbing pipes are holding bronze sculptures that evoke animal shapes, mythological characters, and abstract bronze clusters. If this installation forms narratives of human and more-than human relationships, who is supporting whom? Who feeds on whom? Again, I feel like I am encountering a feedback loop whose dynamics and workings I cannot quite pin down.

In *n0thing* (2018), a rectangular concrete pedestal supports a wishing well guarded by an ancient deity that has taken an earthly form in aluminum. I toss a coin and make a wish while I watch the piece of metal sink in the water. Magical beliefs and talismanic figurines, ritual objects and spaces for contemplation—these are all recurring motifs in Lene's oeuvre. She is curious towards the meanings and power carried by rituals, even in secular communities.

FIGURE 1

Following the Italian philosopher Federico Campagna's thinking around two conflicting reality systems, Lene seems to be playing with the tensions between the "cosmogonies" of Technic and Magic.[5] In very subtle ways, Lene's oeuvre points to the limitations of the scientific and technological world order to address many cosmic unknowns. Lene carves and holds space for those realms of life that do not easily fit into the scientific systems of description.

FEELING THE REVERBERATIONS

A multifaceted public commission for KORO at UiT Narvik university campus (2021–), one of Lene's latest projects, combines many of the artistic and philosophical concerns mentioned above—and introduces a whole new scale. The three-folded artwork titled *hôtel*, is an architectural, sculptural, and sonic installation that consists of fragments dispersed across space and time yet are conceptually interwoven.

Lene's intention with this commission has been to foster experiences of connectedness—to one's environment and to one's self. As her point of departure, Lene had been looking into how spaces of worship, such as temples and shrines, evoke meditative and spiritual experiences. But whereas religious architecture is often designed to make the devotees feel small, and to blow the non-believers off their feet, Lene was keen to create something more humble and more grounded to daily life on the campus. She decided to create a space for solitary contemplation that would transgress the boundaries between different belief systems.

A research trip to Japan in early 2020 proved to be important to how the commission developed. In Japan, Lene was impressed by how worship was integrated into the everyday life of many locals. Shinto and Buddhist temples and shrines were ubiquitous, and rites and rituals could happen sometimes quite spontaneously. Lene shares with me a memory that left a lasting impression:

> Once I was invited to join a small ritual for the fire gods in a rural area north of Kyoto. We were six people gathered around a shrine that was located next to a bus stop, bowing, clapping our hands and giving offerings of sake.

These kinds of experiences made Lene think about how the sacred and the quotidian experiences could be brought closer together in the rather different cultural context of northern Norway. The artwork that was born out of these questions consists of three parts. The central element is located outdoors on the campus grounds, a large concrete sculpture realized in collaboration with the architecture office KFA Arkitekter. From the outside, the sculpture's form brings to my mind a giant tardigrade. In the local vernacular, the piece is also called "the elephant." The sculpture's purple-brown shade is derived from the iron pigment characteristic of the Narvik region. During a site visit to the town, Lene noticed how there is iron dust gathering everywhere, naturally giving a coat to many surfaces, and wanted to highlight this local element in her piece.

To find the second element, one must look beyond the surface. Inside the sculpture, there's a tall and narrow space that fits only one visitor at a time. Those entering the chamber will become immersed in a site-specific sound piece developed in collaboration with composer, microtonal tuba player, and sound engineer Peder Simonsen. The third element is a series of six small wall sculptures cast in bronze. They are installed indoors, on the walls of a corridor painted black. The sculptures shimmer and emerge just slightly from the dark walls, reminding after-images or reverberations. If the giant concrete sculpture is the mothership, then maybe these are shuttle crafts, or escape pods?

FIGURE 2

To build the layered, site-specific sonic environment inside the concrete sculpture, Peder, for his part, also combined three elements. He started by playing the small bronze sculptures like percussion instruments, hitting them as if they were gongs. Through multiple steps, each sculpture's unique sonic signature became part of the composition. The acoustic environment of the concrete chamber, its so-called room modes, and the ways sound reflect from its walls, form another element. The composition also incorporates sounds of the local environment.

Through a moment spent listening and sensing the resonances of the space, Lene hopes that staff, students, and the community will visit something larger than themselves. In this moment of fast-forward culture obsessed with memes and other communication formats that provide instant gratification through fast fixes of dopamine, Lene would like to encourage people to take some time to sit with something they might not quite be able to wrap their head around.

1 Karen Barad, *Meeting the Universe Halfway: Quantum Physics and the Entanglement of Matter and Meaning* (Durham, NC: Duke University Press, 2007).
2 Vanessa Watts, "Indigenous place-thought & agency amongst humans and non-humans (First Woman and Sky Woman go on a European world tour!)," *Decolonization: Indigeneity, Education & Society* 2, no. 1, (2013): 20–34.
3 Deboleena Roy, *Molecular Feminisms: Biology, Becomings, and Life in the Lab* (Seattle: University of Washington Press, 2018), 35, 131.
4 David Abram, *The Spell of the Sensuous* (New York: Vintage Books, 1997), 186–89.
5 Federico Campagna, *Technic and Magic: The Reconstruction of Reality* (London: Bloomsbury Academic, 2018).

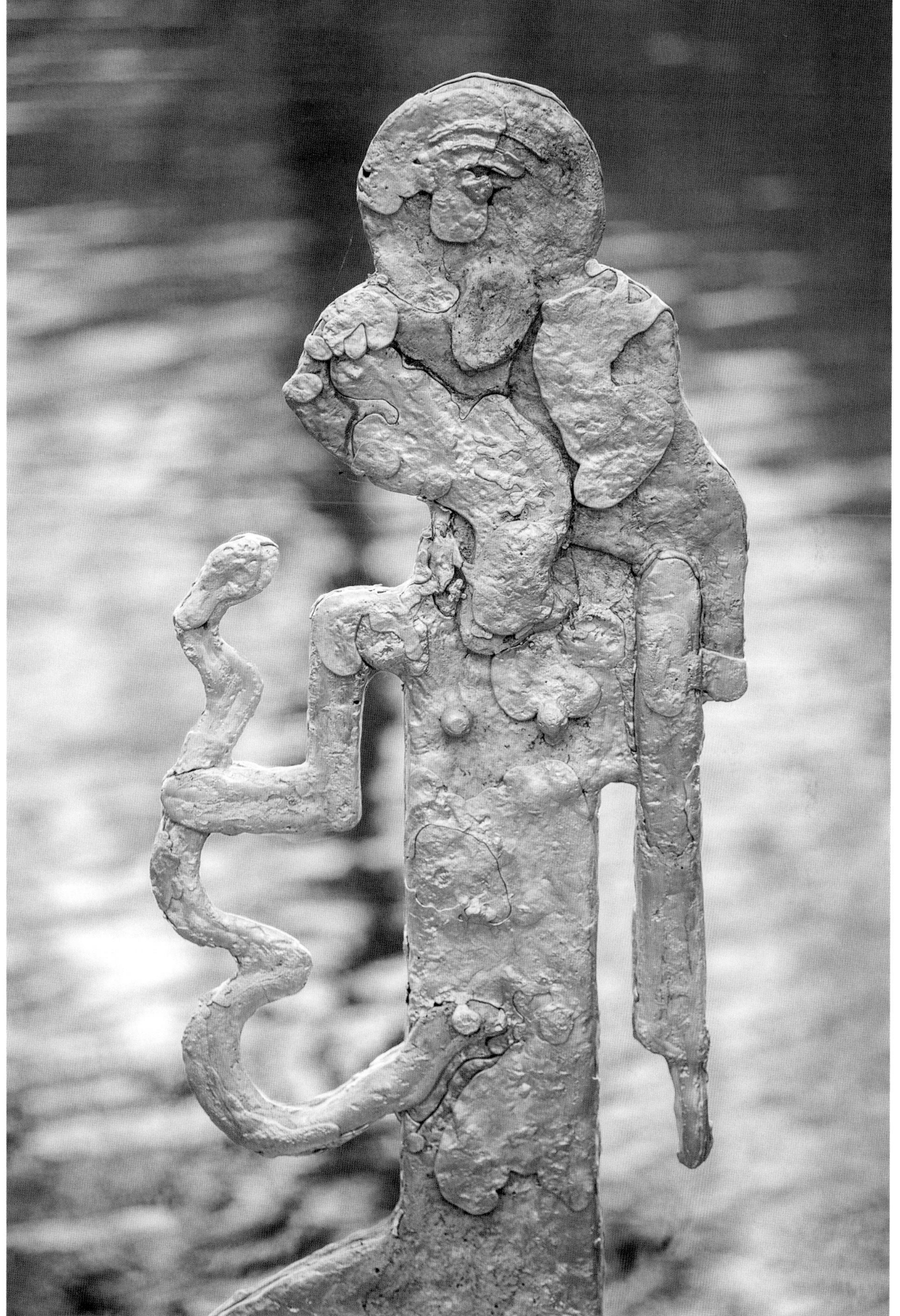

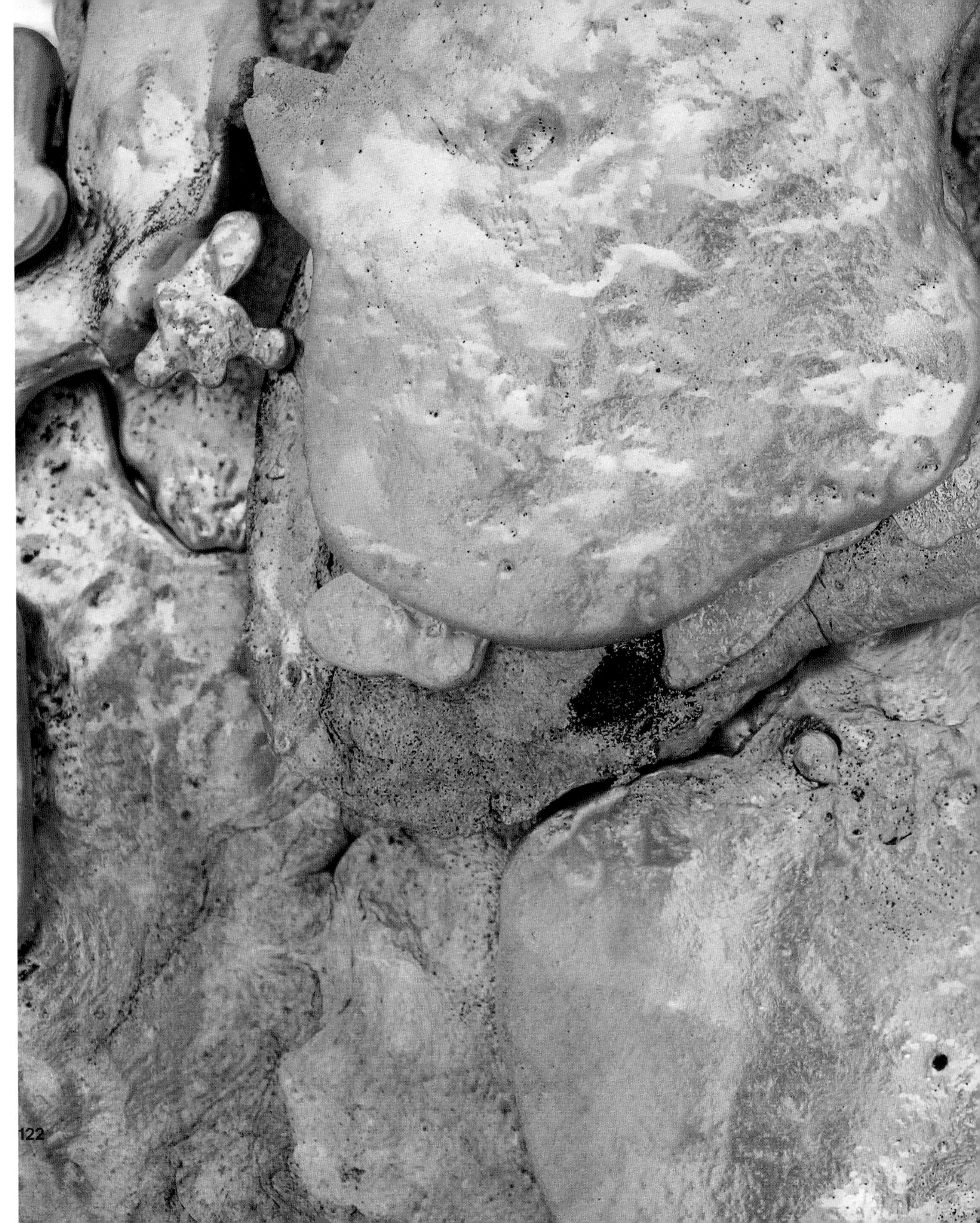

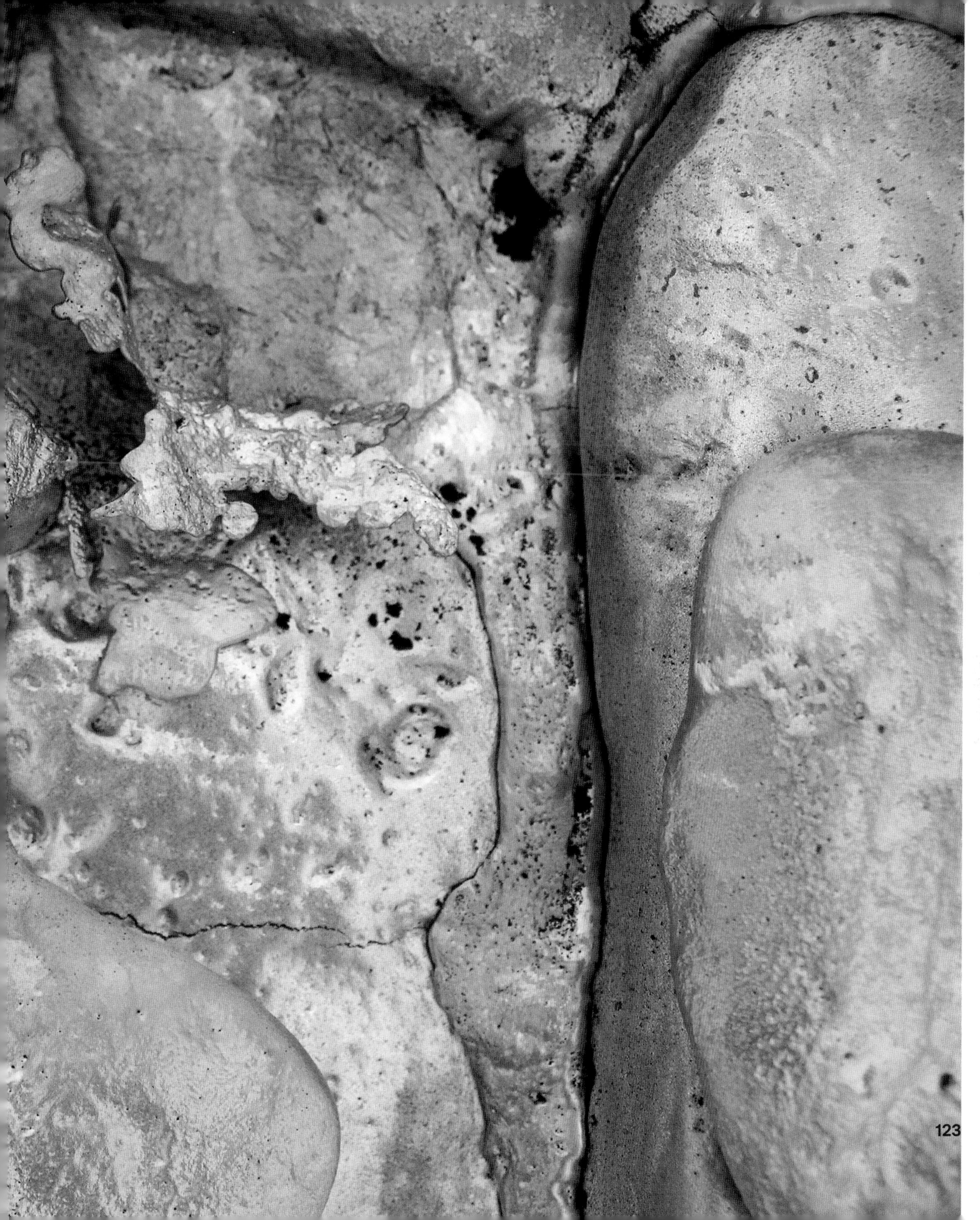

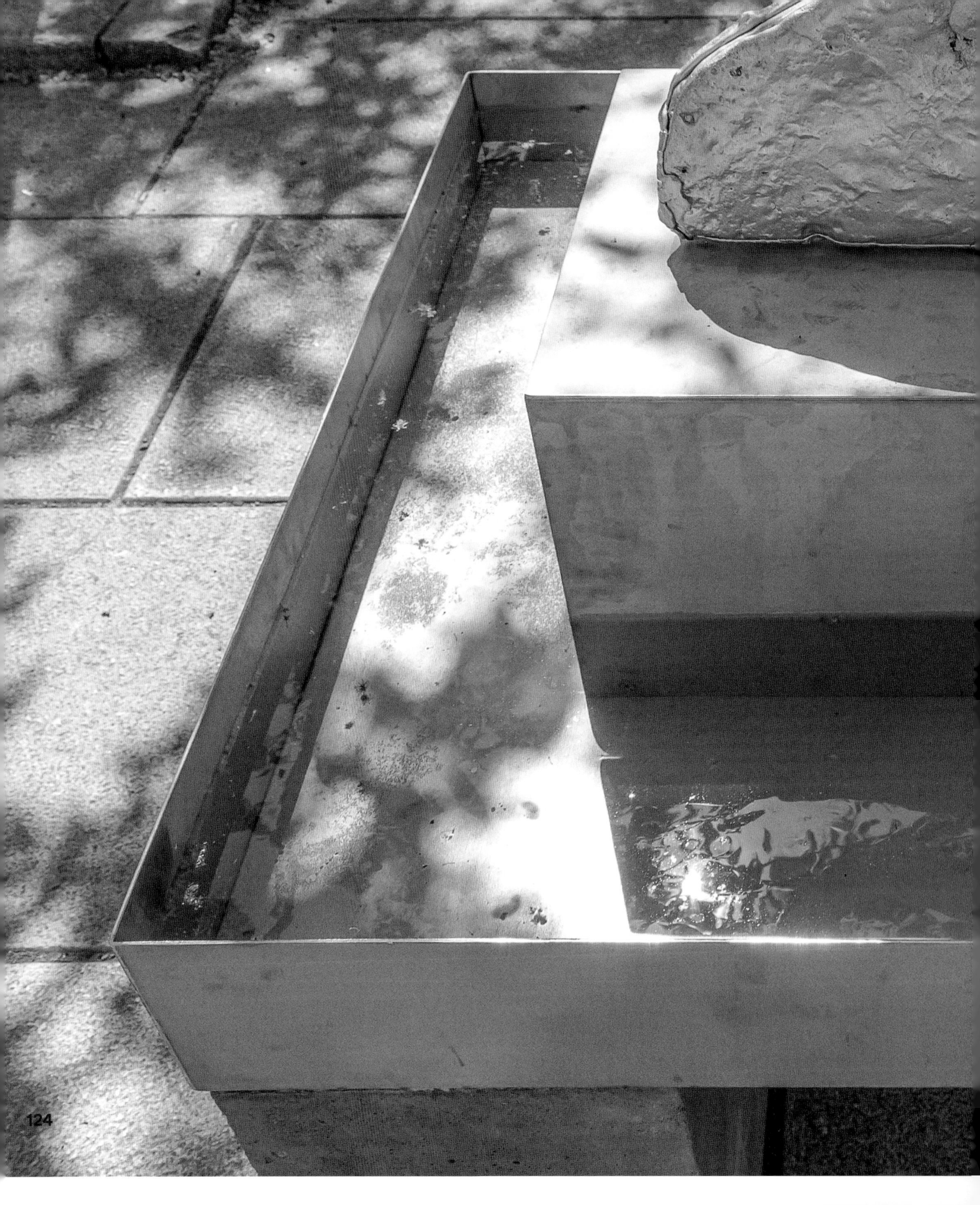

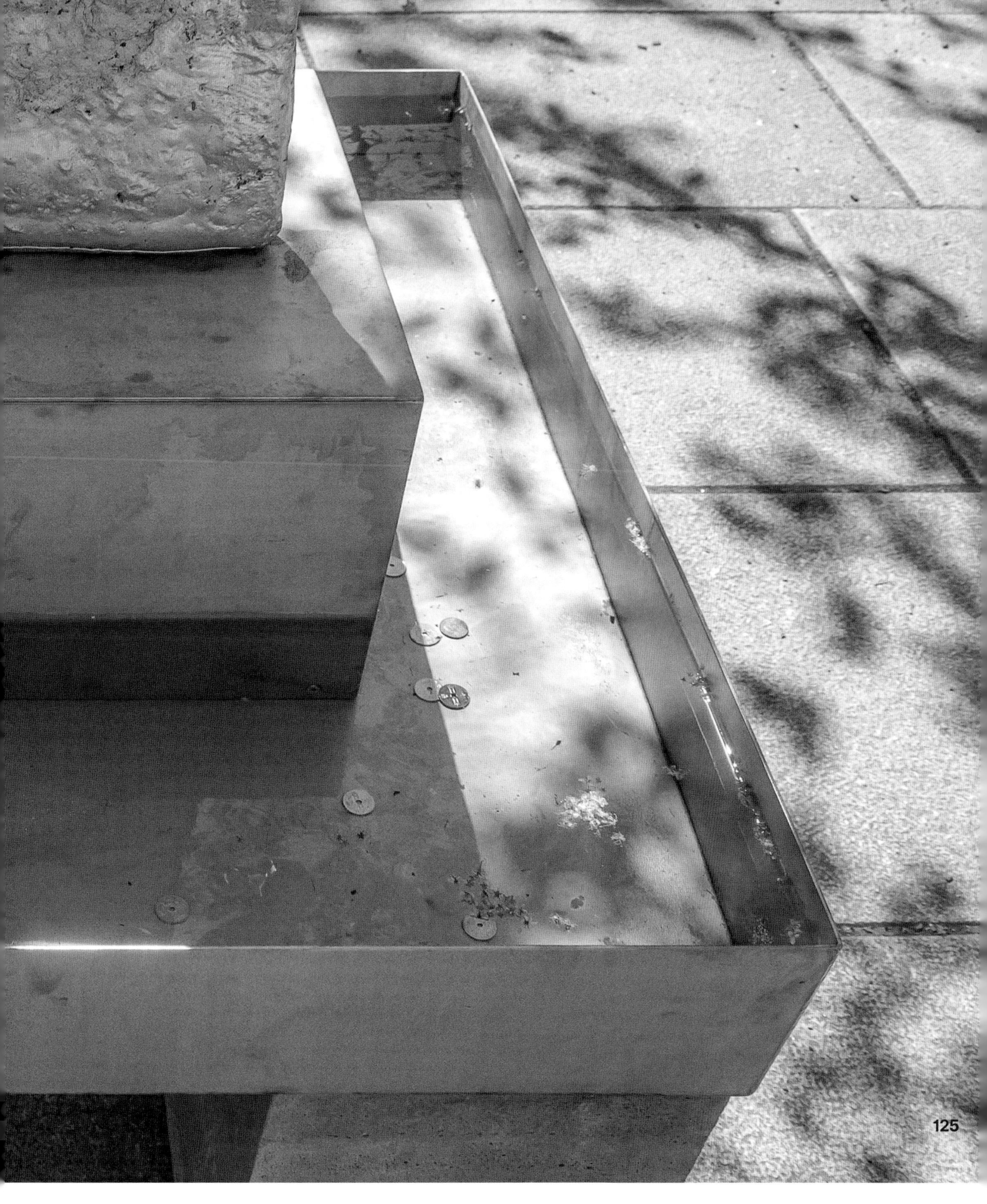

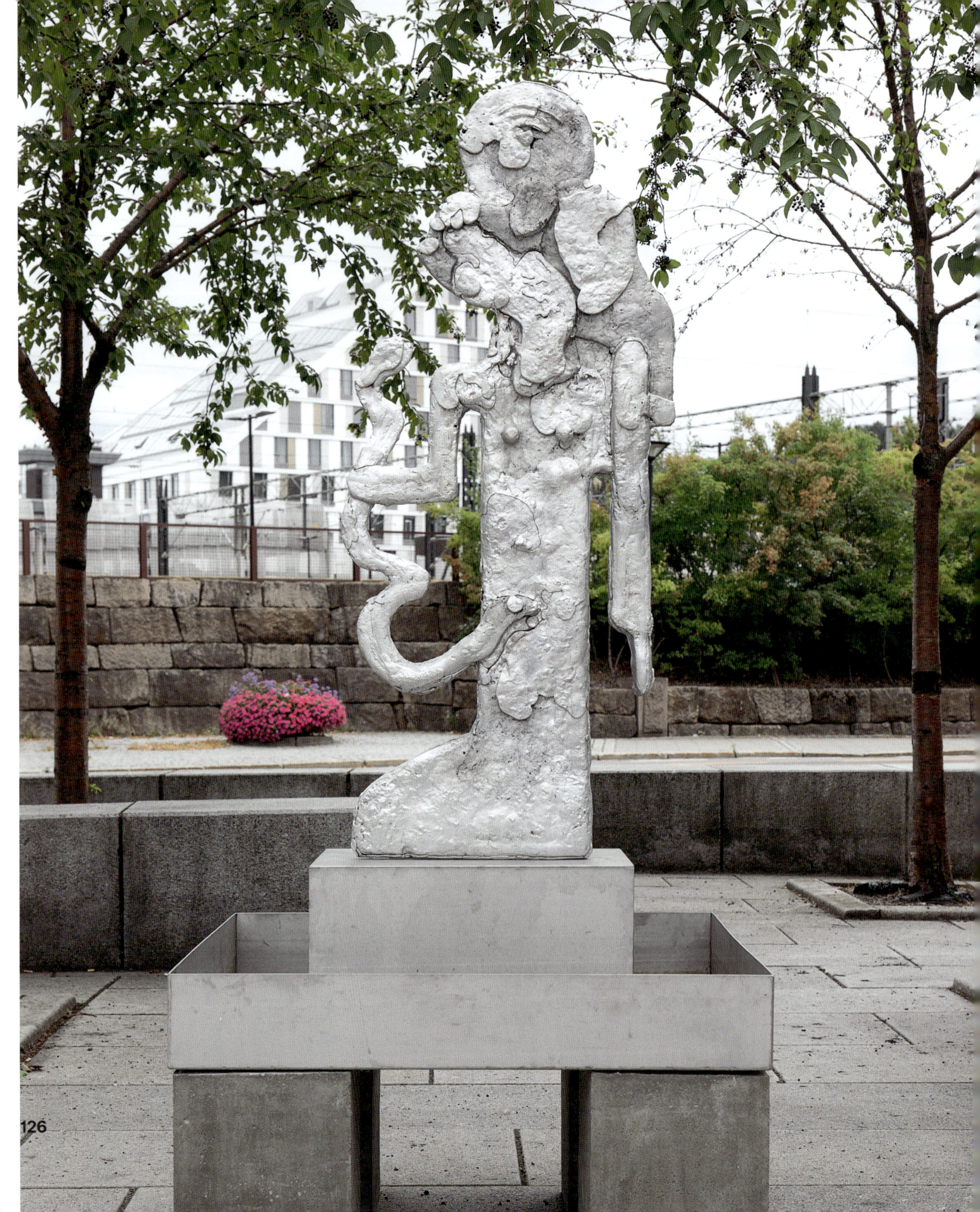

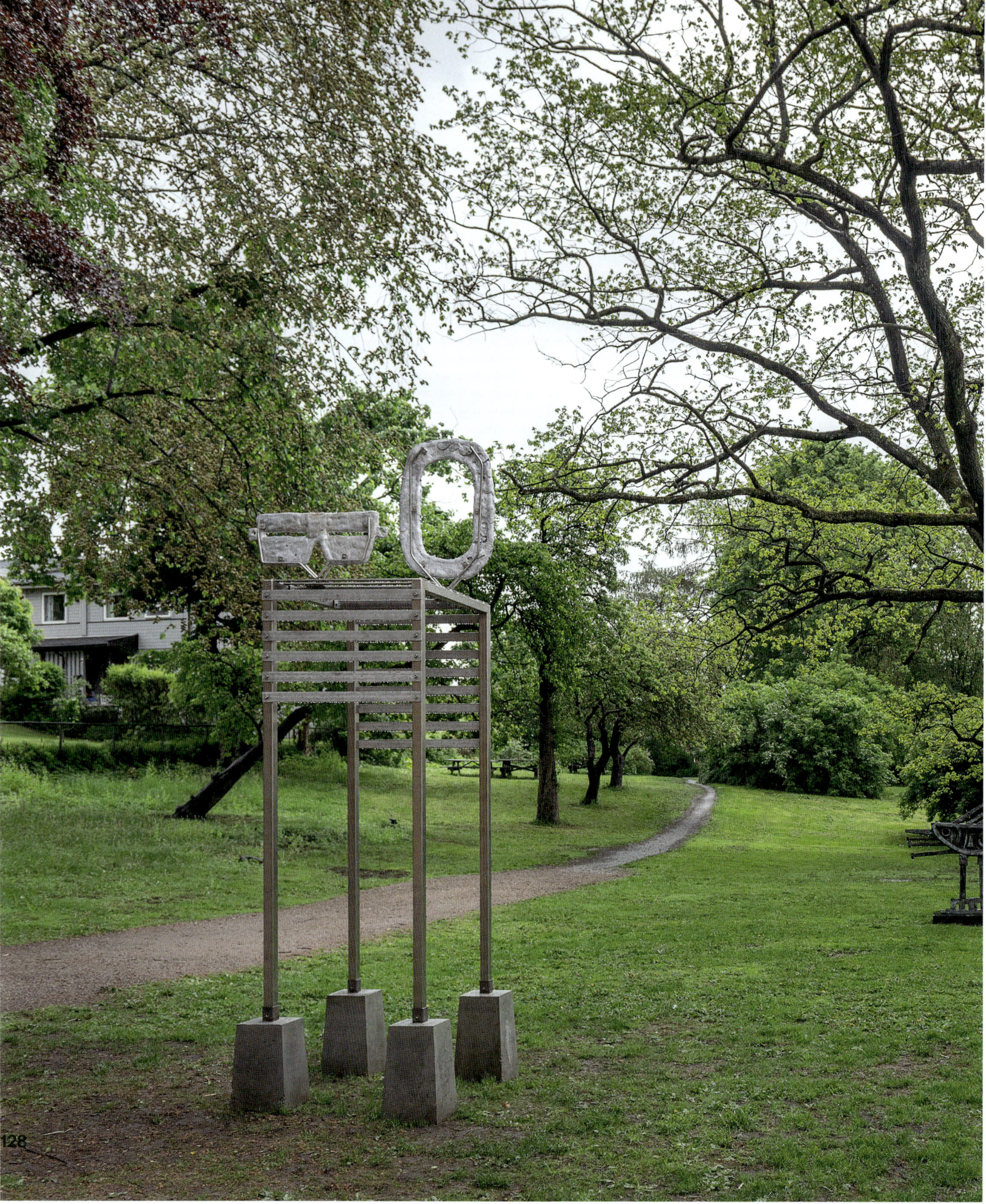

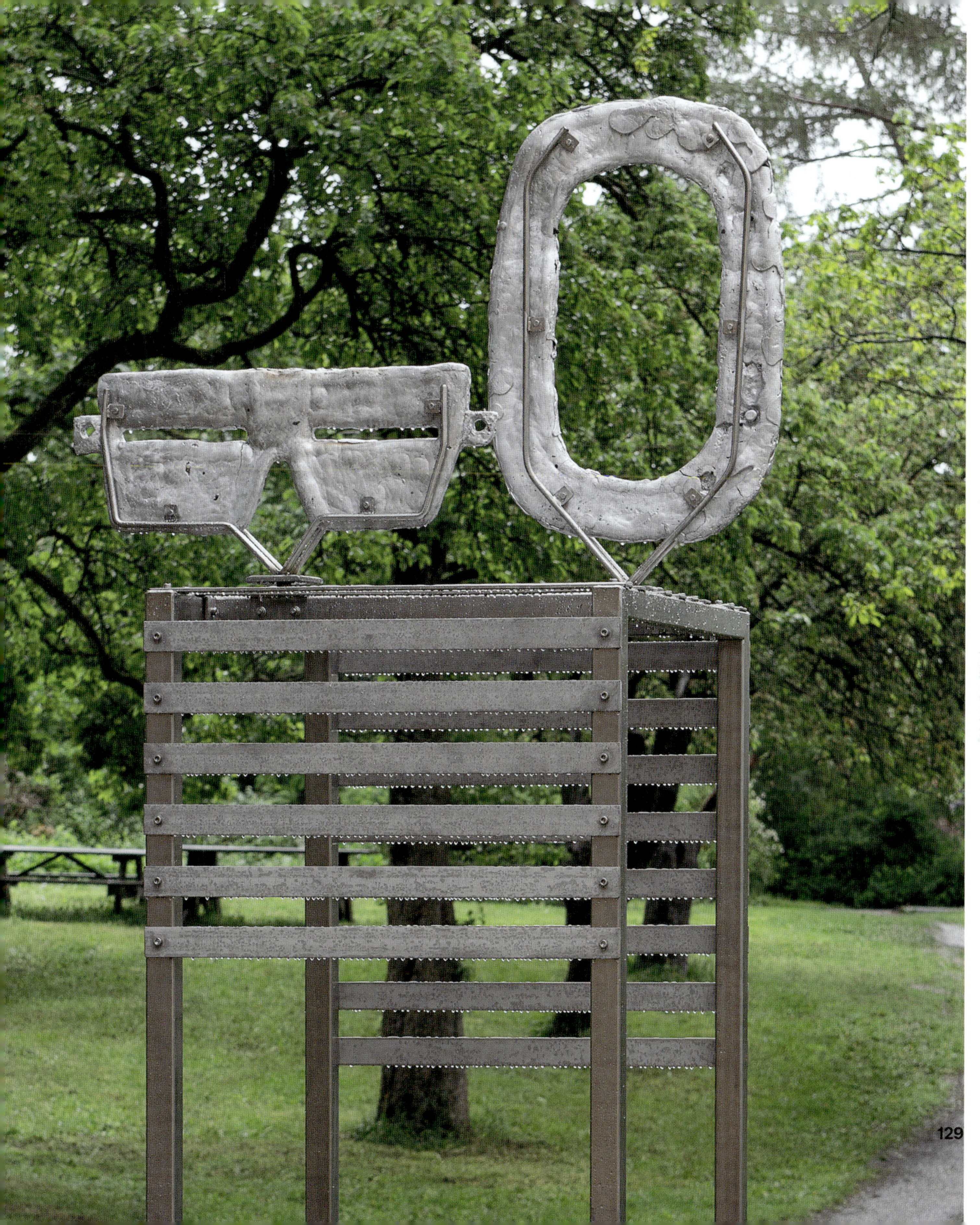

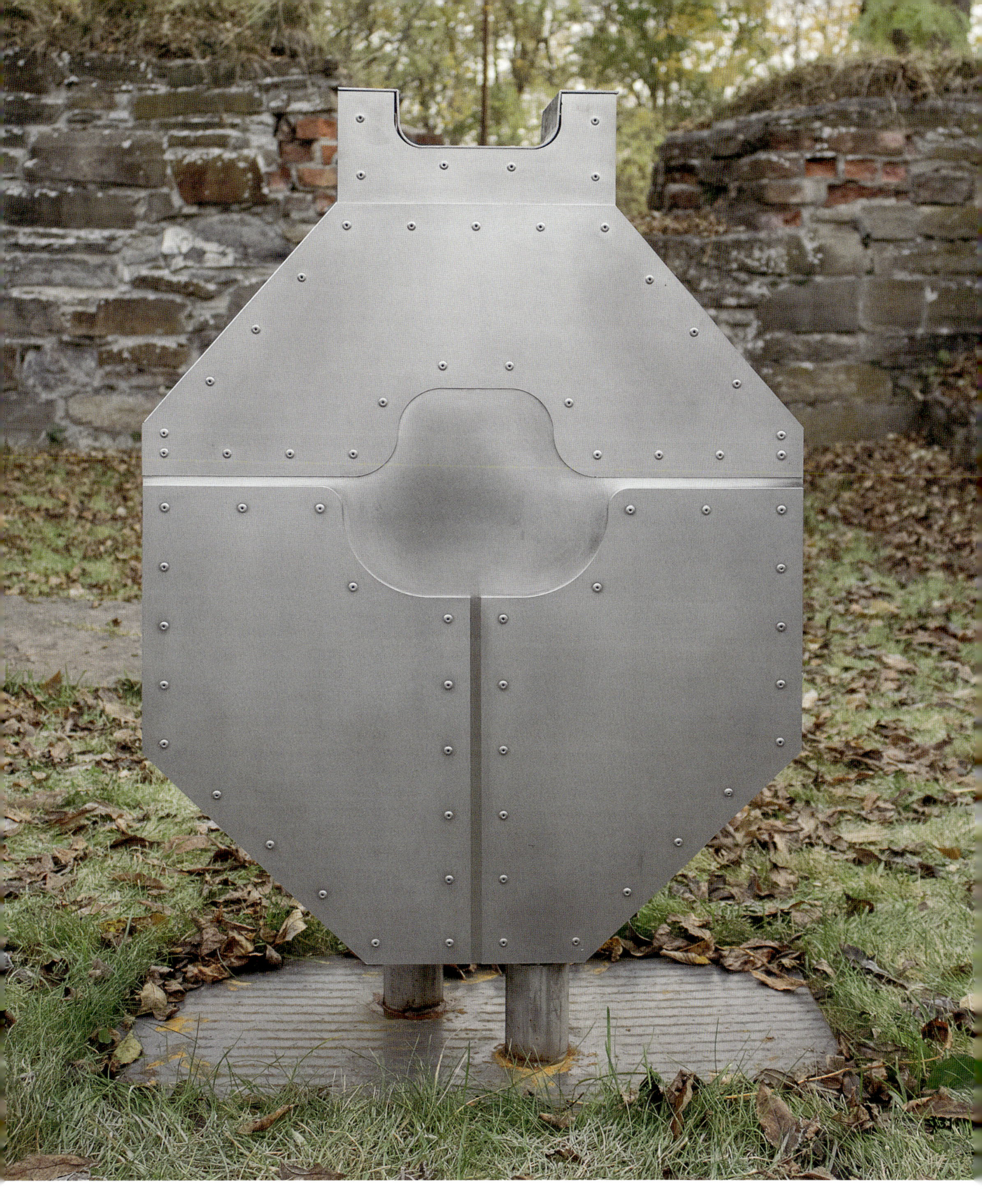

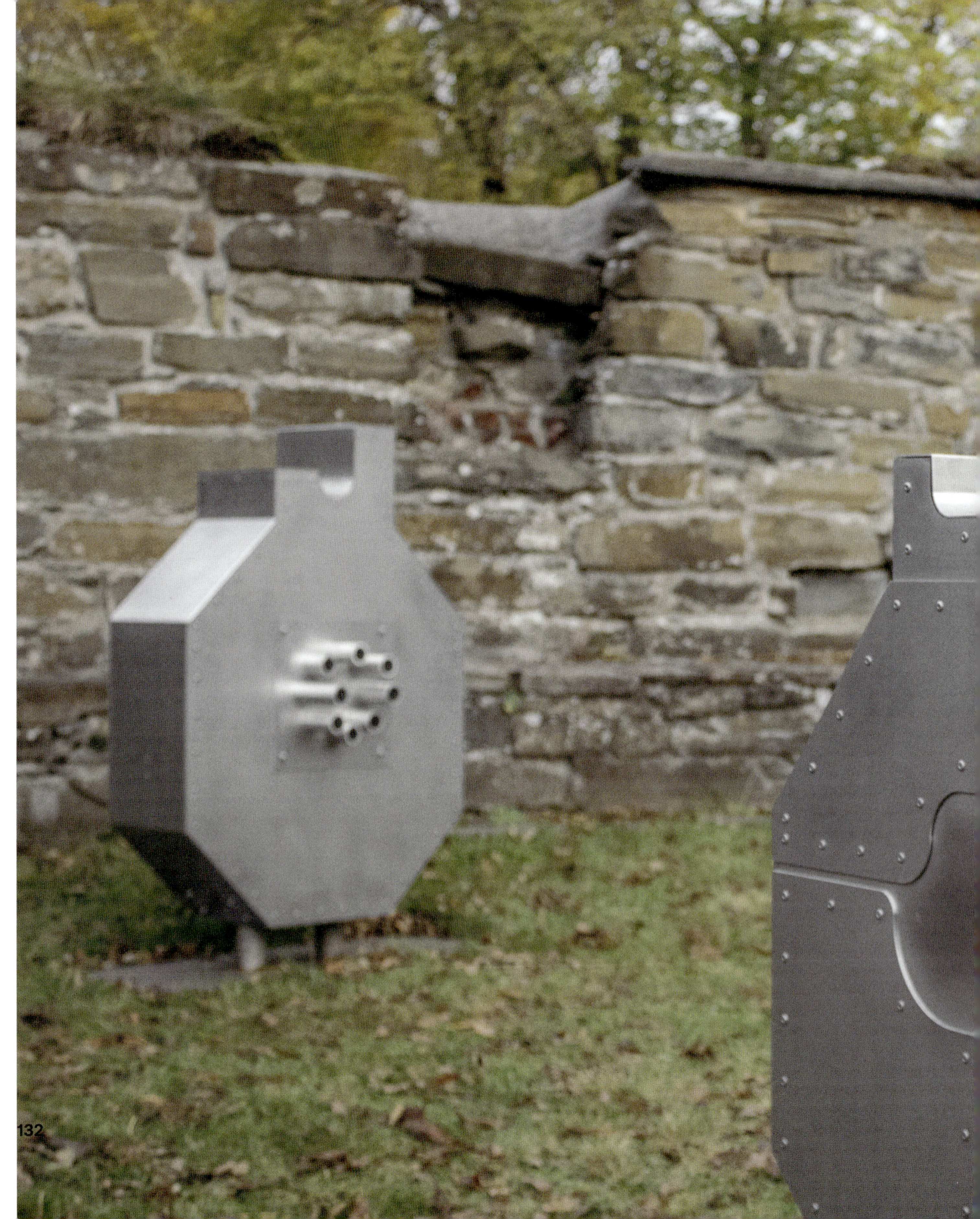

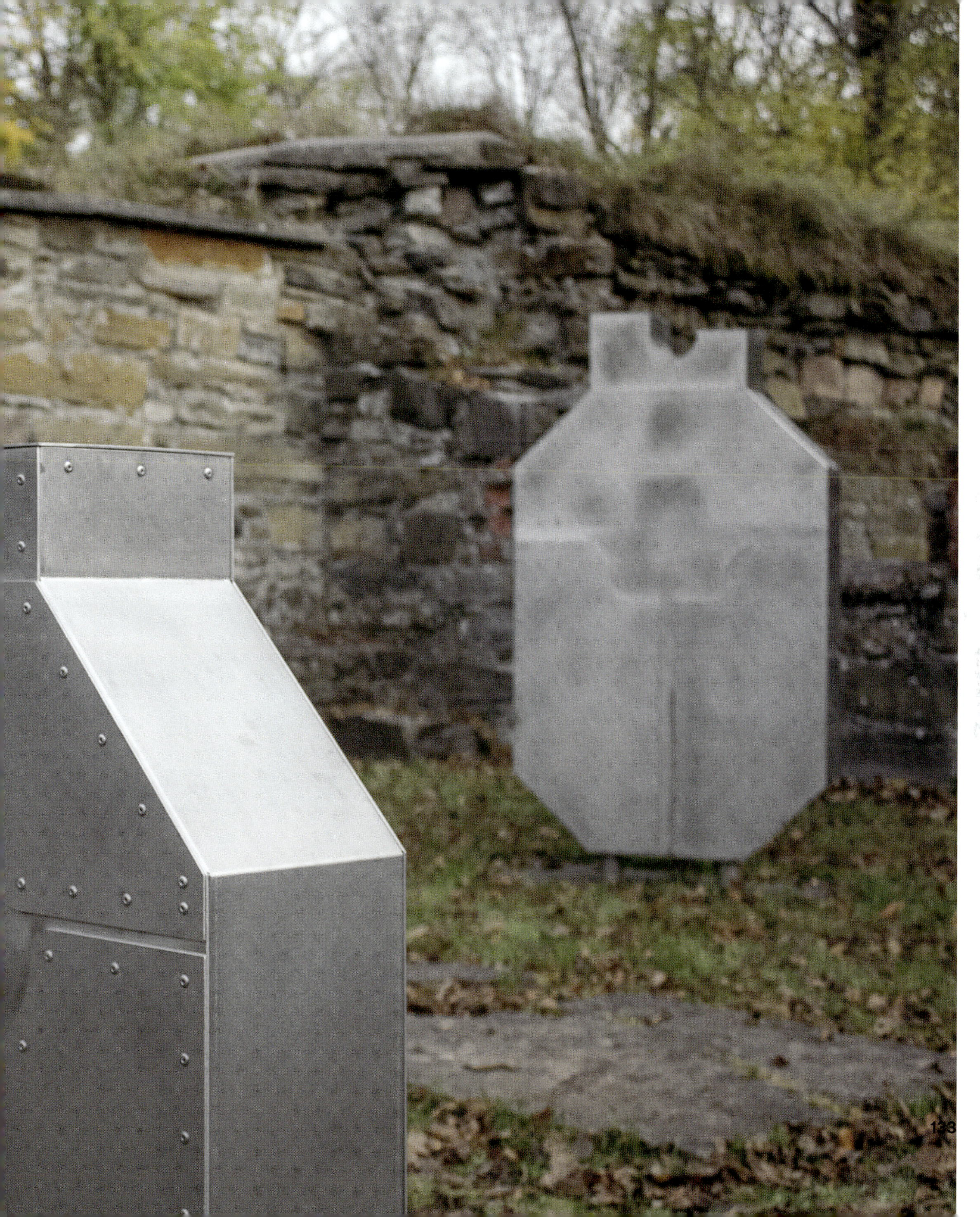

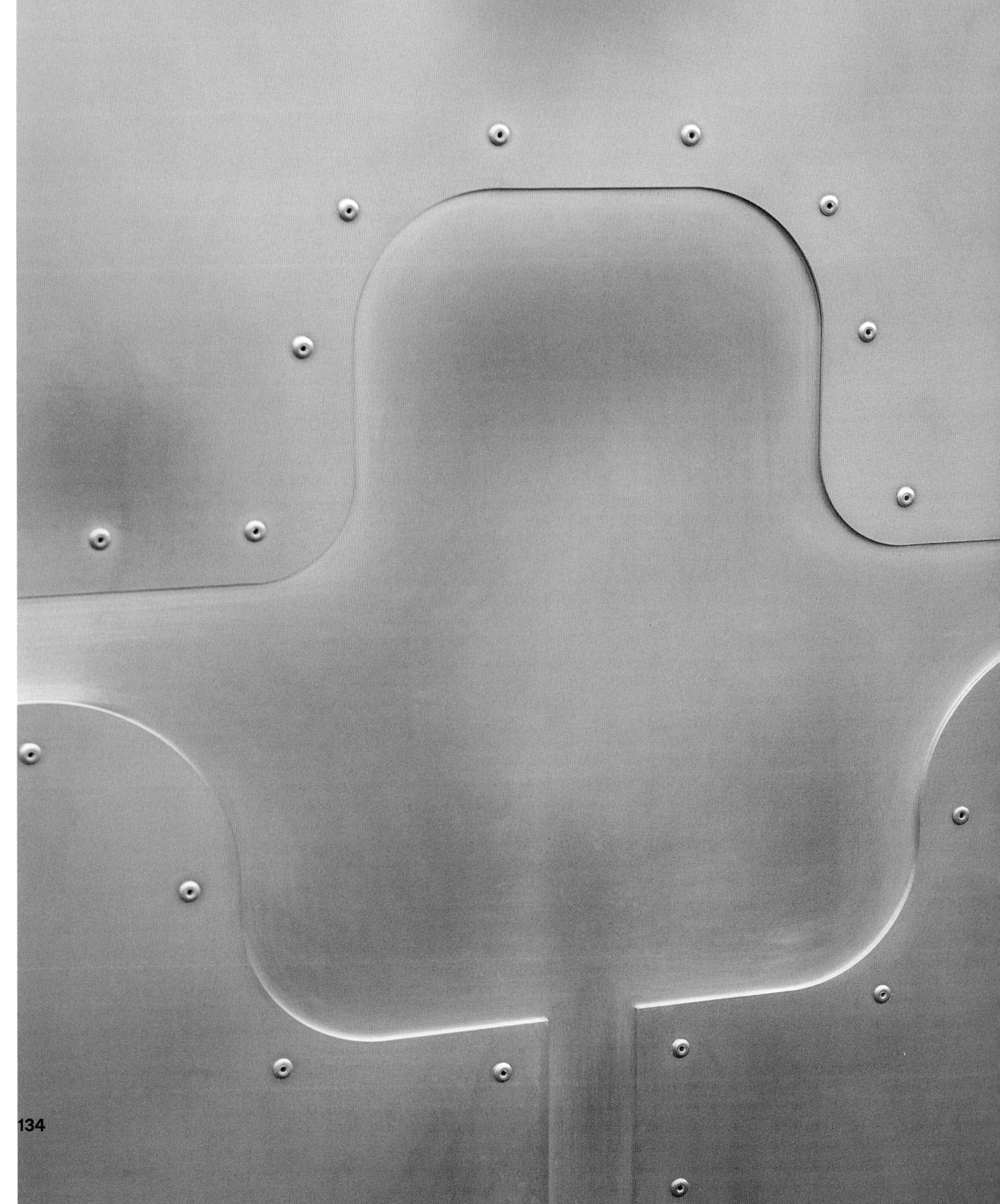

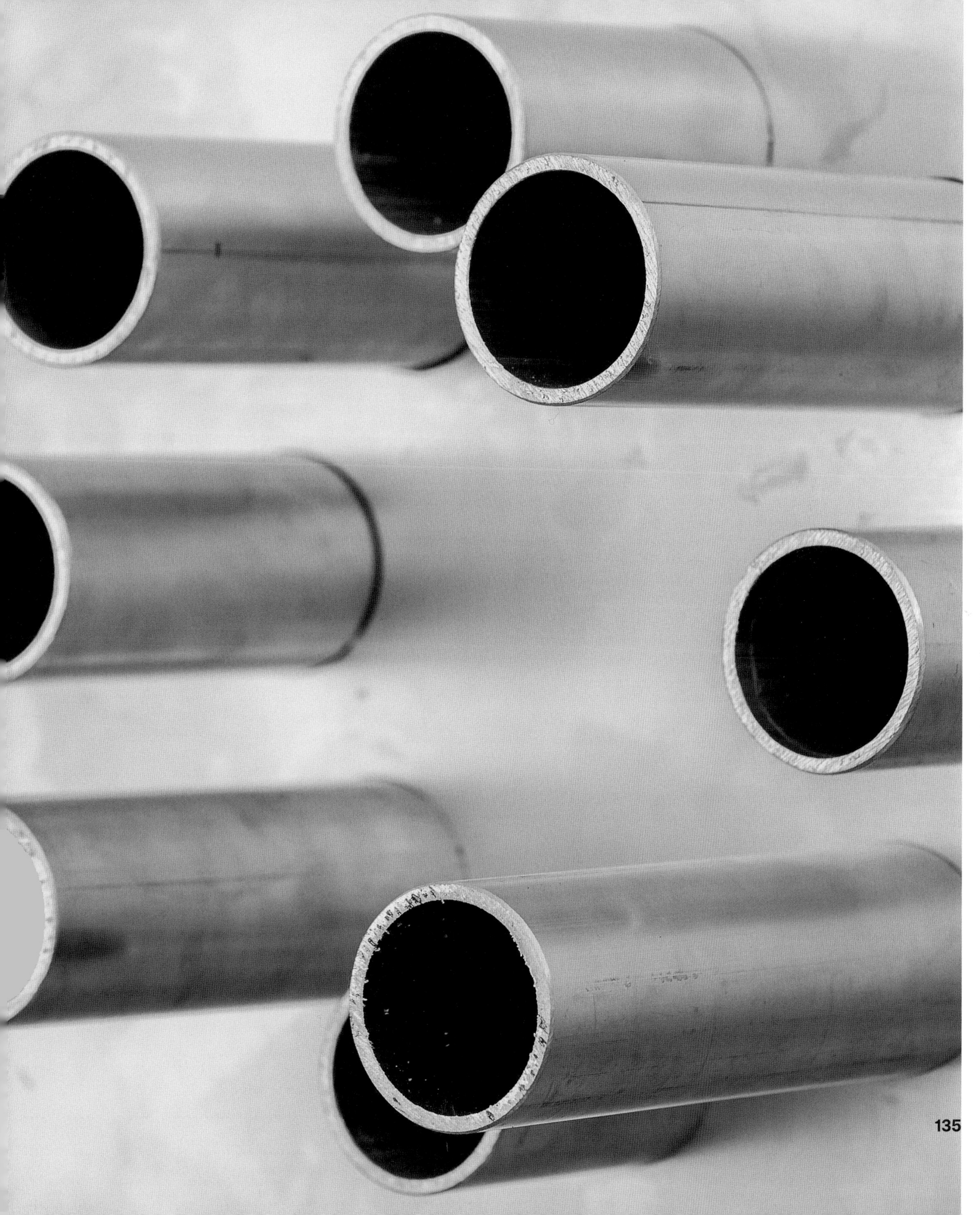

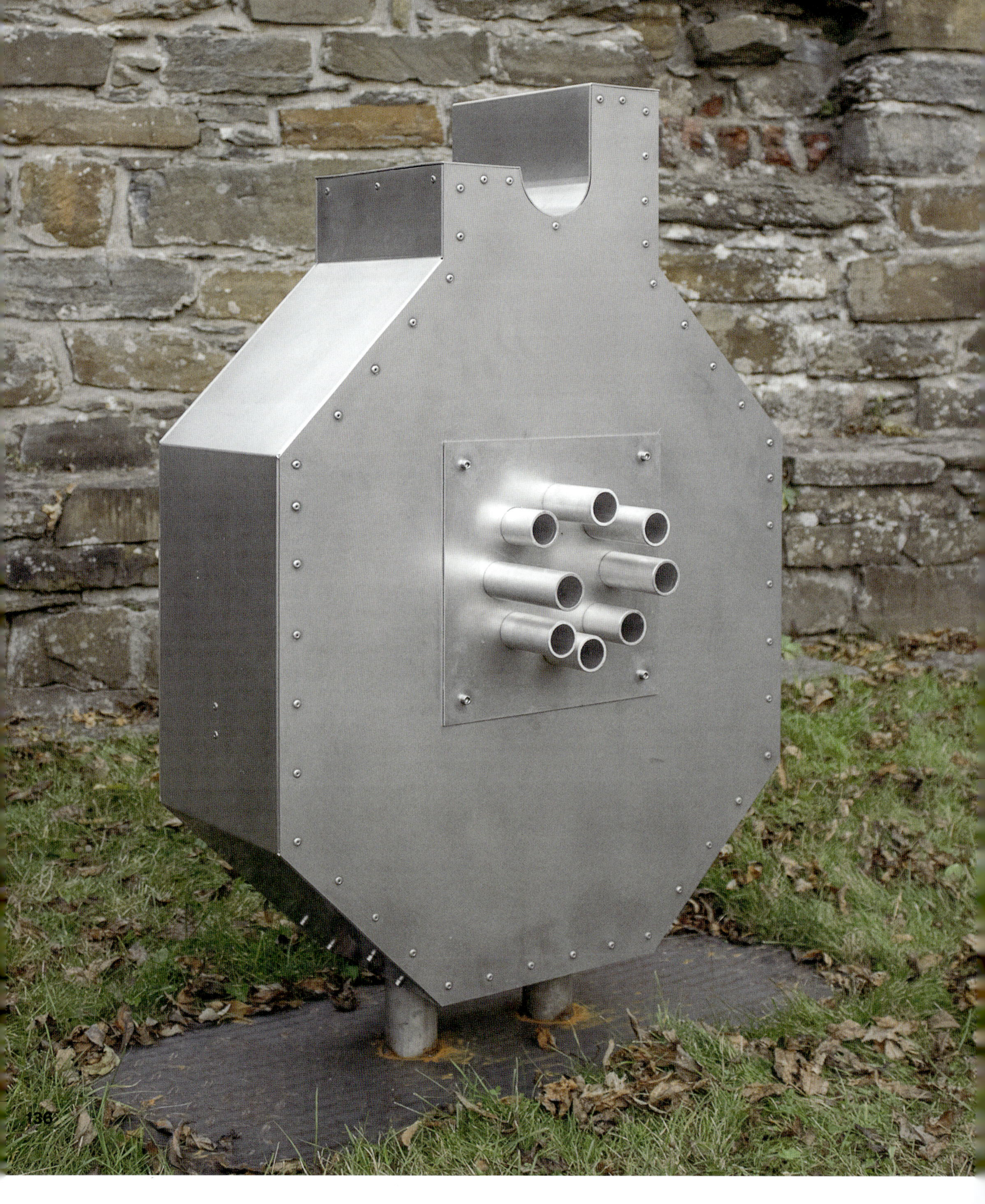

INDEX OF WORKS

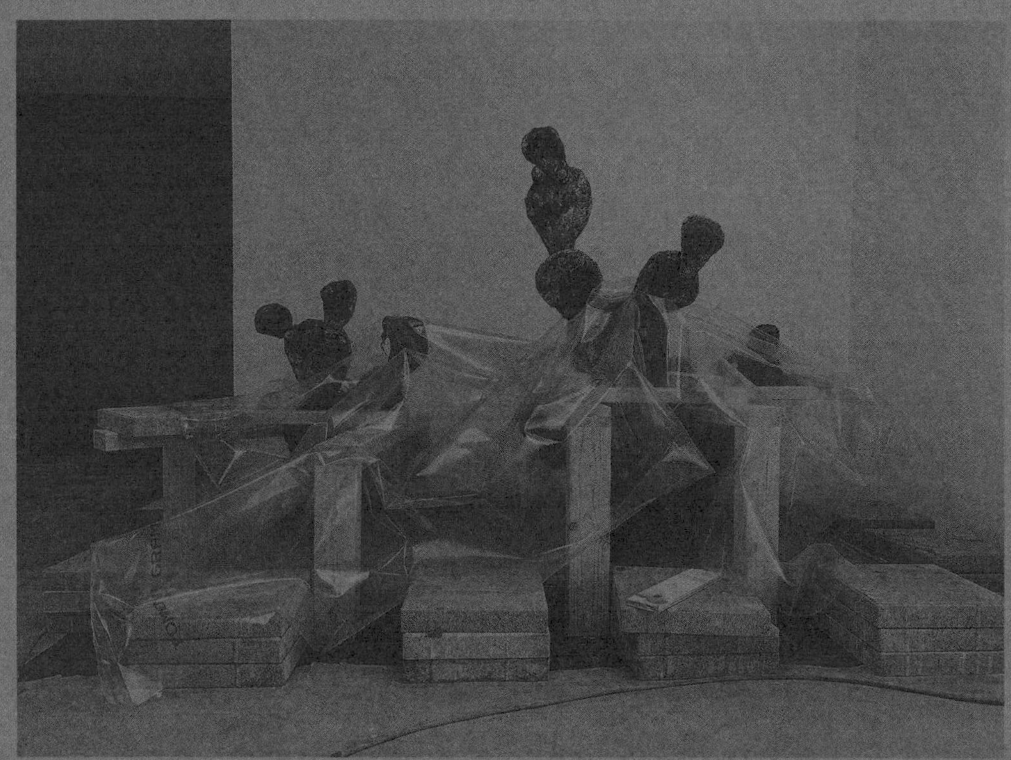

Installing a bronze sculpture to a concrete plinth made in situ for the exhibition *Subterranea* at Hordaland Kunstsenter.

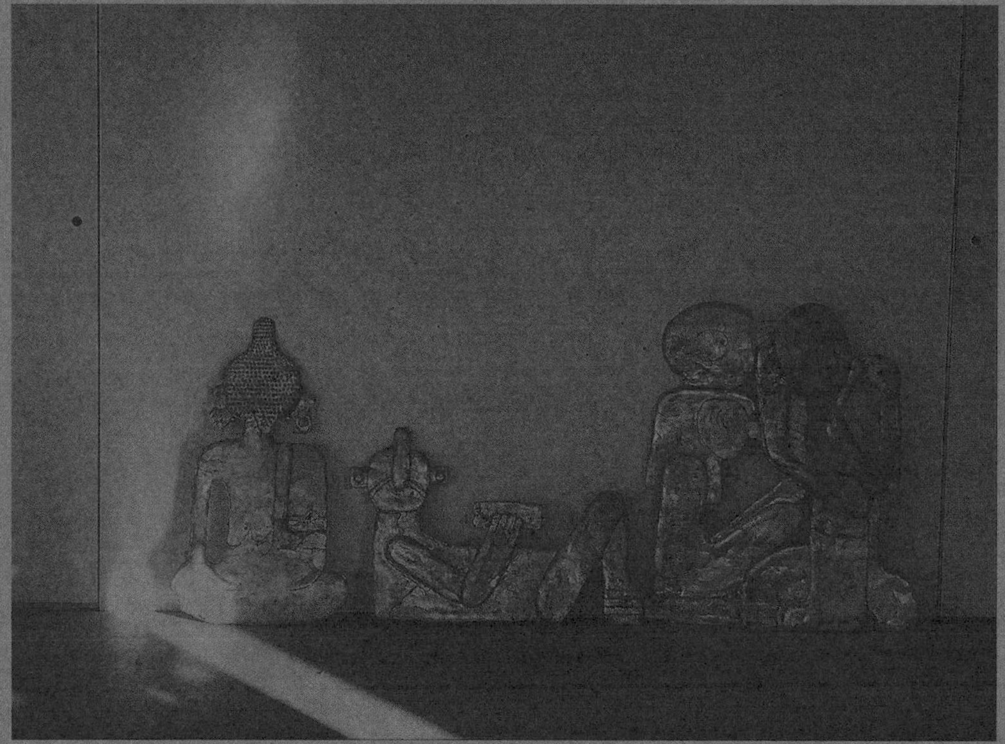

Documentation from Lene's studio, left out details from the process of making the sculpture *(w)hole*.

PAGE 1
Title: *Dear Darkling*
Year: 2015
Materials: Concrete, pigment, earth
Dimensions: Variable
Exhibition title: *Dear Darkling*
Curator: Johanne Nordby Wernø
Location: UKS, Oslo
Courtesy: The National Museum of Art
Photo: Lene Baadsvig Ørmen

PAGES 2–3
Title: *Dear Darkling*
Year: 2015
Materials: Concrete, pigment, earth, MDF, glossy oil paint
Dimensions: (platform) 478 × 327 × 12 cm
Exhibition title: *x4*
Curator: Hanne Mugaas
Location: Kunsthall Stavanger
Courtesy: The National Museum of Art
Photo: Maya Økland

PAGE 4
Title: *Dear Darkling*
Year: 2015
Materials: Concrete, pigment, earth
Dimensions: Variable
Exhibition title: *Dear Darkling*
Curator: Johanne Nordby Wernø
Location: UKS in Oslo
Courtesy: The National Museum of Art
Photo: Lene Baadsvig Ørmen

PAGE 5
Title: *Dear Darkling*
Year: 2015
Materials: Concrete, pigment, earth, MDF, glossy oil paint
Dimensions: (platform) 478 × 327 × 12 cm
Exhibition title: *x4*
Curator: Hanne Mugaas
Location: Kunsthall Stavanger
Courtesy: The National Museum of Art
Photo: Maya Økland

PAGE 6
Title: *Dear Darkling*
Year: 2015
Materials: Concrete, pigment, earth, MDF, glossy oil paint
Dimensions: Variable
Exhibition title: *Dear Darkling*
Curator: Johanne Nordby Wernø
Location: UKS in Oslo
Courtesy: The National Museum of Art
Photo: Lene Baadsvig Ørmen

PAGE 7
Title: *Dear Darkling*
Year: 2015
Materials: Concrete, pigment, earth, MDF, glossy oil paint
Dimensions: Variable
Exhibition title: *Dear Darkling*
Curator: Johanne Nordby Wernø
Location: UKS in Oslo
Courtesy: The National Museum of Art
Photo: Lene Baadsvig Ørmen

PAGE 8
Title: *Foresee Thy Tingling Thumb*
Year: 2016
Materials: Fiber concrete, pigment, sand, copper
Dimensions: 150 × 60 cm
Exhibition title: *Tegnebiennalen 2016*
Curator: Elise Storsveen
Location: Tegneforbundet, in Oslo
Photo: Jon Benjamin Tallerås

PAGE 9
Title: *Fickle Finger*
Year: 2017
Materials: Fiber concrete, pigment, sand
Dimensions: approx. 50 × 35 cm
Exhibition title: *It Might Be Cold Out There But It's Warm In Here*
Curator: Kenneth Alme
Location: Altanen, Vestfossen
Photo: Kenneth Alme

PAGE 10–11
Title: *Fickle Finger*
Year: 2018
Materials: Aluminum, concrete
Dimensions: approx. 35 × 14 × 8 cm
Exhibition title: *Klorofyll og kapital*
Curator: Monica Holmen
Location: Akershus Kunstsenter
Photo: Ingrid Eggen

PAGE 12–13
Title: *Lady Bird*
Year: 2018
Materials: Aluminum, concrete, steel wire
Dimensions: approx. 50 × 35 × 15 cm
Exhibition title: *Klorofyll og kapital*
Curator: Monica Holmen
Location: Akershus Kunstsenter
Photo: Ingrid Eggen

PAGE 14
Title: *Foresee Thy Tingling Thumb*
Year: 2016
Materials: Concrete, pigment, sand, copper
Dimensions: Close up
Exhibition title: *Skissen*, Tegnebiennalen 2016
Curator: Elise Storsveen
Location Tegneforbundet, in Oslo
Photo: Jon Benjamin Tallerås

PAGE 15
Title: *Off-Course*
Year: 2018
Materials: Aluminum, concrete, steel wire, earring
Dimensions: approx. 70 × 35 × 22 cm
Location: Akershus Kunstsenter
Exhibition title: *Klorofyll og kapital*
Curator: Monica Holmen
Photo: Ingrid Eggen

PAGE 16
Title: *Off-Course*
Year: 2018
Materials: Aluminum, concrete, steel wire, earring
Dimensions: Close up

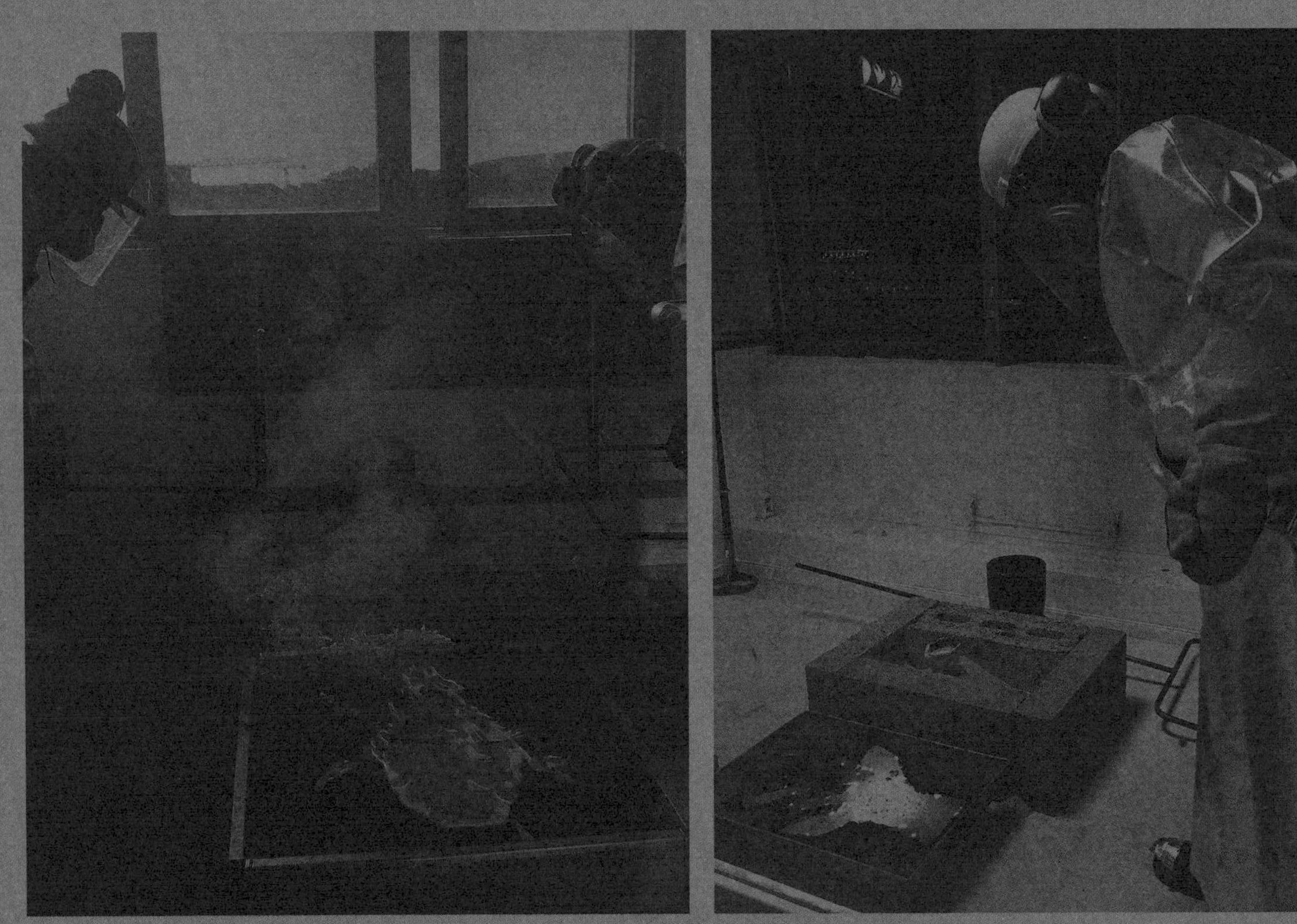

An assistant and Lene in process of sand casting bronze sculptures in Lene's studio.

Exhibition title: *Klorofyll og kapital*
Curator: Monica Holmen
Location: Akershus Kunstsenter
Photo: Ingrid Eggen

PAGE 25
Title: *Heads and Tails*
Year: 2017
Materials: Acrylic one, green and black sand, spray paint, stainless steel and textile
Dimensions: Variable
Exhibition title: *3D Female*
Curator: Louise Sparre
Location: Viborg Kunsthall in Denmark
Photo: Lene Baadsvig Ørmen

PAGE 26–27
Title: *Heads and Tails*
Year: 2017
Materials: Acrylic one, green and black sand, spray paint, stainless steel and textile
Dimensions: Variable
Exhibition title: *3D Female*
Curator: Louise Sparre
Location: Viborg Kunsthall in Denmark
Photo: Lene Baadsvig Ørmen

PAGE 28
Title: *Heads and Tails*
Year: 2017
Materials: Acrylic one, green and black sand, spray paint, stainless steel and textile
Dimensions: Variable
Exhibition title: *3D Female*
Curator: Louise Sparre
Location: Viborg Kunsthall in Denmark
Photo: Lene Baadsvig Ørmen

PAGE 29
Title: *Heads and Tails*
Year: 2017
Materials: Acrylic one, green and black sand, spray paint, stainless steel and textile
Dimensions: Variable
Exhibition title: *3D Female*
Curator: Louise Sparre
Location: Viborg Kunsthall in Denmark
Photo: Lene Baadsvig Ørmen

PAGE 30–31
Title: *Heads and Tails*
Year: 2017
Materials: Acrylic one, green and black sand, spray paint, stainless steel and textile
Dimensions: Variable
Exhibition title: *3D Female*
Curator: Louise Sparre
Location: Viborg Kunsthall in Denmark
Photo: Lene Baadsvig Ørmen

PAGE 33
Title: *Beat*
Year: 2019
Materials: Black steel, falconry glove, concrete, plastic
Dimensions: (steel structure) approx. 210 × 300 cm
Exhibition title: *Subterranea*
Curator: Silja Leifsdottir
Location: Billedhoggerforeningen
Photo: Istvan Virag

PAGE 34
Title: *Beat*
Year: 2019
Materials: Steel, concrete, plastic, falconry glove
Dimensions: detail
Exhibition title: *Subterranea*
Curator: Silja Leifsdottir
Location: Billedhuggerforeningen
Photo: Istvan Virag

PAGE 35
Title: *Subterranea*
Year: 2019
Materials: Bronze
Dimensions: Close up
Exhibition title: *Subterranea*
Curator: Silja Leifsdottir
Location: Billedhoggerforeningen
Photo: Lene Baadsvig Ørmen

PAGE 36–37
Title: *Subterranea*
Year: 2020
Materials: Bronze, concrete, steel, spray paint
Dimensions: Overview
Exhibition title: *Subterranea*
Curator: Mathijs van Geest
Location: Hordaland Kunstsenter
Photo: Bjørn Mortensen

PAGE 38
Title: *Subterranea*
Year: 2020
Materials: Bronze, concrete, steel, spray paint
Dimensions: Overview
Exhibition title: *Subterranea*
Curator: Mathijs van Geest
Location: Hordaland Kunstsenter
Photo: Bjørn Mortensen

PAGE 39
Title: *Subterranea*
Year: 2020
Materials: Bronze, concrete, steel
Dimensions: approx. 90 × 35 × 30 cm
Exhibition title: *Herfra*
Co-curated with the gallery: Olve Sande and Martin Sæther
Location: Galleri Opdahl
Photo: Galleri Opdahl

PAGE 40
Title: *Subterranea*
Year: 2020
Materials: Bronze, concrete, steel
Dimensions: Detail
Exhibition title: *Subterranea*
Curator: Mathijs van Geest
Location: Hordaland Kunstsenter
Courtesy: Private collection
Photo: Bjørn Mortensen

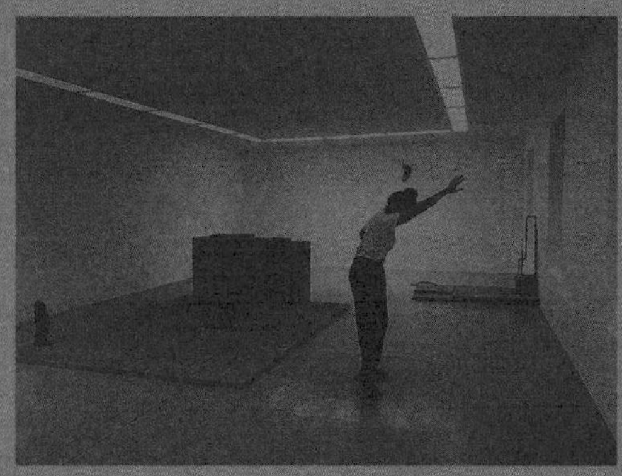

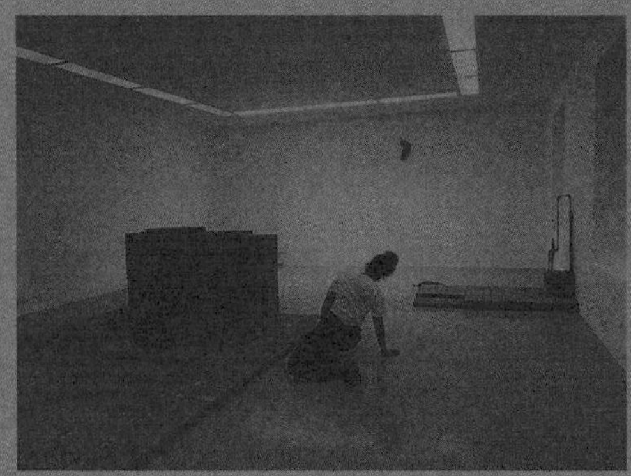

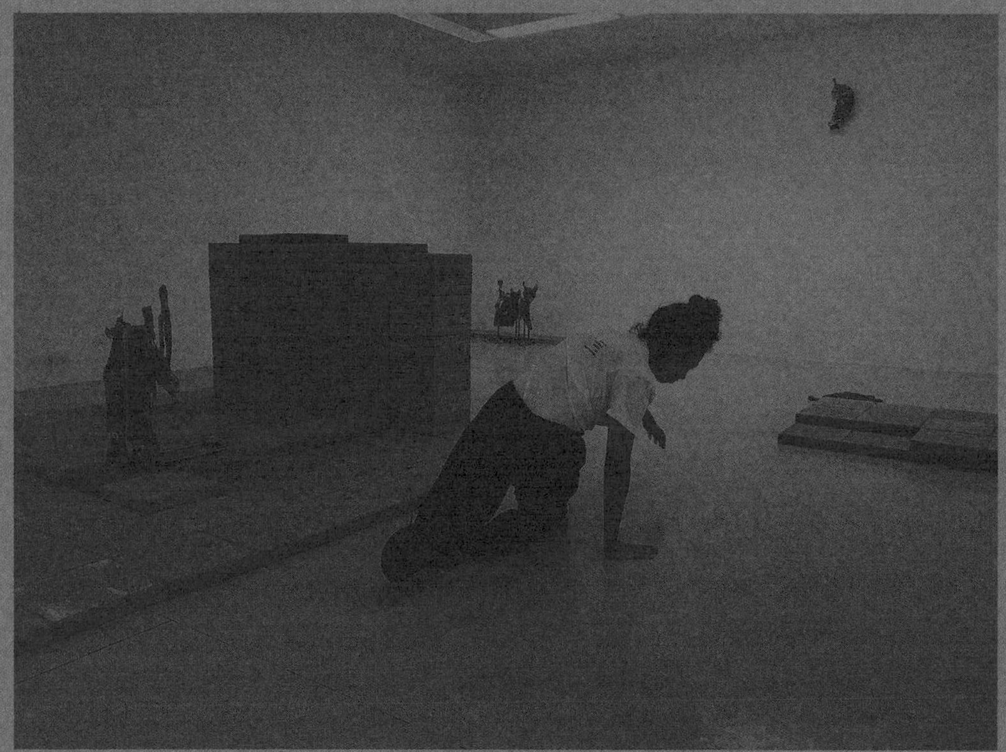

A workshop part of a mediation program for Hordaland Kunstsenter, curated by Daniela Ramos Arias. Carte Blanche dancer Noam Eidelman Shatil's guided experience in the exhibition *Subterranea*, a series of physical and visual exercises that allowed participants to experiment and engage with the room, its shapes and textures through their body.

PAGE 49
Title: *Subterranea*
Year: 2020
Materials: Bronze, steel
Dimensions: Close up
Exhibition title: *Subterranea*
Curator: Silja Leifsdottir
Location: Billedhoggerforeningen
Photo: Lene Baadsvig Ørmen

PAGE 50
Title: *Subterranea*
Year: 2020
Materials: Bronze, concrete, steel, spray paint
Dimensions: Overview
Exhibition title: *Subterranea*
Curator: Mathijs van Geest
Location: Hordaland Kunstsenter
Photo: Bjørn Mortensen

PAGE 51
Title: *Subterranea*
Year: 2020
Materials: Bronze, concrete, steel, spray paint
Dimensions: Detail
Exhibition title: *Subterranea*
Curator: Mathijs van Geest
Location: Hordaland Kunstsenter
Photo: Bjørn Mortensen

PAGE 52, 53
Title: *Subterranea*
Year: 2019
Materials: Bronze
Dimensions: close up / close up
Exhibition title: *Subterranea*
Curator: Silja Leifsdottir
Location: Billedhuggerforeningen
Photo: Lene Baadsvig Ørmen

PAGE 55
Title: *Subterranea*
Year: 2019
Materials: Bronze
Dimensions: Detail
Exhibition title: *Subterranea*
Curator: Silja Leifsdottir
Location: Billedhuggerforeningen
Courtesy: The Municipality of Oslo
Photo: Istvan Virag

PAGE 56, 57
Title: *Subterranea*
Year: 2019
Materials: Bronze, concrete, steel, spray paint
Dimensions: Close up / detail
Exhibition title: *Subterranea*
Curator: Mathijs van Geest
Location: Hordaland Kunstsenter
Courtesy: The Municipality of Oslo
Photo: Bjørn Mortensen

PAGE 58–59
Title: *Subterranea*
Year: 2019
Materials: Bronze
Dimensions: Close up
Exhibition title: *Subterranea*
Curator: Silja Leifsdottir
Location: Billedhuggerforeningen
Courtesy: The Municipality of Oslo
Photo: Istvan Virag

PAGE 60
Title: *Subterranea*
Year: 2019
Materials: Bronze, concrete, steel, spray paint
Dimensions: Detail
Exhibition title: *Subterranea*
Curator: Mathijs van Geest
Location: Hordaland Kunstsenter
Courtesy: Private collection
Photo: Bjørn Mortensen

PAGE 61
Title: *Subterranea*
Year: 2019
Materials: Bronze, steel, concrete,
spray paint
Dimensions: Detail
Curator: Silja Leifsdottir
Location: Billedhuggerforeningen
Photo: Istvan Virag

PAGE 62–63
Title: *Subterranea*
Year: 2019
Materials: Concrete,
spray paint
Dimensions: Detail
Curator: Silja Leifsdottir
Location: Billedhuggerforeningen
Photo: Lene Baadsvig Ørmen

PAGE 64
Title: Subterranea
Place: Billedhuggerforeningen
Year: 2019
Materials: bronze
Size: detail
Curator: Silja Leifsdottir
Photo credit: Istvan Virag

PAGE 73
Title: *hôtel* (part one & part two)
Year: 2021
Materials: Recycled concrete, iron dust,
site-specific sound installation
Sound: Peder Simonsen (29 min 58 sec;
full composition played every Wednesday
at 19:00 and Sunday at 14.00; one of
the six sound sequences are randomly
played every day between 07:00–23:00)
Collaborators: KFA Arkitekter, Bjørn Bygg,
the concrete laboratory at UiT Narvik
and CIRCULUS—Sustainable concrete
recycling and re-use
Dimensions: Close up
Curator: Ruby Paloma
Location: The Arctic University of Norway,
dep. Narvik
Commissioner: KORO
Photo: Lene Baadsvig Ørmen

PAGE 74
Title: *hôtel* (part one & part two)
Year: 2021
Materials: Recycled concrete, iron dust,

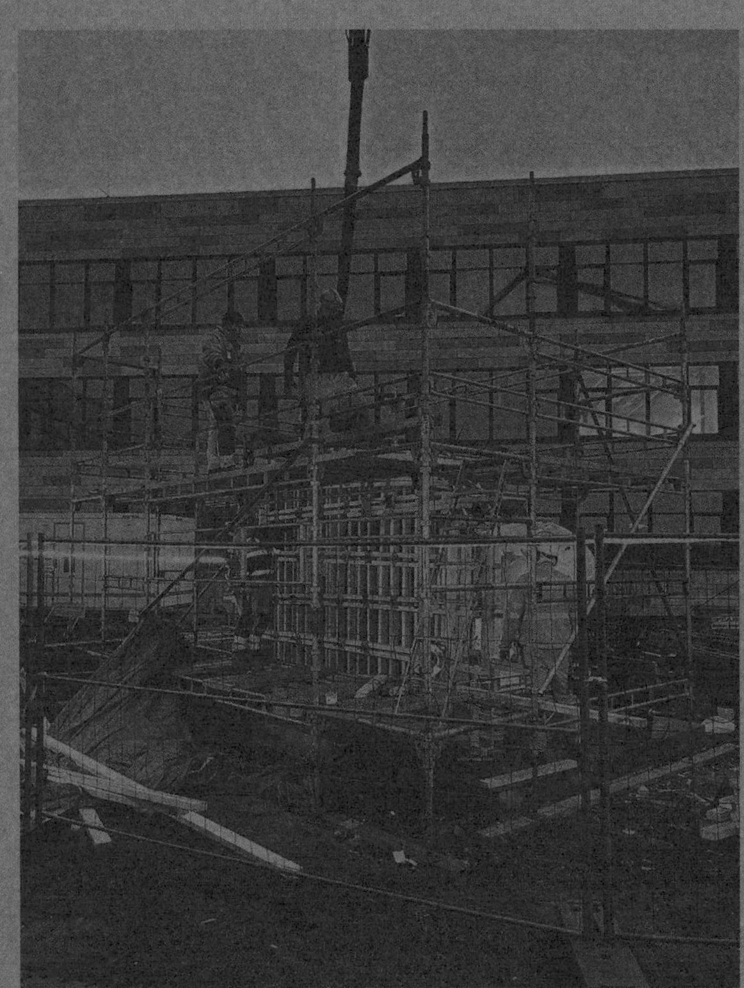

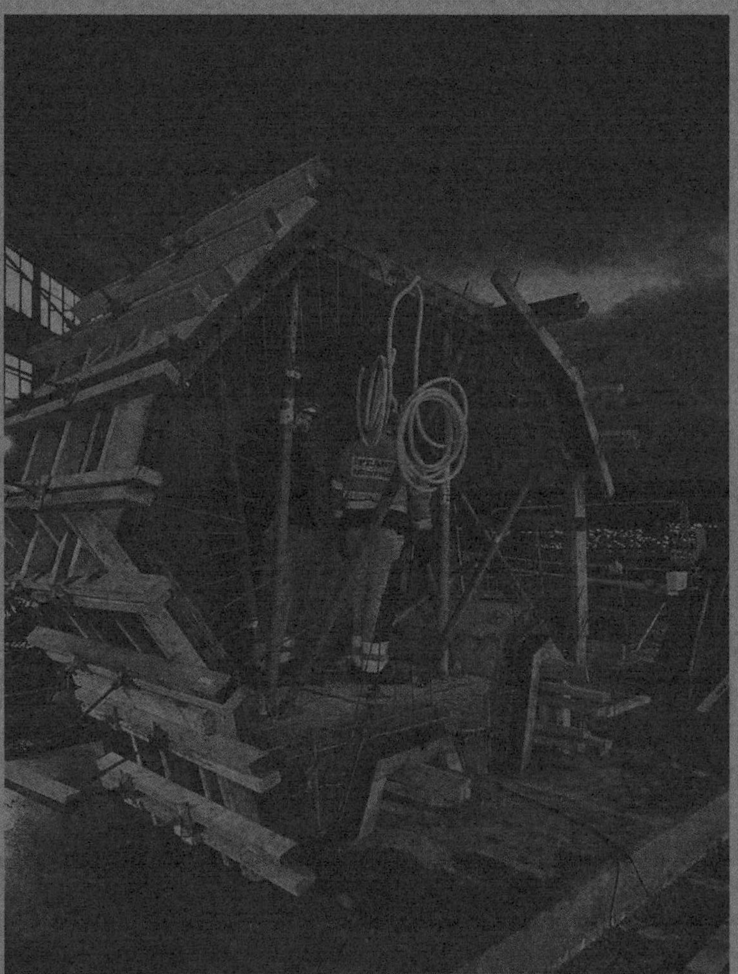

Contractors from Bjørn Bygg making the mold for the concrete sculpture *hôtel*, at UiT in Narvik. Photos by the project manager Stian Søderholm.

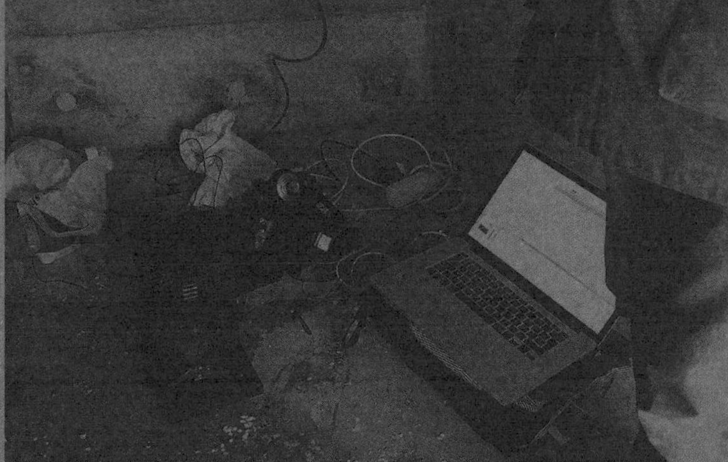

Working on the site-specific sound installation inside the concrete sculpture. The sound in *hôtel* originates from analyzed frequency spectra derived individually from each of the six bronze sculptures. When building upon this, layer by layer, with supportive and amplifying sounds, and fusing this together with further experimentation on how these sound waves physically react with room modes inside the large concrete sculpture, as well as sounds from the local environment, the piece becomes intensely site-specific.

site-specific sound installation
Sound: Peder Simonsen (29 min 58 sec; full composition played every Wed at 19:00 and Sun at 14.00; one of the six sound sequences are randomly played every day between 07:00–23:00)
Collaborators: KFA Arkitekter, Bjørn Bygg, the concrete laboratory at UiT Narvik and CIRCULUS—Sustainable concrete recycling and re-use
Dimensions: 400 × 150 × 310 cm
Curator: Ruby Paloma
Location: The Arctic University of Norway, dep. Narvik
Commissioner: KORO
Photo: Lene Baadsvig Ørmen

PAGE 75
Title: *hôtel* (part one & part two)
Year: 2021
Materials: Recycled concrete, iron dust, site-specific sound installation
Sound: Peder Simonsen (29 min 58 sec; full composition played every Wednesday at 19:00 and Sunday at 14.00; one of the six sound sequences are randomly played every day between 07:00–23:00)
Collaborators: KFA Arkitekter, Bjørn Bygg, the concrete laboratory at UiT Narvik and CIRCULUS—Sustainable concrete recycling and re-use
Dimensions: Detail
Curator: Ruby Paloma
Place: The Arctic University of Norway, dep. Narvik
Commissioner: KORO
Photo: Kjell Ove Storvik

PAGE 76–77
Title: *hôtel* (part one & part two)
Year: 2021
Materials: Recycled concrete, iron dust, site-specific sound installation
Sound: Peder Simonsen (29 min 58 sec; full composition played every Wednesday at 19:00 and Sunday at 14.00; one of the six sound sequences are randomly played every day between 07:00–23:00)
Collaborators: KFA Arkitekter, Bjørn Bygg, the concrete laboratory at UiT Narvik and CIRCULUS—Sustainable concrete recycling and re-use
Dimensions: 400 × 150 × 310 cm
Curator: Ruby Paloma
Location: The Arctic University of Norway, dep. Narvik
Commissioner: KORO
Photo: Lene Baadsvig Ørmen

PAGE 78–79
Title: *hôtel* (part one & part two)
Year: 2021
Materials: Recycled concrete, iron dust, site-specific sound installation
Sound: Peder Simonsen (29 min 58 sec; full composition played every Wednesday at 19:00 and Sunday at 14.00; one of the six sound sequences are randomly played every day between 07:00–23:00)
Collaborators: KFA Arkitekter, Bjørn Bygg, the concrete laboratory at UiT Narvik and CIRCULUS—Sustainable concrete recycling and re-use
Dimensions: Detail
Curator: Ruby Paloma
Location: The Arctic University of Norway, dep. Narvik
Commissioner: KORO
Photo: Kjell Ove Storvik

PAGE 80, 81
Title: *hôtel* (part one & part two)
Year: 2021
Materials: Recycled concrete, iron dust, site-specific sound installation
Sound: Peder Simonsen (29 min 58 sec; full composition played every Wednesday at 19:00 and Sunday at 14.00; one of the six sound sequences are randomly played every day between 07:00–23:00)
Collaborators: KFA Arkitekter, Bjørn Bygg, the concrete laboratory at UiT Narvik and CIRCULUS—Sustainable concrete recycling and re-use
Dimensions: Close up / Close up
Curator: Ruby Paloma
Location: The Arctic University of Norway, dep. Narvik
Commissioner: KORO
Photo: Lene Baadsvig Ørmen

PAGE 82
Title: *hôtel* (part three)
Year: 2021
Materials: Bronze, black set bolts
Dimensions: Overview
Curator: Ruby Paloma
Location: The Arctic University of Norway, dep. Narvik
Commissioner: KORO

PAGE 83
Title: *hôtel* (part three)
Year: 2021
Materials: Bronze, black set bolts
Dimensions: 20 × 50 cm
Curator: Ruby Paloma
Location: The Arctic University of Norway, dep. Narvik
Commissioner: KORO

PAGE 84
Title: *hôtel* (part three)
Year: 2021
Materials: Bronze, black set bolts
Dimensions: 27 × 46 cm
Curator: Ruby Paloma
Location: The Arctic University of Norway, dep. Narvik
Commissioner: KORO

PAGE 85
Title: *hôtel* (part three)
Year: 2021
Materials: Bronze, black set bolts
Dimensions: 32 × 20 cm

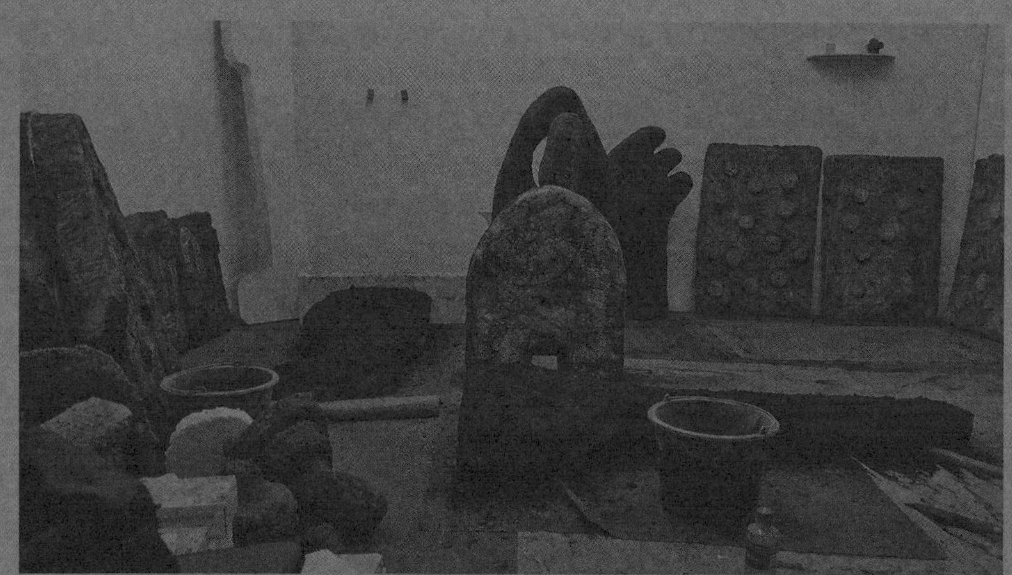

Documentation from Lene's studio, in process of making the exhibition *Fret Not Upon Thy Blue Funk* (2016) at Kunstnerforbundet, in Oslo.

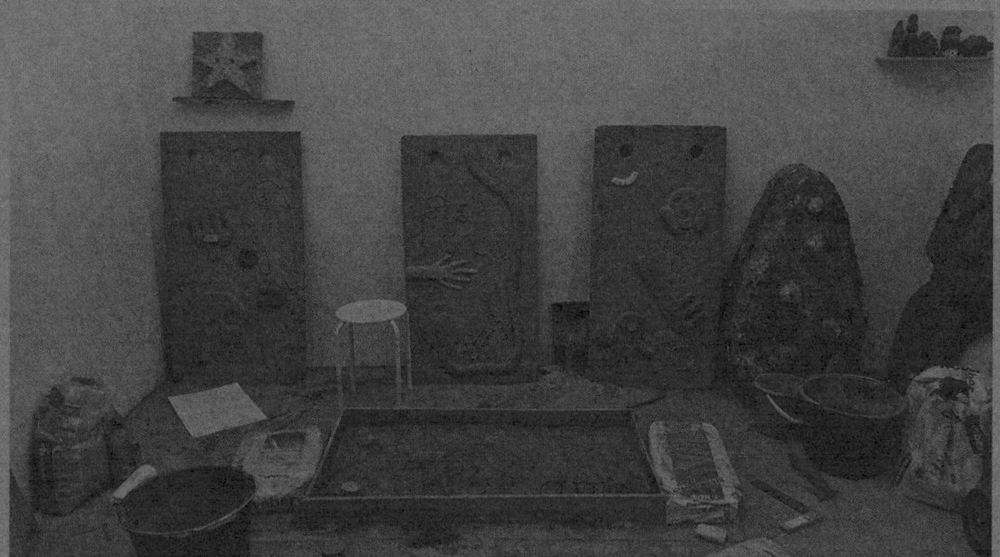

Documentation from Lene's studio, in process of making the piece *Foresee Thy Tingling Thumb* for the Drawing Biennale in Oslo (2016).

Curator: Ruby Paloma
Location: The Arctic University of Norway, dep. Narvik
Commissioner: KORO

PAGE 86
Title: *hôtel* (part three)
Year: 2021
Materials: Bronze, black set bolts
Dimensions: 28×10 cm
Curator: Ruby Paloma
Location: The Arctic University of Norway, dep. Narvik
Commissioner: KORO

PAGE 87
Title: *hôtel* (part three)
Year: 2021
Materials: Bronze, black set bolts
Dimensions: 25×45 cm
Curator: Ruby Paloma
Location: The Arctic University of Norway, dep. Narvik
Commissioner: KORO

PAGE 88
Title: *hôtel* (part three)
Year: 2021
Materials: Bronze, black set bolts
Dimensions: 40 cm×22 cm
Curator: Ruby Paloma
Location: The Arctic University of Norway, dep. Narvik
Commissioner: KORO

PAGE 97
Title: *Heavy Cheers*
Year: 2016
Material: Concrete, pigment, earth
Dimensions: approx. 140×65 cm
Exhibition title: *Fret Not Upon Thy Blue Funk*
Location: Kunstnerforbundet, Oslo
Photo: Thomas Tveter

PAGE 98–99
Title: *Bursting Bubble, Toil and Trouble*
Year: 2016
Material: Concrete, pigment, earth
Dimensions: approx. 45×30 cm each
Exhibition title: *Fret Not Upon Thy Blue Funk*
Location: Kunstnerforbundet, Oslo
Courtesy: The Norwegian Parliament
Photo: Thomas Tveter

PAGE 100, 101, 102, 103
Title: *Puncture Patch 1–4* (of 5 in total)
Year: 2016
Material: Concrete, pigment, earth
Dimensions: approx. 95×60 each
Exhibition title: Fret Not Upon Thy Blue Funk
Location: Kunstnerforbundet, Oslo
Photo: Thomas Tveter

PAGE 104
Title: *Conundrum Sanctuary*
Year: 2016
Material: Concrete, pigment, earth
Dimensions: approx. 150×50 cm
Exhibition title: *Fret Not Upon Thy Blue Funk*
Location: Kunstnerforbundet, Oslo
Photo: Lene Baadsvig Ørmen

PAGE 105
Title: *Subterranea*
Year: 2020
Material: Bronze, concrete, stainless steel, spray paint
Dimensions: Detail
Exhibition Title: *Subterranea*
Curator: Mathijs van Geest
Location: Hordaland Kunstsenter
Photo: Bjørn Mortensen

PAGE 106–107
Title: *Subterranea*
Year: 2020
Material: Bronze, concrete, stainless steel, spray paint
Dimensions: approx. 150×240×110 cm
Exhibition Title: *Subterranea*
Curator: Mathijs van Geest
Location: Hordaland Kunstsenter
Photo: Bjørn Mortensen

PAGE 108
Title: *Subterranea*
Year: 2020
Material: Bronze, concrete, stainless steel, spray paint
Dimensions: Detail
Exhibition Title: *Subterranea*
Curator: Mathijs van Geest
Location: Hordaland Kunstsenter
Photo: Bjørn Mortensen

PAGE 110–111
Title: *Foresee Thy Tingling Thumb*
Year: 2016
Material: Fiber concrete, pigment, sand, copper
Dimensions: 150×250 cm
Exhibition title: *Skissen*, Tegnebiennalen 2016
Curator: Elise Storsveen
Location: Tegnerforbundet, Oslo
Photo: Jon Benjamin Tallerås

PAGE 112
Title: *inflating Heap*
Year: 2017
Material: Concrete, sand, oil paint
Dimensions: approx. 140×40×40 cm
Exhibition title: *Nothing you have to understand*
Co-curated with the gallery: Kristian Touborg
Location: Galereie Mikael Andersen, in Copenhagen
Photo: Jan Søndergaard

PAGE 121
Title: *n0thing*
Year: 2019
Material: Aluminum, stainless steel, concrete, water, coins
Dimensions: approx. 210×90×90 cm

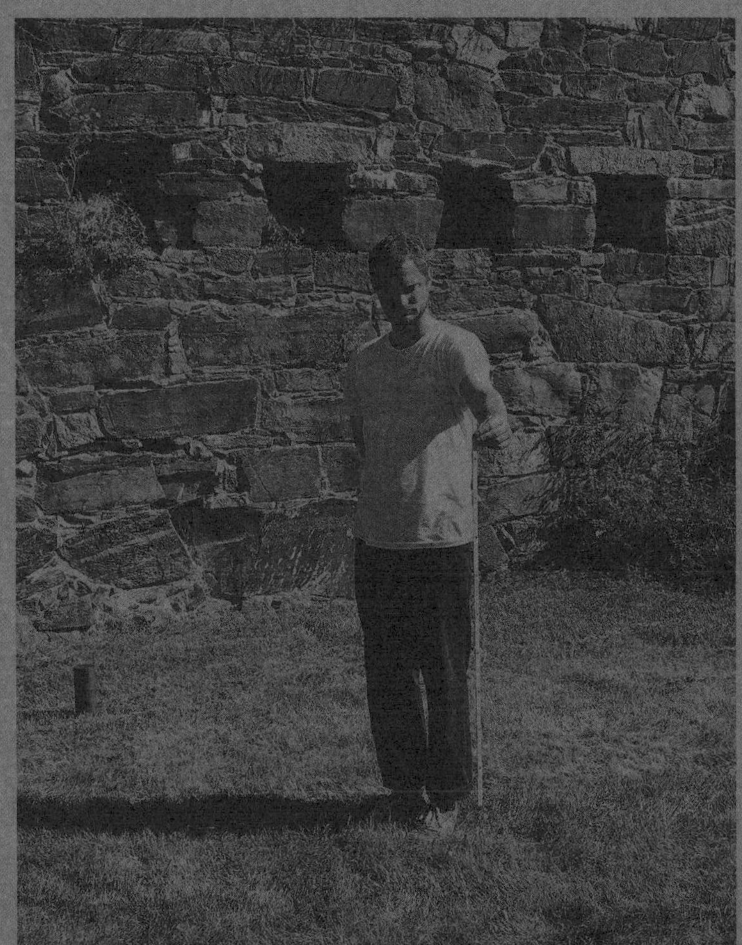

Composer and tuba player Peder Simonsen exploring the site inside the monastery ruins at Hovedøya in Oslo, in process of making the piece *AA11XXX* that took part in Coast Contemporary 2020.

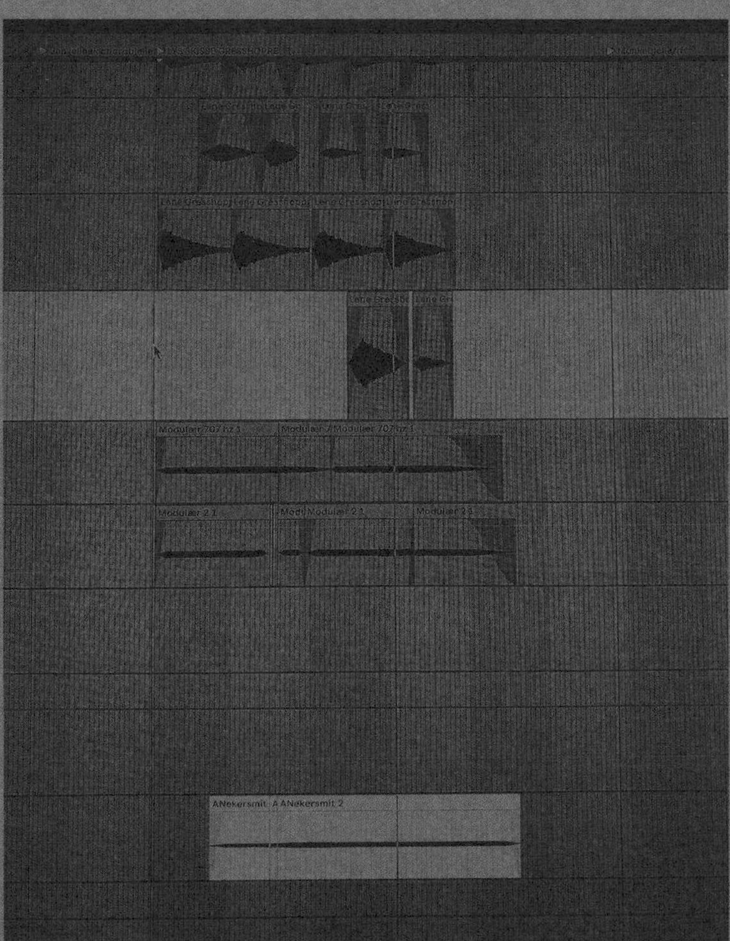

The sound originates from the recordings of an aluminum plate, similar to those used for the sculptures. The frequencies we hear are all harmonies numerically related to the fundamental tone of this. The three sculptures figure as resonance chambers where the materiality of each individual helps to determine both the tonal starting point and the selected frequencies which are emphasized. Loudspeakers are placed inside the sculptures and create an auditory web of vibrations invisibly connecting the three sculpture.

Exhibition title: *Beings With*
Curated by: Ki Nurmenniemi
Location: Fiskars Village Art Biennale
Photo: Kerttu Penttilä (Luovi Productions)

PAGE 122–123
Title: *n0thing*
Year: 2018
Material: aluminum, stainless steel, concrete, water, coins
Dimensions: Close up
Location: Akershus Kunstsenter
Photo: Lene Baadsvig Ørmen

PAGE 124–125
Title: *n0thing*
Year: 2018
Material: Aluminum, stainless steel, concrete, water, coins
Dimensions: approx. 210 × 90 × 90 cm
Location: Akershus Kunstsenter
Photo: Lene Baadsvig Ørmen

PAGE 126
Title: *n0thing*
Year: 2018
Material: aluminum, stainless steel, concrete, water, coins
Dimensions: approx. 210 × 90 × 90 cm
Location: Akershus Kunstsenter
Photo: Ingrid Eggen

PAGE 128
Title: *(w)hole*
Year: 2019
Material: Aluminum, stainless steel, concrete
Dimensions: approx. 80 × 100 × 310 cm
Exhibition title: *Subterranea*
Curator: Silja Leifsdottir
Location: Billedhoggerforeningen
Photo: Istvan Virag

PAGE 129
Title: *(w)hole*
Year: 2019
Material: Aluminum, stainless steel, concrete
Dimensions: Close up
Exhibition title: *Subterranea*
Curator: Silja Leifsdottir
Location: Billedhoggerforeningen
Photo: Istvan Virag

PAGE 131
Title: *AA11XXX*
Year: 2020
Material: Aluminum sheets, nails, steel, site-specific sound installation
Sound: Peder Simonsen (27 min 12 sec)
Dimensions: Detail
Exhibition title: *Constructing Structures*
Curator: Tanja Sæter / Coast Contemporary
Location: Monestary Ruins, at Hovedøya in Oslo
Photo: Lene Baadsvig Ørmen

PAGE 132–133
Title: *AA11XXX*
Year: 2020
Material: Aluminum sheets, nails, steel, site-specific sound installation
Sound: Peder Simonsen (27 min 12 sec)
Dimensions: Overview
Exhibition title: *Constructing Structures*
Curated by: Tanja Sæter / Coast Contemporary
Location: Monestary Ruins, at Hovedøya in Oslo
Photo: Lene Baadsvig Ørmen

PAGE 134, 135
Title: *AA11XXX*
Year: 2020
Material: Aluminum sheets, nails, steel, site-specific sound installation
Sound: Peder Simonsen (27 min 12 sec)
Dimensions: Detail
Exhibition title: *Constructing Structures*
Curator: Tanja Sæter / Coast Contemporary
Location: Monestary Ruins, at Hovedøya in Oslo
Photo: Jan Khür

PAGE 136
Title: *AA11XXX*
Year: 2020
Material: Aluminum sheets, nails, steel, site-specific sound installation
Sound: Peder Simonsen (27 min 12 sec)
Dimensions: Detail
Exhibition title: *Constructing Structures*
Curator: Tanja Sæter / Coast Contemporary
Location: Monestary Ruins, at Hovedøya in Oslo
Photo: Lene Baadsvig Ørmen

LENE BAADSVIG ØRMEN lives and works in Oslo. She is educated from the Academy of the Arts in Bergen (BA) and Oslo (MA). During her BA she also attended an exchange program at the Estonian Academy of the Arts in Tallinn.

Solo exhibitions include: Hordaland Kunstsenter, Bergen (2020), Billedhoggerforeningen, Oslo (2019), Gallery Augusta, Helsinki (2016), Kunstnerforbundet (2016), UKS (2015), Kunsthall Stavanger (2015), and Another Space, Copenhagen (2014).

A selection of group exhibitions 2013–2020 include: Galleri Opdahl in Stavanger, Fiskars Village Art Biennale in Finland, Galerie Mikael Andersen in Copenhagen, Autocenter in Berlin, Viborg Kunsthall in Denmark, Akershus Kunstsenter in Lillestrøm, the 2016 Drawing Biennial in Oslo, Kunsthall Oslo, Kunstnernes Hus, GAD and Podium in Oslo. She has also participated in residency programs at HIAP, in Helsinki (2017) and Residency Unlimited, in New York (2015).

Ørmen's work is represented in private and public collections, including the National Museum, the Norwegian Parliament, KORO/UiT Narvik and Oslo Municipality.
— lenebaadsvig.com

JAN VERWOERT is a critic and writer on contemporary art and cultural theory. He is a contributing editor of Frieze magazine and his writing has appeared in different journals, anthologies and monographs. He teaches at the Oslo National Academy of the Arts, the Piet Zwart Institute Rotterdam, and the Appel curatorial programme, Amsterdam.

MILENA HØGSBERG is a curator and writer. She is the Director of the Museum of Contemporary Art in Roskilde, Denmark, a museum currently exploring what it means to be an itinerant institution.
— milenahoegsberg.com

LEAH BEEFERMAN is a visual artist based in the U.S. She is an Adjunct Lecturer at Brown University and a Critic at Rhode Island School of Design.
— leahbeeferman.com

KI NURMENNIEMI is a Helsinki-based curator of contemporary art, art writer, and doctoral researcher in interdisciplinary sustainability sciences. Ki also shares a creative practice with artist Tuomas A. Laitinen, under the name Myriagon (est. 2018).
— kinurmenniemi.net
— punos.org

MATHIJS VAN GEEST is an artist and curator based in Bergen, Norway. Since 2018 he is director of Hordaland Kunstsenter, a regional resource centre for contemporary art.
— mathijsvangeest.com
— kunstsenter.no

Lene Baadsvig Ørmen
0

Edited by
Mathijs van Geest

Texts by
Leah Beeferman
Milena Høgsberg
Ki Nurmenniemi
Mathijs van Geest
Jan Verwoert

Graphic design by
Indrek Sirkel

Embossed illustrations by
Pärtel Eelmere

Language editing and
proofreading by
Bryne McLaughlin

Photos by
Lene Baadsvig Ørmen, Maya Økland,
Jon Benjamin Tallerås, Ingrid Eggen,
Istvan Virag, Bjørn Mortensen,
Kjell Ove Storvik, Thomas Tveter,
Jan Søndergaard, Kerttu Penttilä,
Jan Khür

Colour correction by
Stuudio Stuudio

Typeface
Ladna Sans by Andree Paat

Paper
Munken Polar Rough 120g
Arctic the Volume 130g

Printed by
Tallinn Book Printers

Special thanks to
Cecilie Løveid, Camilla Martinsen,
Ruby Paloma and Gunnar Moen

Supported by
Norwegian Art Council
Norwegian Visual Artists Fund

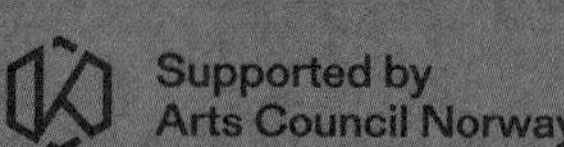

BKV

Published by
Lugemik & Hordaland Kunstsenter

www.lenebaadsvig.com
www.kunstsenter.no
www.lugemik.ee

ISBN 978-9949-7381-8-2

SOM OM DU VAR EN TISTL

Cecilie Løveid

Jeg øvr meg ennå som Satn for å se på froskene henns
eller henn so om hun var en tistl i hagen, ikke falk
Det går ikke an å tegn henn epsk som mennesk fugl eller tistl
fordi

Kan ikke si annt enn at hun må ha hatt problm med fremtidn
og hun
må få problm i ventetidn og i nåtidn har hun angst
og fortidn henn er truend

Paradists tid. Bronsns tid. Kanskj kloakksystm i undergrunns-
stasjonr i nåts tid.
-Hva skal vi med kunst når vi har kalendr?
skrv en vittg på veggn

Hun vrr seg i sin industr tid og håper å ha nok varme til
voks og smelt ferdigbål
Tid er renn for henn, tistl eller kvinn eller dyr
eller sand, smelt og drypp; prill

Brons prill, skapt midt i luftn er som hun selv elv
Livgiv kunne vært navnet henns men Livgiv er enn ikke no
navn

Ettrhvert bretts hun som tistl ellr fugl
Jeg vil si til tistlne: tistl du er vakrst knekkt
men kanskje er det som falk du brekks?

Hoet trykks med størst kraft mot magn, nakkeknakk
som tistl brekt

Hvor trofst falkn er, kongelg flitig og trent til å lande
på falkonérhansn med høstn i nebbet
Sår hun som en ikke ferdigtegnt tistl i en
mølj av materialr: tarm, fibrr, blod, urn fra avløp og rør

Tilsølt. Sugd. Tistl. Mistl. Tåredrp

Du, bronsdrypp fra det tapte Paradist. Prill
Vis deg for meeg som en tistl. Prill!

A poem written by Cecilie Løveid as a literary response to the exhibition *Subterranea*, initiated by Hordaland Kunstsenter as an alternative way of experiencing the exhibition during lock down under the COVID-19 pandemic.